Aubade

Other books by Wallace Fowlie

Journal of rehearsals: a memoir
Letters of Henry Miller and Wallace Fowlie
Characters from Proust: poems
A reading of Dante's Inferno
A reading of Proust
Mallarmé
Rimbaud: a critical study
André Gide: his life and art
Paul Claudel
Stendhal
The French critic
Climate of violence
Dionysus in Paris
Age of surrealism
The clown's grail (Love in literature)

TRANSLATIONS

Complete Works of Rimbaud
Two dramas by Claudel
A poet before the cross by Claudel
Seamarks by Saint-John Perse
Don Juan by Molière
The miser by Molière

Aubade

a teacher's notebook

Wallace Fowlie

Duke University Press   Durham, N.C.   1983

Printed in the United States of America
on acid-free paper

Library of Congress Cataloging in Publication Data

Fowlie, Wallace, 1908–
  Aubade: a teacher's notebook.

  Includes index.
    1. Fowlie, Wallace, 1908–   . 2. French
philology—Study and teaching (Higher)—United States.
3. Philologists—United States—Biography. 4. College
teachers—United States—Biography. I. Title.
PQ67.F65A33 1983   840'.9 [B]   83–14095
ISBN 0-8223-0566-6 (cloth)
ISBN 0-8223-0588-7 (paper)

Contents

Aubade

Introduction

Today I feel a clearer will than ever before to write about myself: not as much a memoir-autobiography as in *Journal of Rehearsals*, but a reconstruction of events and thoughts that have formed me. It will have to be "me" as one among trillions of men who have lived and are living and who testify to the same illusions, to the same stultifying hopes, to the same defeats.

The life of each man: a myth. The effort of each writer: to give meaning to his myth, whether he be poet, biographer, critic, historian, scholar, novelist, scientific researcher, or autobiographer. Man is the subject always, never one individual man. One starts there, of course, in the breathing, thinking body of one man, and then moves toward what must be called, if it is conceived with any success, an artifact.

As I choose from my past the few episodes that may give substance to this book, Angelo's words in *Measure for Measure* come to my mind, and I say them to myself in this present moment of quiet in North Carolina, as I remember saying them forty years ago on a stage at Bennington as spring came suddenly to cold Vermont:

> When I would pray and think, I think and pray
> To several subjects. Heaven hath my empty words.

Thought and prayer: for which words were invented. Thought: jumbled words spoken back to one's mind from which they originally came. Prayer: words more planned and rehearsed, spoken to that Mind beyond us, to that Being of quiet and love we can scarcely imagine, and to whom, because He always will be, we continue to pray.

3

But Angelo, in his anxious state in act 2, just before Isabella comes to him, speaks of praying to several subjects. Thus prayer is diluted and wasted when it supplicates or praises powers within us and loves outside of us. "Empty words," says the deputy in Shakespeare's play. All those words that are merely pretense and construction and illusion.

I would like to believe that any attempt to write autobiography is self-interpretation, not for the self writing but for others reading. There is no way to write in the past. It is an occupation solely for the present. Present time—now—is always, inevitably, fleeting. It is being constantly emptied—unless unbidden memories come to fill and fulfill it. Yes, it is a fulfillment I am after. Whenever I write, I am turned into a sleuth verbalizing experience into fiction. Facts are nothing by comparison with the truth of fiction. Aristotle calls this the truth of poetry as opposed to the lies of history.

We alter the present by thinking of the past. Every writer of fiction reveals his inner life in which errors and omissions count. The issues at the heart of every novel and every autobiography are three: memory, love, and death. In that order, as if those three were three acts of a drama. Memory is the experience, the florid engaging act one; love is the action, the growing stress and conflict of act two; and death is the dénouement of act three which had been present but invisible in act one, and which became by act two clearly discernible, and which in act three is celebrated as the fatal epiphany of every life.

I have now moved beyond the canonical age of threescore and ten years, and hence the book I want to write herewith is merely the sketch of a program for survival. The word *candid* keeps coming into my mind as I choose and plan the episodes, the memorable ones on which I can focus whatever skill I may have acquired in the discipline of literary interpretation. It comes from the Latin "white"—*candidus* —because a Roman candidate was a man dressed in a white toga. A candid man is indeed a candidate today for calumny and ostracism.

The noun *candor* also pushes its way into my mind, and suddenly I realize why I juxtapose noun and adjective. They are in a poem of Wallace Stevens and designate the power a poem can have, and I substitute the word *poem* for the more modest writing I am attempting:

> The poem, through candor, brings back a power again
> That gives a candid kind to everything.

Notes Toward a Supreme Fiction

To write, for Rousseau, was to free himself of shame and anxiety. In my own, less paranoid case, I am aware of the shedding of some anxiety, but do not always remember the moments of shame or the causes. But they are in my subconscious memory, and they return in my dreams especially if I have been trying to resurrect them. A dream can arrange such a moment and present it in spectacular fashion. In the dream itself I recognize what I had sought after and called after down through the years. And I relive that experience which I had first felt when I was very young. There is no growing old from shame.

A memoir begins with memoranda—a note-taking on memory—and then gradually the words take form. I am first the observer of myself, and then the writer of those observations. But interpretation—hermeneutics as it is now called—is a destructive art, and hazardous. The act of interpreting oneself or a poem or some sacred symbol is to become a performer and to obey the dictates of an audience. As the interpretation continues, it is saying to the audience (real or imagined) "this is what it is like to believe—in myself, or in this Mallarmé sonnet, or in the sun symbolism that gives us life."

Our multiple impersonations would be fewer if we adhered more closely to our native soil. I am thinking of Cellini's Florence, of Sean O'Casey's Dublin, of William Carlos Williams' Paterson, New Jersey, and of Ernest Renan's Brittany. When attached to such sites as those, a man's self-portrait appears more authentic to a reader and more fully realized to himself. The site fuses with the inhabitant. At times in *Walden* the pond seems to be a human personality.

Derisive synonyms are often used to define an autobiographer. I have heard Rousseau called an egomaniac, Gide an immoralist, Henry Miller a pornographer, T. E. Lawrence and Saint Augustine mystics. And I have heard these same autobiographers called by opposites of those terms: Rousseau and Gide, writers of sincerity and frankness; Miller the pioneer in the new wave of literary expression; T. E. Lawrence and Saint Augustine analysts of the subconscious.

Such conflicting responses arise from the relationship existing between a text and a reader. Reading may be a drama, a struggle going on between the effort to read a text and to read into the text. Most days of my life I feel incapable of any bright or adventurous destiny. The reading of a book may point the way to some unspent force that my life can release. The psyche, then, has its own mysterious methods of restoring a balance. Life in a man, in order to keep unfolding, does not always need events. It is made up also of signs and images, of sayings and parables.

I have often noticed a pattern of three moments that succeed one another in the course of twenty-four hours and that seem controlled by my psyche. The first is an experience of dread that emerges from dreams occuring just before dawn when sleep is heavy. It might be a sense of dread coming from a reluctance to understand the message of the dreams or to interpret them in terms of my present life. Then during the course of the morning with its light, the dread dissipates and is replaced by desire. Not always erotic desire—although that is frequent—but it may be quite simply an overwhelming desire to live —without the haunting sense of dread. This desire to live is always in my case the desire to work, to write, to reorder my thoughts as preparation to write.

The day continues with this strong sentiment in me until it gains such power that it creates of itself a third moment, a third movement, I might say, best characterized by belief. The desire to write has become a belief in myself, so firm a belief as to embrace all pitfalls and hopes, all forms of dread and desire. The pattern of those three— dread, desire, belief—forms the structure of my clearest days.

What do I make out of these changing moods that form and dissolve within twenty-four hours? The design must have something to do with the ultimate elusiveness of human identity. This very elusiveness I have watched and followed and tried to comprehend in the two authors I have taught the most assiduously and admired over the longest period of time: Dante Alighieri and Marcel Proust.

Is it a contradiction or a sign of nobility of spirit—the variousness of sentiments in these two creators of characters? The compassion Dante shows for his Francesca and Bertrand de Born is equal to Proust's compassion for Swann and Mme Sazerat. But the Italian poet demonstrates as much cruelty in his depiction of Filippo Argenti and Vanni Fucci as the French novelist does in his treatment of Morel and Albertine. In several of the Italian and French portraits there is a mixture, an alternating revelation of compassion and cruelty. I am thinking of Ulysses and Ugolino in *The Inferno*, and of Oriane de Guermantes and Charlus in Proust.

When puzzled by my own life, with its contradictory drives and dreams, with the thoughts that obsess me and that are so infrequently realized in actions, I turn gratefully to a canto of the *Commedia* or to a scene in *A la recherche* and read it out loud. And always the same lesson comes clear: to write about experience is to erect a larger context of experience. The man who writes is not the same as the man who experiences. If Dante is the pilgrim, then Alighieri is the poet. If Marcel is the small boy waiting at the top of the staircase for his mother's goodnight kiss, then Proust is the semi-invalid writing in bed in his cork-lined room.

Writing, like living, is a process of constant exploration and discovery. As I try to write each morning during the first hour of the day, I face my own unvarnished likeness. That is the moment when I feel I am setting the record straight. Later in the day, with occupations involving other people—friends, students, colleagues, tradesmen—I know that I will shift from part to part and do my best to avoid any repetition as I make those shifts. There will be moments of diffidence and uncertainty. At the end of the day I will try to return to a moment of self-regard, a recall of the first hour of my day, and that self-regard will strengthen me.

That steadying look at dawn which I often call to myself my *aubade*, and in which I can usually discern a curious mixture of snobbery and eros, comes soon after my night of dreams. As I try to come to terms with myself and my world, I am relocating my conscious self with respect to my dreams that have just ended. Living and dreaming are two modes of repetition. Both modes must be reestablished within the sacred.

During the course of the dreams I am fully aware of the animal buried in my being, of the sexual drive deepest within me, whereas during my conscious life throughout the day I can feel at the highest moments the awakening of myself toward aspiration. Thus dreaming and living are my eros and agape, the two ways, which, if they are prolonged, lead me to panic. I have known myself, at the end of a long dream, to think if not to say: "Pan is here!" And I have known myself to feel, at high noon, a touch of the sun.

When it is still night, at that hour of predawn, I have to lie prone, quietly, in order to recover from unconsciousness. When the sun is at the zenith of the sky, I have to walk, at least mentally, toward slopes alive with flowers and green grass, toward an enchanted place where the psyche of my being will meet with ecstasy. My dreams awaken in me a phenomenon I have never quite understood—a need, felt then when I am alone, to reach stability by means of belongingness and connections.

Guises and disguises: are these the realities that will emerge from my writing this new autobiography? I am not so much concerned with a search for meaning as for the experience of memory. I have already fixed in my mind most of the episodes to come that will make up this book. But I do not know how I am to write them or what I will say about them. Everything depends upon these words I am using now, upon human speech thanks to which we utter truth and falsehood, half-truths and truthful lies. Do words control everything: documents, poems, sermons, contracts, promises, lovemaking, medical reports, scenarios?

I have no answer to this question, only the will to write more words, which are old words I have already used. One of these words from time to time will be Ariadne's thread that will help me trace back a moment of the past and discover there a half-forgotten shape. At times it will be the Minotaur; at other times, an angel.

And once again, as I did at the beginning of these pages, I feel that I am Angelo on the stage in Vermont adding to his lines already quoted, the words that follow fast in his soliloquy:

> Heaven in my mouth
> As if I did but only chew his name.

Oh! the bemused vanity of human beings that will arise in bidden and unbidden memories!

From the past

Histrionics

As a boy I had to cross the town line from Brookline to Allston in order to see my first films, showing at the Allston Theater. At Saturday matinées I would see a short Chaplin film, a chapter from a Pearl White serial, and a feature film: a Western with Bill Hart, or an oriental fantasy with Sessue Hayakawa. Such extravagances became a weekly fare. Worlds of wonder for me, those films! I learned to keep the humdrum, unimaginative schoolwork in its place during five days of the week, but Saturday, for the walk to Allston, and Sunday, for reminiscences of Saturday's revelations, offered another life I discussed with no one, eager as I was to preserve within myself its mysteriousness.

Not until years later did my native Brookline allow a movie theater. Allston was normally off bounds for me, and therefore movies too, tainted as they must be, I thought, with some form of immorality not easy for me to define. Brookline, more puritanical, allowed no such indulgence in the viewing of adventure, violence, and lovemaking. So Allston, more decadent just two miles away, was the goal of my earliest liberation.

My grammar school years were more dominated by films than my high school years, during which I did not get to the movie theaters very often. Music, and especially opera (The San Carlo Company and the Chicago Opera Company turned up regularly in Boston) aroused excitement in me over performances on a stage. The exoticism of *Lucia di Lammermoor*, *Aïda*, and *Tosca* easily replaced Francis X. Bushman in *Ben Hur* and Buster Keaton. Then in my junior year of high school a good friend and I tried out for parts in the spring production of *Taming of the Shrew*. William Humboldt, a stocky German fellow and a senior, was a Latin enthusiast (I was a comparable French enthusiast) and helped me often in translating Cicero. He won the glamorous part of Petruchio and I won the totally minor role of Petruchio's servant with the gloomy-sounding name of Grumio.

My few minutes on the stage during the actual performances rushed by so fast that I was left hungry for more. The costume, the makeup and lights, the almost invisible public on the other side of the footlights, and my voice I could not recognize when I spoke my few lines —all of that seemed an experience my moviegoing days had prepared. I tried out for the two plays of my senior year, and was given only a small part in each. Quickly I learned the few scenes I was in, practiced them at home until I felt fully confident, and then was free to watch during rehearsals how the director put the play together for the performance. In my mind I acted the parts I watched being rehearsed. Thus I played all the parts and encouraged in myself innovations in movements on the stage and imaginative tricks with which to bring out this and that interpretation.

The two years of waiting for the chance to play a part that might give me a real sense of acting were rewarded in the spring of my freshman year at Harvard. The faculty club of Brookline High had decided to put on Shaw's play *Man of Destiny*, and extended an invitation to me to play young Bonaparte. I read the play avidly and accepted on the spot. This would give me the chance to know what the experience of acting really was.

My memory of the play is very vague, except for a scene or two of violence, scenes that excited me both sexually and psychically. The actions of those scenes, set, as I remember them, in an inn in Italy (young Bonaparte was conducting his Italian campaign) demanded that I dominate and tame a strong-willed girl. She wore a yellow dress that billowed like a sail as I chased her on the stage, grabbing her and whirling her about until I forced her to heed me and obey me. Was she a young teacher or a student like myself? I can't recall, but I can still see her swirling yellow skirt as I bent her to my will. And I can hear her voice shouting at me, denouncing me.

George Bernard Shaw, that wily old dramatist, provided me with an early victory over a female, provided me, in fact, with a tense, exciting relationship with a girl. On the stage I had a savage tongue. The text I followed and the part I played gave me the upper hand over my partner. In young Bonaparte I lived out whatever violence had been latent in my nature, and thereafter I could live beside women without attempting to dominate them or submit to them. A coward's stance? Perhaps! My reign of terror was over early, and it was only a performance.

From *Man of Destiny* I learned, what I already half knew, that acting can give me a total kind of enjoyment, and I also learned from that play that women are mythical creatures, like centaurs, who have to be bridled. During the hour-long performance on the stage I was sundered from myself. And after the last performance was over, I sat easy for a few days, glowing with a sense of accomplishment.

Today I see that event as the beginning of a drama that will last my entire life: the infatuation with acting as a profession. Had I chosen this course, I would have been free to roam the world like Ishmael, to play this character and that character on this stage and on that one. But I am a creature of habit, as regular as a monk. I too have my prime and compline. I forced that dream of a profession into a very subordinate place.

To play a character other than myself was to experience on the stage absolute power without the slightest remorse of conscience. In real life I would have been conscience-stricken. In growing up very little was ever said to me about the meaning of "character." I learned about it as I learned about sex and religion, by piecing together references from books. Character? If I learned my Latin conjugations and all about the ablative absolute, character would take care of itself.

During the remainder of my undergraduate years, I had to take a leave from acting because of the demands of my courses and a large amount of tutoring in French. But the need for it was there, and to placate the need each year I studied with a French actor, Monsieur Perrin, who directed French plays in and around Boston, especially at Harvard. An able teacher, a true man of the theater, he had me memorize scenes from Molière. Then when I began teaching at Harvard as a graduate student, Eliot House asked me to put on a French play. I chose Molière's *L'Amour Médecin* because of its farcical scenes and its Lully music. There was no stage in Eliot House. We used the dining room and devised as best we could a production that was well attended and warmly applauded. All the players spoke good French and seemed to enjoy acting in French before their American audience.

But from directing a play I derived far less pleasure than from acting. The director's responsibility for so many details and for the general effects a good production is supposed to produce—all of that weighed on me and worried me through rehearsals and performances. I decided that evening at Eliot House that I would rather play Horatio or a gravedigger than direct *Hamlet*.

Bennington College was first and foremost for me a world where the stage counted. On my arrival there, Francis Fergusson invited me to read one of the two speaking parts in a production of *The Eve of Saint Agnes* that he was directing. A girl student and I were seated at each end of the proscenium and recited the lines of the Keats poem. Each of us was responsible for half of the text. The action of the poem was danced on the stage. For my part, only the voice counted. I was more singer than actor as I mouthed those over-rich lines of Keats. I pretended to myself that I was the poet creating the lines and watching on the stage the coming to life of his fantasies.

This performance was my introduction to the Bennington College community, and thereafter I held an alliance with the stage. So far was I from appearing the heroic-looking guy or the lover that I accepted everything else: a drunken captain in Turgenev's play *Where It Is Thin, There It Breaks,* a husband harassed by his wife and mother-in-law in the medieval *Farce du cuvier.* These were typical roles, and I grew to enjoy the variety, the unpredictable invitation to be this or that, in French or English, as the case might be. My repertory, almost never repeated, grew steadily to include Oedipus in the third act of Cocteau's *La Machine infernale,* Kent in act 4 of *Lear,* Angelo in act 2 of *Measure for Measure,* the French ambassador, a singing part in *Of Thee I Sing,* Chrysale in *Les Femmes savantes,* Tartuffe, and finally Caesar in Shaw's *Caesar and Cleopatra.*

Caesar was my last role at Bennington. The year before, I had decided to do no more acting and to give full attention to whatever acting was required of a teacher in the classroom where he belonged. Then, a new drama teacher at the college asked me to take on the role. I declined at first, but as he argued with me, I began reviewing in my mind scenes I remembered from the film based on the Shaw play, with Claude Rains as Caesar. It had been an expertly acted part. The old desire to act grew in me. I accepted guiltily, sheepishly, as if I were resuming a vice.

Rehearsals had already begun when one day a new drama fellow arrived from New York. We all shook hands with him and welcomed him to Vermont. Because of his late arrival, he was given a small walk-on part. He took the script, moved off the stage to a corner in the theater and began work on his part. I could see in no time that he was authentic, the real actor. A conflict engaged me then: shouldn't I relinquish my role of Caesar to that young fellow whose name was Alan Arkin, and let teaching again take over my life? The bad part of me won over by telling me that Alan Arkin would have in his life many fine parts, and this Caesar was my last fling.

I enjoyed knowing Alan briefly at Bennington where, after *Caesar and Cleopatra*, we worked on a few scenes together in drama workshop. He left Vermont before I did, and a few years later, in Chicago, I attended a show at *Second City* and was delighted to watch him perform—admirably—in several of the skits. We spoke afterward and he remembered me. Soon after that his big chance came with the film *The Russians Are Coming, The Russians Are Coming*. I knew then that his future was assured and became one of his fans in film after film, notably *Catch 22* and *The Heart Is a Lonely Hunter*.

Alan Arkin was one of several drama students with whom I worked at Bennington, and who later became professional men in the theater. Larry Arrick, Barry Primus, Allen Leavit, and Chandler Cowles, one of the first producers of Gian-Carlo Menotti's operas and of the verse adaptation of *Billy Budd*. I cherish the memory of hard work in the theater done with those men in an atmosphere of dedication and enthusiasm.

Even in the earliest Bennington years I was struck by the theater's paradox: its need of living men and women to demonstrate its fictions. To reenact crimes they never committed, to struggle against obstacles invented by the mind of a poet, to speak language that was never spoken by real people, the theater demands of its players that they forget their own lives and personalities in order to put on the immortal cloak of an Orestes or a Medea, or the costume of some eternal type of clown or prostitute or miser.

The actor lives for the enchantment of metamorphosis. Movement of the human body is at the origins of the theater: a man dancing for his gods. All acting is exhibitionistic: the woman playing Phèdre, as well as boxers, gladiators, clowns.

The dance form tends to divest the theater of its intellectuality. But the theater was born out of dancing, which is, according to Valéry, "the pure act of metamorphosis." A drama secretly inhabits the ballet and imposes its form, its architecture, its limitations on the movement of the dance. Even in such ballets as those of *L'Amour Médecin* and *Le Bourgeois Gentilhomme*, the form does not exist separate from the text. Each time a group of dancers come upon the stage and make their circular walk preparatory to the real beginning of the ballet, we know that we are about to witness a work of organized perfection from which all chance has been removed. We watch the seeming frailty of each girl, and know that in reality she is a monster of strength and skill. A salamander, she lives in the two worlds of fire and air.

I remember my first visit, in the winter of 1938, when I was thirty, to Charles Dullin's theater, L'Atelier. Everything seemed diminutive or worn out: the shaded Place Dancourt in Montmartre where the theater was located and where Dullin had been presenting plays ever since 1921; the small auditorium; the rickety seats from which the paint was peeling off. But when the house lights were lowered and the curtain went up, a miracle took place. Never had I beheld such an impeccable troupe of actors. I tried to recall the few facts I knew of Dullin: his great poverty in Paris during his early years, his reciting of Villon and Corbière at the *Lapin agile* in Montmartre, his first real engagement at the Théâtre des Arts for the role of Smerdiakov in *Les Frères Karamazov*, directed by Copeau.

For ten or twelve years after the war Jean-Louis Barrault appeared in Paris, in his Théâtre Marigny as a kind of archangel, as Pan at the head of a group of actors. His temptation was poetry, a poetic stylization of every role he played. In his Hamlet we saw the mime, and in his literal characterization of a mime (in the film *Les Enfants du paradis*) we saw a man tormented by poetry and ideas.

The actor is the mask, the sacred magical instrument forged very early in the history of man to counteract the pain of living by transcending it.

Partage de midi

The title of this Claudel play represents an important episode in my life, centering about the première (*la générale*) of the play, which I had the good fortune to attend in Paris, on December 17, 1948. No single event in my life has ever brought together so many themes, so many connections, so many illuminations. So many strands in my life were caught up together as I watched the actors and listened to their voices and followed an admired text I knew intimately that I despaired of ever unweaving and explaining those strands.

In September 1948, thanks to a Guggenheim Fellowship and a leave of absence from the University of Chicago, I had settled into a most satisfactory hotel in Paris, Le Paris-Dinard, on the rue Cassette. Several months lay ahead of me to be used in writing a book on Mallarmé. I had met the biographer of Mallarmé, the celebrated physician Henri Mondor, who insisted that I pay him a visit every Tuesday evening through the winter, to report to him what I had discovered about Mallarmé during the week.

Work went smoothly during September and October. Then to have a little respite, I went to Royaumont for a weekend in November with my friend Alice Coléno, a professor at the Lycée Victor Duruy. At that time Royaumont was a *centre culturel international*. There must have been a conference going on that weekend because there were many guests. The large refectory was well filled at each meal. But I no longer remember the subject of the meetings, nor have I any memory of attending them. Alice and I were entranced by the beauty of the ruins of the Cistercian abbey founded in 1228 by Saint Louis. Their beauty, as well as the beauty of the trees and shrubbery and lawns, were enhanced by an ice storm on Friday night. The sun came out on Saturday and the entire landscape, the ruins of the abbey and the newer building where the guests were lodged, glittered with the morning light on the ice covering every twig and every stone.

Almost through a sense of duty we decided to pay our respects to the director of Royaumont. I had come across his name in a bibliography of Ronsard: Gilbert Gadoffre. The hour we spent with him was filled with a stimulating literary discussion. In order to initiate our conversation, I confessed my inability to appreciate fully the art of Ronsard. M. Gadoffre, without the slightest trace of pedantry, told us what he believed to be the greatness of Ronsard.

This was the beginning of a friendship that has continued through the years. I have met him on only one other occasion—in San Francisco —where I was speaking at the Modern Language Association meeting and when he was a professor at Berkeley. I was seated in the audience, as Jacques Hardré was introducing me. Gilbert Gadoffre sat down beside me and gave me news of himself that he thought would interest me. He was writing his "thèse pour le doctorat" on *Claudel et la Chine*. That thesis was completed and published by Gallimard as *Claudel et l'univers chinois* in 1968. That was a violent year for the university world in France. During the defense of the thesis at the University of Paris the students, largely motivated by a dislike for Claudel and what he represented to them, created an uproar outside the building. The clamor was such that the proceedings of the ceremony inside became inaudible, and Etiemble, one of the jurors, a man fully capable of violence himself, rushed outside to denounce the offenders.

"Tas de voyous," he shouted at the jeering crowd, "you are impeding the functioning of a ceremony that marks the culmination of twenty years work by a first-rate scholar and who deserves the recognition the university intends to give him. Like you, I have no sympathy for Paul Claudel, but I respect the scholarly work carried out by Gilbert Gadoffre. I ask you to stop this rumpus and go away."

The *soutenance* was continued and the scholar received his degree. During the last years of his teaching career, he was a professor of French literature at the University of Manchester. In the seventies one of my Duke students, Bob McCutcheon, spent a year at Manchester where, on my recommendation, he took Gadoffre's course, and where the French professor showed him courtesy and hospitality as well as expert instruction. Through the mediation of McCutcheon, Gadoffre and I sent messages to one another. He has continued in summers at Loches to direct international literary colloquia.

The 1948 November weekend at Royaumont (situated not far from Paris, in the department of the Val D'Oise, north of Saint Denis and south of Chantilly) was a stimulating interlude in my labors on Mallarmé. I followed with great interest in the newspapers and weeklies the many articles that began appearing in December on Barrault's announced production of Claudel's play *Partage de midi* whose première was scheduled for the 17th of the month. The first-night audience was by invitation only. It would be, as it was traditionally, a gala social event. I had planned to purchase a ticket for later during the play's run.

The interviews with Barrault or Claudel during that month of December emphasized in particular two facts of which I was already aware: Barrault's attempts, several times repeated, to secure permission from Claudel to produce the play, and Claudel's hesitations because the play was based on a personal event in his own life, a love that had taken place before his marriage. Heretofore the text of the play had not been generally available. During the early forties when I was teaching at Yale, Henri Peyre lent me his mimeographed copy of the first version of the play (1905), and Mabel Lafarge, who had once received Claudel in her home outside of New Haven, had told me of Claudel's account of this early love in his life. As they walked one day through her garden, the poet spoke with unusual candor about this important episode which he claimed to be the genesis of *Partage de midi*

In my mail one day in December, close to the opening date of the play, I received an invitation from Henri Gouin, owner of Royaumont, to a soirée in his Paris home to which all those who had attended the November conference were invited. It was a large gathering where I recognized almost no one, but M. Gouin and M. Gadoffre did their best to introduce the guests to one another. I had about decided to leave when I found myself talking to an attractive young woman. When she learned I was a professor at Chicago, she spoke warmly of a friend of hers in Chicago, a poet, teacher, and editor.

Then simultaneously, each of us recognized the other. Her friend was my friend too, Henry Rago, editor for several years of *Poetry*. He had spoken of me to her because of my profession of French teacher and my particular interest in Claudel. And Henry had spoken to me of Renée Nantet, one of the daughters of Claudel and godmother of Henry's first daughter. The conversation between us picked up, joyously, thanks to the many discoveries we made about one another. At the end of the evening, as a parting question, Mme Nantet asked: "You will be there, won't you, on Friday night at the *générale*?"

I shook my head: "Alas, no, that night is by invitation only, as you know. I plan to go later to one of the regular performances."

The next morning in my hotel room, my telephone rang early. It was Mme Nantet who quite simply said: "We have one ticket left for *Partage de midi*. It is yours if you meet me in the foyer of the Marigny. You will be sitting between me and my brother Henri."

My lifelong interest in the theater and in France seemed to culminate that evening, memorable on many counts and which had come about through so many seemingly chance encounters: the first lecture in French I heard at thirteen in the Copley Plaza in Boston when Paul Claudel spoke to the Alliance Francaise; my study of Claudel at Harvard under André Morize; my early study of *Partage de midi* at Yale thanks to Henri Peyre's copy of the play; Mabel Lafarge's account of Claudel's visit and his confession about the play's origin; my meeting with Henry Rago in Chicago and our friendship; my decision, urged by Alice Coléno, to spend a weekend at Royaumont; Gilbert Gadoffre's interest in Claudel, and Henri Gouin's invitation to his soirée and the invitation he must have extended to Renée Nantet; the chance moment when I began talking with her at M. Gouin's house; her kind offer of a ticket for the *générale*. Behind that long series of events and chances was the Guggenheim Fellowship, the project on Mallarmé, and my presence in Paris for the year 1948–49.

I arrived early that evening at the Marigny, but Mme Nantet was already there in the foyer greeting friends and celebrities. In the most gracious way, she kept me by her side, introducing me to a friend when she felt it would be appropriate. Finally it was time to go to our seats. I followed her to the door leading to the orchestra center. We were delayed momentarily by the crowd, and she turned her head to speak to me behind her as we waited: "Do you know that this play is about an event in my father's life, about his meeting a young woman on a boat?"

Slightly embarrassed that she raised this question at this particular moment, I replied that I did indeed know about the background of the play. Then Mme Nantet uttered a sentence that was unexpected: "Cette femme est ici ce soir, et ma mère est furieuse" ("That woman is here tonight and my mother is furious").

I pondered that bit of knowledge as we made our way down the center aisle to the third row. We were on the right side. My seat was the sixth from the aisle. A man was in seat seven on my right, Henri Claudel, to whom Mme Nantet introduced me as she sat down on my left. The three of us seemed equally eager to survey the crowded theater. Two young boys occupied the first two seats in our row, grandsons of Claudel. The grandfather himself, the real center of tonight's spectacle, sat in front of them, in the aisle seat of the second row. I had not seen Claudel since I had heard him in Boston when I was thirteen. His profile was clear, but never through the evening did he turn his face to the row behind him. He moved once between acts 1 and 2, when he slowly made his way to the first box on the right of the stage. Before the first curtain Mme Nantet had pointed out to me the occupants of the first boxes: a drama in itself in contrasts. The queen mother of the Belgians sat in the first box, and in the second the black singer Josephine Baker, clothed in a shining white dress, and waving to friends in the audience. Henri Claudel, at my side, was attracted to her and nudged me two or three times during the performance when his concentration on his father's play faltered, and his gaze was fixed on the beauty in box two: "Dites donc, elle est bien, Josephine Baker!"

During the first intermission the singer was admired at a distance, whereas a line of men, headed by Paul Claudel himself, made their way to the box of the queen mother of the Belgians, bowed before her, kissed her hand, and left, each making way for the man behind him. I recognized in the line waiting to pay homage, François Mauriac and Jules Romains. Traditionally the forty members of the Académie Française were invited to such a *générale* as this. Mme Nantet told me that such an audience was feared by the players. If they were the stars on the stage, the orchestra and the boxes were studded with other stars accustomed to places of eminence. This was the case, for their coughing and whispering grew in intensity through the three acts. The nervousness of Edwige Feuillère, playing Ysé, and of Barrault, playing Mésa, was evident to me at the beginning of the play. Feuillère's hand was shaking visibly as she took hold of the railing on the ship's deck, and Barrault's voice was not clear in his first speeches.

Edwige Feuillère's appearance, after the first exchange of words between Amalric (played by Pierre Brasseur) and Mésa, was spectacular in her facial beauty and in the poise of her body. I remembered at that moment an interview Claudel had given a journalist in which he spoke of coming to one of the early rehearsals before he had met Feuillère. When she appeared on the stage in the scene that was being rehearsed, he was momentarily overcome by the resemblance she bore to the Polish woman the poet had met on the deck of the *Ernest Simmons* in 1900.

This meeting between the poet and the woman came at a moment in Claudel's life which he describes both in the final passage of the ode, *Les Muses*, and in *Partage de midi*. The writing of the work was indeed the exteriorization of a personal drama.

When, in 1948, almost half a century after the event itself and the writing of the first version of *Partage de midi*, Claudel acceded to the request of Barrault and began work on a new version of the play for the Marigny production. During the months of revision and early rehearsals, *Partage de midi* grew into a new work for Claudel. The long passage of time had resolved the initial dilemma in his life. The rewriting of the play made it, once again, into a work of importance for him. Barrault's understanding of the text and the constant consultations with him on problems of mise-en-scène helped the poet to complete the acting version of the play.

Actually two new versions were written. The first, for Barrault, was used by him in the 1948 production. The second, completed when rehearsals had begun, is a further modification, especially of act 3, and is the text which Claudel looked upon as definitive. It was this text I translated in 1960 for Henry Regnery. Barrault was reluctant in 1948 to incorporate at the last minute the newer changes, and Claudel did not insist.

Many matters—linguistic, literary, histrionic, autobiographical—went through my mind that extraordinary evening at the Marigny as I watched the performance. The general meaning of *Partage de midi* is that of a separation or a turning point. When, in 1960, I was working on my translation of the play, I wished it had been possible to keep the French title in the English translation. "Divide of Noon" occurred to me first as a possibility, but it was too peaceful for the dramatic connotation of *Partage de midi*. This aspect of the title is perhaps carried over into *Break of Noon*, which I finally chose. "Transfiguration of Noon" would be a fuller translation, but I preferred the short simple word *break* to the long Latin vocable.

As I watched that initial performance, I somehow felt the play would become for me a center of study at some future time. The play is about the meaning of love, and especially about the role of woman in the experience of love. Ysé is not happiness for Mésa, but she is there in his life in the place of happiness. Their long scene in the second act is a love duet reminiscent of the love duet in the second act of *Tristan*. The woman becomes in this scene the means by which man will understand the concept of paradise.

Claudel has often said, with the seeming arbitrariness and rigor for which he has been castigated, that only the Christian knows the full experience of desire. In such a statement, he implies that the Christian, when he is fully aware of the metaphysics of his faith, knows in the experience of desire what he really desires. For such a man, what is often called human tragedy can never be thus limited. It inevitably moves into the dimensions of a cosmic tragedy where centuries form the setting and all of humanity the actors.

Balandraou

By the summer of 1936 when I made my fifth visit to France, I knew, largely because of my dissertation on Ernest Psichari, several French people in Paris who had become friends and whom I was anxious to see again and restore with them the habit of frequent visits in their homes or in cafés or restaurants. The first days were too filled with such visits, and I had little time for work. I foresaw an entire summer given over to what would have been for me an exceptional life of talking and café sitting and endless walks in Paris. I feared most of all that I would end by performing perfunctorily in terms of friendship.

So, one morning I went to the Bureau de tourisme at the Gare Montparnasse, approached a man behind a long desk, and asked him to suggest some quiet, out-of-the-way place in a province where I might live peacefully for two weeks. It was a slack moment at the bureau, and he talked haphazardly about the characteristics of a few provinces. They were too near Paris. I wanted to get as far away as possible, and forced the man into suggesting a place which I had wanted an excuse to see: the Pyrenees. This desire had been in me ever since reading *La Chanson de Roland* and learning of Roncevaux. "Which do you wish," he asked, "Les Basses Pyrénées or Les Hautes Pyrénées?" I replied, "Les Hautes Pyrénées." Whereupon, with the utmost assurance, he proposed that I go to Argelès-Gazost and underlined in the pamphlet in the list of pensions, La Pension Balandraou, where he himself had once stayed.

I had never heard the name of Argelès-Gazost before, but it struck me as being the most resonant of all those recited by the tourist agent. When, in my pedantic manner, I asked him the meaning of "Balandraou," he shrugged his shoulder and said, "Ask when you get there. I never thought of asking."

By this time I was intrigued by the pure chance of the enterprise. On each occasion when I had allowed myself to be guided by whim or by some unpremeditated project, enlightenment had come to me. Each activity in my life had been so painstakingly planned that a spontaneous free choice, like this decision to go to Argelès, was comparable to revolution. I accepted this "chance," to go to a place where I knew no one, and encounter—what I would encounter.

During the night train ride, I watched in myself—it was a sleepless night—a new kind of excitement focusing my perceptions and drawing me outward to a newness of scenes and people.

I arrived at Argelès early in the morning, checked my bags at the station, and started out on foot to find the Pension Balandraou. That meant crossing the small town. Everyone I asked knew where it was and kept pointing ahead, always in the same direction. The street leading off from the station was straight and lined with evenly shaped trees. It resembled every other station street I had seen in small French cities. Then, a few narrow, curving streets, lined by the high walls of houses, led me to the square from which I had my first glimpse of the valley. From the terrace of the Centre Touristique the view of the huge valley and the mountains against the sky was unexpected and boundless. Even before more modest scenes of nature I had felt uneasiness, and now I found myself before a view of exceptional grandeur and proportions. I turned back into the square, passed by shop windows, and lost myself in the open market spread out around the church.

From there I kept on the back road that led from the church through the rest of the town. Overhead I was becoming more and more conscious of the glowing sky suffused with a sharp whiteness. During this first crossing of Argelès, I kept saying over and over to myself the name of Balandraou, first in order not to forget it, and then because I had become hypnotized by it and was unable not to say it.

The house itself was disappointing. It was a tall, narrow building, completely unattractive. On the other hand, Mlle Chomette, who ran the pension, was a very attractive young woman, with abundant golden hair and a deeply tanned complexion. Business about my room was quickly settled and then she told me about winter skiing in Argelès and mountain climbing. When I filled out the slip for foreigners, she showed surprise at my not being a Frenchman and spoke a sentence I have always cherished: "Mais vous avez une tête française."

My speech was fairly well disguised in accent and tone. By that time, in my study of French, what I said sounded like French, but occasions still arose, trivial occasions usually, when I doubted that I knew what a born Frenchman would have said. I was never troubled over talking about my reaction to a book, but when it was a question of reacting to food and wine, for example, my references and judgments were all insecure.

Balandraou, Mlle Chomette told me, was the old name of this part of Argelès, or rather of this section of the mountainside. Farther up, if I continued on the road that had led me to the pension, I would come to an open flank of the mountain where a large rock jutted out. She believed that the rock, a kind of dolmen, was originally called Balandraou. I seized the suggestion of climbing higher. It was midmorning by then, and it would be some time before my bags would arrive from the station. So I set out again, on the same road, which, just beyond the pension, became a rocky path and turned upward.

At the first bend I almost collided with a donkey that was coming down laden with two piles of brushwood. The animal forced me off the path into the bushes. The woman who tagged on after the donkey spoke to me in a shrill voice. Her accent was strange and a few seconds elapsed before I realized what she said: "Attention aux vipères qui sont dans les broussailles." This warning of vipers was sufficient to make me leap back into the center of the path and wonder whether it was worth while risking my life to reach the dolmen Balandraou.

The path continued to narrow as I mounted. Abruptly, several yards beyond my encounter with the donkey, the high hedge on my right disappeared. Spread out in a semicircle lay a fantastic woodland scene, so perfect that it seemed unreal. Large chestnut trees surrounded the semicircle and formed a dense background for the green grass of the open space. A brook crossed the entire expanse.

I had been in the grove a few minutes before I realized there were some moving figures at the farther end. I came out from behind a tree where I could see more clearly, and there on a little knoll, quite at the extremity, were two women gaily clad in bright summer clothes. They made a strong contrast of color against the green of the setting: their dresses, their large hats, wraps, and blankets on which they sat, were all colorful. As soon as I looked at them, they resumed their work with a studied attentiveness. One was painting what I imagined to be a watercolor, and the other was reading a book.

Two opened parasols, adding further color, were beside them. The scene was too perfect. From my distance I looked at it fixedly as if it were a painting in the great French tradition of Renoir or Courbet.

They had brought with them the attributes of civilization: large flowered hats, a paintbox, a book of verse, and had arranged them decorously in the center of a rather wild corner of a forest. There they were: two women of France disciplining a chestnut grove on the mountainside of one of the Pyrenees!

I must have appeared insolent in my gaze on the living picture I was confusing with a painting. The attentiveness of the two women to their sketching and reading finally turned into irritation. From under the broad brims of their hats they darted rapid glances in my direction. At the moment when I realized I had looked too long and too deliberately, they began gathering up their belongings with excitedly nervous gestures. They communicated quite easily to me across the grove that I had been importunate and that my staring had dislodged them. As they began moving, I moved too. Our relationship became more complex. As I strolled up the brook on one side, they came down on the other side, and kept making little reconnoitering sallies out from the brook. Their furtive glances at me and their half-submerged sentences made me feel exactly what they wanted me to feel: that I was an intruder, uninvited to the sacredness of this forest grove, and that perhaps I was even to be feared, a dangerous intruder with evil intent. This latter they did not literally believe, but pretended to, in order to enliven the scene.

I marveled at the moving array of color and brightness they carried with them. The shorter woman, who was the painter, came first. Her speech was high-pitched and fiery. The taller one, who was the reader, appeared more timid. Her hat completely covered her face, and the brim flapped up and down as she walked. She even wore large, dark glasses for further concealment, I suppose, although the light in the grove was subdued and filtered. We enacted a kind of sparring scene. I knew they would not settle down in any spot until I had left. How I wanted to speak to them and make peace! Then, just when I had decided to recognize my defeat and leave the grove, they made a grandiose exit, carrying their large flowered bags and opened parasols.

I left, too, and went a bit farther up the mountainside. The rock Balandraou, which I came upon before I expected to, was not impressive in size, but it did detach itself from the earth in a spectacular way. It pointed out over the valley that spread for miles before turning up to very high peaks at both ends.

Mlle Chomette met me at the door of the pension to show me my place for lunch. The rooms on the ground floor were used as dining rooms. The room on the left of the entrance was humming with the voices of the pensionnaires, but the room on the right, into which I was ushered, was quiet and dark. I was seated at a small corner table, and there opposite me, just a few feet away, eating lunch and speaking in subdued tones, were the two women of the chestnut grove, the only other pensionnaires in the room.

Again we were caught together, this time in a dining room. But this time they showed no irritation and improvised no fear. They did refuse, however, to look in my direction, and I wondered again all through the meal how I could break into conversation with them. It became more difficult as time went by and the reserved silence grew between us.

When they ordered camomile tea at the end of their lunch, I almost did likewise in order to make that the excuse. But I really wanted coffee. Finally, in desperation, I flung out a sentence involving a new word I had learned since coming to Argelès. It was the word *chamois*, a kind of antelope in the Pyrenees I had seen on a postcard in the railroad station. The word had remained in my mind all morning and when I said it for the first time, asking the ladies whether the animals were ever seen in Argelès, it came out ludicrously changed into *chaminois*.

If I had pronounced the word correctly, they might have answered me bluntly, and the silence would have been resumed, but my comic error induced a smile on the face of the grave, tall woman and a quickly repressed chuckle in the shorter woman. But they both turned toward me and while one corrected my mistake, the other explained the rarity of the animal in this part of the Pyrenees. The cold reserve was broken and I leaped into the conversation as eagerly as a *chamois* might leap from a dark, lonely crag to a higher, more friendly peak.

The next morning, at the same time, I returned to the *châtaig-neraie*: that was the name used by my pension friends in referring to the magic grove. But there was no sight of them. And quite rightly, I reasoned with myself. Friendly conversation in a pension dining room was no proof that the ladies would be friendly in a supernatural *châtaigneraie*.

I made the same circuit as the day before. Toward the end of my walk I suddenly knew I was being watched. At the entrance to the grove stood the diminutive figure of a young boy. He was watching me in deep seriousness as if I actually were performing a scene. I smiled and waved, in order to assure him I was an ordinary person, just a casual tourist. He smiled back and began walking slowly and cautiously toward me. He was very small and completely covered by a black *sarrau*, a kind of apron dress that closed in the back and which I had noticed most of the children wore.

The little fellow seemed more Italian than French. He had large black eyes and an olive skin. As we walked back together into the *châtaigneraie*, I asked him his name. "Dominique," he replied. It happened to be the fourth of August and, since I had attended mass that morning, I knew it was the feast of St. Dominic. Everything that happened there had some strange coincidence connected with it.

I asked Dominique if he knew about the day, and he said in solemn fashion that, yes, it was his *fête* and there would be due recognition of it that evening at home. I was struck by the lack of jubilation and childishness in Dominique. Perhaps he was older than he seemed, or perhaps I had forgotten how wise and grave very young children can be. I asked him why he came to the *châtaigneraie*, and he explained that he waited here for his mother either to come up from the village with their donkey or to come down from the mountain when the donkey's back would be well laden with brushwood. I could see no resemblance between the woman who the day before had laconically warned me about vipers and this cherub looking Dominique.

A few days went by without my being able to extract from the two ladies any more friendly signs than engaging bits of conversation in the dining room. If other tables were occupied, I would have to wait until camomile tea time before the room was left to the three of us when we would talk about the valley of Argelès and literature. Then one day they invited me to go on an afternoon expedition with them to a chapel that overlooked the valley at several kilometers from Argelès. From then on, during the rest of my stay, I became an assiduous, enthusiastic companion of Mlle Yvonne Omnès, director of the *école normale* at La Roche-sur-Yon, and of Mlle Hélène Collot, director of the *lycée de jeunes filles* at La Roche-sur-Yon. They taught me how to look at the valley from all angles, how to watch the light change, and to single out at a great distance the moving forms of sheep and cows.

On the quiet afternoons at Balandraou, they taught me the names of flowers, or rather taught me what real flowers corresponded to the words I had learned in reading French books: *scabieuse, genêt, bruyère, marjolaine, oeillet, thym*. I learned that the swift-flowing mountain stream where I went swimming was a *gave*, and that the rich, yellow cake at pastry shops, a *spécialité du pays,* was called *pastis*.

Returning from the late afternoon walks, we often stopped at a terrace of a small hotel in the village, from which we had a broad view of the valley, to refresh ourselves with hot chocolate and *tartines*. There, one day when the valley was bathed in a thin mist that gave it a marine aspect, Yvonne Omnès, whom I had first seen reading a book, began reciting Valéry's *Cimetière marin*. Her voice was low, but resonant and rich. Each word took on for me a new value in pure sound. *Palme* also she recited with equal fervor.

A new pattern of life was created for me by my two friends of the Pyrenees whom I had stalked first in a chestnut grove. The three of us were exiles: they from their *lycée* and *école normale* in La Roche-sur-Yon, and I from across the Atlantic. The exhilarating change we discovered in the valley of Argelès-Gazost came from the attentiveness we bestowed on the sunlight, on the tiny romanesque chapels, on the modest flowers, on the legends of the countryside, and on the children in their black *sarraus*.

From the first word I said to my new friends, from my miserable mangling of *chamois*, they knew how untrained I was in matters of the outside world, and they brought me to it, with the patience of charming pedagogues, by relating it always to books, by reciting Valéry when my eyes were tired from looking and trying to distinguish, by stimulating me in a more familiar way with their appreciation of the French writers by whom I had lived. They illuminated for me, during my major adventure of chance and coincidence, the great French ideal which combines exercise of thought with a love of nature.

Partly to relieve my new friends of my presence, thus interrupting the steady routine we had reached, and partly to satisfy my curiosity, I decided to go on two day-trips to visit places not far from Argelès and which were easily accessible. Both, more famous than Argelès, had brought distinction to the Pyrenees.

Lourdes was the first of these trips. Ever since coming to les Hautes Pyrénées, I had wanted to visit the shrine and dreaded going. I had read about it first in Zola and more recently in tracts that had provided statistics on the recorded miracles. I was prepared for the rampant commercialism I would find in the streets and shops, and not too well prepared for the spectacle of sickness and hope that spread out on a huge square under a gray sky at four o'clock in the afternoon when a priest, holding a monstrance containing the sacrament, blessed each sick person as he passed by the cots—hundreds of them. Lourdes: a city devoted to pain—and hope for the recovery from pain.

I boarded the train in Argelès, in the early morning. The ride was brief and noisy, a rhythmic clangor of wood on metal. The cavernous railway station at Lourdes seemed to me dominated by a huge clock. It was an appropriate introduction to my day's visit because there I had the first sight of the handicapped and the sick pilgrims. Some had just arrived and others were waiting to be put back on trains to return home. Small groups of them were singing the *Ave Maria*, a prayer I was to hear throughout the day and into the night until I, too, took my train back to Argelès.

The town, as I walked away from the station, seemed wrapped in heavy clouds. Melancholy waters of the mountains oozed through the walls that lined the sidewalks. Even here in this place of prayer, shopkeepers were pushing up the metal covers that had guarded their windows through the night, and opening their doors in order to begin selling religious frippery. From time to time the sun would break through the clouds as I passed by the church and the grotto. Although it was still early, a line of the sick was already forming at the entrance to the pool. A little girl whose body was badly deformed was held by her mother. As I went by, she waved at me and dropped the rosary her hand had been clutching.

The air was warm and motionless. There were signs of suffering all about me, and signs of hope too. A world in itself, this Lourdes, where peasants and people of great wealth gathered, each suffering differently from all the others. No one wanted to be pitied. Their concentration was not on people around them but on the invisible presence of the Blessed Virgin, who was going to intercede for them.

Even early in the day—and the sentiment grew in me throughout the day—I felt guilt over being a tourist in such a place as Lourdes, a scrutinizer. I almost envied the sick because they were here with a purpose, and I certainly envied the helpers of the sick: the boy scouts and the nuns. I felt amorphous and globular on a strange planet where cancer reigned and where prayer had become an addiction.

During the day I spent at Lourdes the sky never quite declared itself as blue. It was a small mountain city in a mist and wrapped in humid clouds. My eyes were on the sick and the maimed as I watched them being moved here and there. Their thoughts were on the Healer as they prayed to his Mother. My own thoughts kept changing as I watched one heartbreaking scene after another. I wondered what it is like to live in suffering like a salamander in the flames. And then I would think of the dead I had once known who, being substanceless, needed my thoughts. Above all, I was conscious of a bittersweet sense of time passing. It was not hard for me to take the night train back to Argelès-Gazost.

The second of my two escapes from the Pension Balandraou was a bus trip to Roncevaux, five miles into Spain. This time the sun was out all day. When we reached our destination, close by the abbey church, the real center of the Roland legend, the sun almost blinded me as I got off the bus. It seemed to fill the entire sky in an attempt to blot out its blue with sheer gold. The grass was still green and lush. The hot, sultry air smelled of hay. Craggy peaks were everywhere looming above melancholy forests where Roland died fighting the Saracens.

Here I was on the site of the battle fought in 778 where the army of the young King Charles—Charlemagne—was attacked—not by Saracens as claimed in the eleventh-century poem—but by Basques. Spontaneous memories of a lost happiness swept over me. I was back in an old classroom in Sever Hall in Cambridge where J. D. M. Ford endlessly discussed the changes that had taken place between the historical battle and the epic poem of *La Chanson de Roland*. The only other topics he discussed were philology and morphology—the changes in sound and form of Old French words. If we wanted to enjoy the poem as a literary work, that was up to us in the class. Professor Ford did not concern himself with such trifling matters.

I remembered best the middle section of the poem, the battle itself —colossal in its fierceness where all the fighters were strong and all the horses magnificent. Not until I taught passages from the poem, in the survey course on French literature I have given countless times, have I enjoyed the poem as a poem. It is always, in such a course for college freshmen, the first text, read in part and discussed briefly. What does a poet—unknown in the case of the *Roland*—do when he transposes history into an epic? How does Roland's devotion to Charlemagne illustrate feudalism? What is that sentiment of *gloire* that keeps Roland from blowing his horn, his *olifant*, until he knows that the battle is lost? Was the poem composed to be recited and sung at stopping places for pilgrims on their way to Saint James of Compostella: Blaye, Bordeaux, Roncevaux, Pampelune? What theory concerning the origins of the *chansons de geste* was now in favor? Pamphilet or Gaston Paris? Bédier or Rayna?

These were only a few of the questions my mind resuscitated as we walked through the church, guided by and lectured to by a most amiable and intelligent priest. I asked him a few simple questions about ornaments in the church and even about the poem. He was pleased to answer. An ideal guard and guide who began reciting in modernized French a few of the lines:

Roland est preux, Olivier est sage

. . . .

Préserve mon âme de tous périls

. . . .

Gabriel et Michel portent l'âme du comte au paradis

As we came out from the semidark and cool of the church, the priest continued to speak about the landscape. The sun, still shining powerfully, had burnished the scene until it looked like a paradise out of some medieval book of hours. I walked farther on, in order to escape the sun, toward a few luxuriantly leafy trees. Under them the sky paled to a lightless hazy white. A pure clarity entered my head and then flowed through me in a cleansing stream. I thought of paladins and the mystical aspect of feudalism. I thought of the power of the medieval Church when it founded sanctuaries containing relics. I thought of the most enduring of the French epics whose central action had unfolded here on this spot where I stood, and I thought especially of how terribly complete death is, how strangely clean.

Before the afternoon visit was over, I went back into the church, alone, where this time the air was too thick and breathless, smelling of dust. I sat in a corner and was glad that the walls of the church cut me off from the awesome view of the Pyrenees and the expanse of land where Roland and Olivier and Archbishop Turpin had once fought the Saracens. I was glad that the bus would soon be heading back to Argelès and the Pension Balandraou.

On my last day I presented my two friends with a mysterious sonnet I had written about them in celebration of the *châtaigneraie*. The title was "HYCO" which for some time they did not realize was the intertwining of the initials of their two names: Hélène Collot and Yvonne Omnès. The next year they wrote me about building a villa on the flank of the mountain not far from Balandraou, where they planned to spend the rest of their lives.

The war years intervened before I was able to return to Argelès. Between the end of the war and 1948 when I returned to France for the first time since 1939, we resumed correspondence. They wrote sparingly of the trials during the Occupation, and stressed their good fortune at having the villa overlooking the valley they loved. Yvonne wrote the letters. She was the more literary of the two, a French teacher before she became Mlle la directrice, whereas Hélène had taught science.

The exchange of letters strengthened our friendship. They seemed eager to know about the teaching I was doing at Chicago and my attempt to write a book on surrealism. And for my part I enjoyed learning about the villa and the resumption of a more normal life in France after the war years. They were insisting that on my return to Argelès, which I planned for the summer of 1948, I stay with them. They had designed a guest room and bath on the first floor where I would have isolation and quiet for work. During our last exchange of notes from Paris, we chose a specific date for my arrival and Yvonne asked for the exact time of the train arrival. They would meet me at the station and the three of us would walk to the villa which might be difficult for me to find alone.

Ten years had gone by since our fortuitous meeting in the chestnut grove. Physically they had changed very little. Hélène, always more effusive than Yvonne, greeted me warmly and embraced me as if I were a prodigal son. Yvonne, a familiar solemn expression on her face, embraced me with more reserve but was obviously pleased I had returned. After a few minutes of talk in the station, I felt there had been no interruption in our conversations of ten years earlier. Since I was to be their house guest for a week, their plans for taking care of me had been worked out in detail—even to the hiring of a young fellow with a cart and donkey standing outside the station to carry my bags up to the house.

They led the way. There was little change in the town. The parasols they carried had the same bright colors of those I had seen the morning of my first arrival in Argelès. Soon we took a path that was new to me. It mounted gradually between rows of houses. At a sudden turn my friends stopped and I too. There ahead of us at some distance, and high up on the side of the mountain, was a large white house with a veranda running the full length of the façade. I guessed instantly it was theirs even before I saw its name in gold letters: HYCO. The sonnet title welcomed me back to the Pyrenees and to my friends who through a long war had not forgotten their intruder friend.

That week at Hyco was different from the weeks spent at the Pension Balandraou. We were ten years older and enjoyed the comfort and spaciousness of the villa itself, and the veranda from which there was a magnificent view of the valley. We talked of the old memories of our explorations: Balandraou, the tiny chapels scattered through the valley, the hot chocolate drunk on the way back to the pension and Yvonne's reciting *Le cimetière marin*, the habitual camomile after lunch.

My room was off the veranda. When that first night Hélène and Yvonne retired to their apartment on the second floor—it was a combined living room-bedroom-study that occupied the entire floor—I turned my lights out and walked on the veranda facing the darkness of the valley. Below me was the town of Argelès where some scattered lights were still on, and beyond that a hollow, silent expanse of space still visible against the night sky. I left open the French doors of my room to let in the cool of the night, full of smells which the hot sun had elicited from the leafy slopes of the Pyrenees surrounding Argelès.

Hyco seemed to me a house of contentment. Then, as the days and nights of my week passed, I knew that it was more than that. The two lives of my friends were so joined, so mingled, one so complementary of the other, that I at last realized it was a house of love. No direct allusion was ever made to the reality of that love, but I learned soon through our conversations that the house had been built as a *barrage*, a refuge against the world's hostility. Brief references and innuendoes had convinced me that their high roles of *directrices* had aroused feelings of envy. Envy easily turns into enmity. Such a word as *ostracism* had not been used but it was implied. Their relationship had been suspect, not on the part of their students who worshiped them, but on the part of teachers, administrators, townspeople, and their own families.

Retirement was synonymous with Hyco. I felt proud they had accepted me into their life of greater freedom and happiness. The hours we spent together, the meals we ate together, and the *tisanes* we drank together on the terrace after the meals were hours of an intense friendship. The teacher's vocation and the teacher's life were permanent topics in our conversations. At that time I could not have realized how much I was to be influenced in later years by their philosophy of education, by the example they gave me of a lived humanism.

Two or three years went by after that visit to Argelès, when, at Bennington where I was then teaching, I received Yvonne's letter telling me of Hélène's sudden death. It was a brief, almost starkly written letter, giving me mainly the medical facts concerning the heart attack that had taken her friend's life. She announced another letter to come that would speak of her own plans. My fears grew not because of the grief Yvonne must be experiencing but fear of what the "plans" would be. With the second letter my fears were justified.

Between the lines, Yvonne was saying to me: "You lived here once, you saw how we lived for one another, with one another, and you must know how impossible it is for me to face life alone."

The immediate words of the letter were practical. She was sorting out papers and objects, and announced she was sending me all the letters I had written to them and the notebooks containing her poems and other literary efforts. These were for safekeeping in my files, *en dépôt chez vous.* At the end of the letter were the ominous words, "You will hear a bit later from the housekeeper (*notre femme de ménage.*)"

I wrote three or four letters, one after the other, pleading with her not to carry out her plan. She ignored the letters, as I knew she would. A long month went by before the letter came from Madame R. who briefly told me how Yvonne had taken her life by swallowing a large amount of gardenol on a Saturday after the mailman had passed, so that no one would try to enter the house until Monday. She was dying on that Monday. It was too late to prevent her death. She had carefully made all the preparations for her suicide and the disposal of the house, for the ending of the happiness the two friends had found in Argelès.

In my last letters I had made no reference to any religious reasons for opposition to suicide. Yvonne was a stoic, in the ancient sense. We had once spoken of the "sacrament of suicide" that Baudelaire discusses, and she had made her philosophical stand clear at that time. From the beginning, I knew that no one and nothing would change her will and her plan. Her grief had been set aside, and all that counted was the plotting for her suicide. By totally ignoring my pleas, she had made me feel useless, sentimental, and sad. Never before in my life had I felt so sharply the loneliness of the living and the awful deadness of the dead.

I have not returned to the Pyrenees since the death of Hyco.

Duke University 1964–79

_____

The rock

I was teaching in Boulder at the University of Colorado when in 1964 the first letter came from the Department of Romance Languages at Duke. Clifton Cherpack's letter was followed by others, and we set a date for a day of interviews in Durham.

At the airport I was met by Professors Cherpack and Wardropper who seemed to be my principal sponsors. Bruce Wardropper, the eminent Hispanicist, I had met several years earlier at Penn State during my first stint of summer school teaching, when he and I served as "visiting professors." Between the airport and the university these two emissaries expressed words of welcome and exchanged with me information about friends we had in common. Both men had taught at Johns Hopkins. I remember that the name of Leo Spitzer was referred to with reverence. Two days later, on the drive back to the airport, they spoke to me in practical terms about the advantages of Duke and urged me to accept the offer which they claimed would come immediately.

A few days after my return to Boulder, the formal offer came, and I accepted with pleasure at the thought of living again on the East Coast and teaching at Duke University.

In late August I drove from Colorado to North Carolina. On arriving in Durham I found a motel not far from the university. Eden Rock was its name, and I felt that was in keeping with Boulder, which I had just left. I knew there would be a wait at Eden Rock before my furniture would reach the new apartment I had rented in Durham.

On the day of my arrival, a Saturday, I dropped my bags in the motel and found my way to my office in the language center, a fine building close to the library. The office, on the top floor, seemed bare to me. I left the door open—there seemed to be almost no one in the building that afternoon—and I opened my typewriter with the intention of typing a few letters. The shift in my Olivetti had caught, and I was bending over the machine to see what was wrong when I sensed that someone was standing in the doorway.

A very tall young fellow was watching me and smiling. He asked, "Can I help you?" I invited him in to fix the typewriter, which he did immediately, and then we introduced ourselves. He was Townsend Ludington, called Towny, and described himself as a graduate student in English, a New Englander like myself, and a Yale graduate. He welcomed me to Duke in affable terms, and then invited me to speak at the October meeting of the English Graduate Club since he was its president that year. I accepted because Towny was the first person to speak to me since my joining the faculty. All of this transpired in a few minutes and culminated in an invitation to join him and his wife, Jane, and a few friends at dinner that very night. I accepted, cheered by the warmth of this first friend at the university.

Jane, a beautiful young woman, was as friendly and simple in her manner as Towny was. Of the other dinner guests I remember only two: an impressive southern gentleman and professor of English, William Blackburn, and another English graduate student, James Applewhite. Jim, as he was called, was fairly quiet throughout the evening, and not until the very end, as we were all getting ready to leave, did he speak to me directly. He moved me into a corner and in a serious voice asked if I would serve on his Ph.D. committee. He was writing his dissertation on Wordsworth. I accepted, and felt that, with the earlier request to speak to the Graduate Club, and this first dissertation assignment, I might have been joining the English Department rather than Romance Languages.

That first evening at the Ludingtons was made memorable by the histrionics and storytelling skill of Professor Blackburn. He was an imposing man, not only by his stature, but by his wit, by the shrewdness of his observations, by his "southernness" which he accentuated and exploited. He spoke with a well-modulated voice and an accent that was only barely noticeable to a northerner like myself. But he quoted, using a strong accent, southern friends and types from the South because he spoke in anecdotes and stories, with constant historical references, thanks to his admirable memory.

That evening Bill Blackburn represented North Carolina for us all, and we fell into the habit of asking him questions, which he encouraged. His stories that evening, his impressive face and bearing, his gift for caricature as well as characterization, the tones of stricture when he was angry and the tones of gentleness when he was compassionate—all of that made me aware that I had come to a part of my country that I did not know and that I was in the presence of a type of man I did not know. Bill Blackburn was both gentleman and critic: these two sides of his nature were never confused and never separated. I listened hard that evening for a possible contradiction in these two traits. There was none.

I gathered from all that was said at the Ludingtons that Professor Blackburn had exceptional success in his teaching of "creative writing," having trained such students as William Styron and Reynolds Price, that he was not always in agreement with his department, and that he had created a kind of department for himself. As I listened to him, it was hard for me not to feel some apprehension entering this scene in the South. Would I be able to function here as easily, as well as I hoped I would? This first encounter with a very strong southern temperament, a person who seemed proud to be somewhat at odds with the university where he taught, forced me at the end of the evening and through the following days into a stock taking of myself.

There were Baptist stories told by Professor Blackburn that evening, and they stimulated in me memories and thoughts that are always ready to surface with the slightest excuse. As I drove back to Eden Rock, I thought of the long drive from that other rock called Boulder, and smiled at the juxtaposition of the two words. (In homage to Fitzgerald's novel *Tender Is the Night*, I had once visited Eden Rock in Antibes.) Echoes of earlier times came to me then until it seemed that the word, or a word resembling it, had pursued me through my years of travel.

Plymouth Rock was a memory from early childhood. Almost every year, because of relatives who lived in Plymouth, Massachusetts, we drove there, and always stopped at the rock, to look down at it and meditate briefly on its significance in our history. And there was, also from childhood, the hymn "Rock of Ages," whose symbol I understood in some very elementary way. Three members of the Harvard Congregational Church in Brookline came each week to sing hymns to my grandmother Adams during the last years of her life. One of my regular duties as a child was to choose for her a few hymns that she would request. Often she would say to me: "Let's have 'Rock of Ages' next week, it's my favorite hymn."

Eden Rock on Chapel Hill Boulevard was not my new home, but it did, for six weeks, provide me with shelter and a bed. I had found an apartment in a new apartment complex in Durham called Four Seasons. I am a renter, not an owner, because I have no desire to be anchored to a house. Consciously, and without effort, I have managed to possess very little. My home is a rented apartment with furniture that is sparse and simple. All that I own can be seen in literally three minutes, or in ten minutes if titles of books are examined and if the pictures on my walls are looked at individually. No television, no record player, no radio. I have seen, perhaps in Europe more than in America, too many houses filled with trumpery, and I turned against such displays early in life. Cleaning my apartment means discarding each week an object, a book, and even a notebook that has served its purpose.

I am, and I illustrate etymologically, an "eccentric." There is no "center" for me in any physical sense. My life might be summarized by a constant and subconscious effort to move beyond any possible center, even that of a university. I enjoy, not a house, but the friendship of the seasons, the undiluted morning air. Am I not, after all, part leaf, part tree, moving toward the inanimate, toward the earth, toward the rock?

Dawn (1964)

My work at Duke began in September 1964 with a program of three courses. Two of these were sections of the same survey course of French literature, a full year course, which I have taught in one form or another throughout my career. Designed primarily for freshmen, it serves as an introduction to all the centuries of French civilization, to the development of the various literary genres, and to the intellectual and esthetic history of France.

I had, by 1964, worked out a kind of technique in the teaching of such a class, and set about at Duke to strengthen and humanize it. I often thought of the first time I gave such a course. It was at Harvard when I was a fourth-year graduate student. At the beginning of that summer my chairman had told me I was to teach a section of the survey of French literature. The fall semester was to go from the Middle Ages through the eighteenth century. That summer I worked every day on the course, preparing the various lessons, taking notes on every major work between *La Chanson de Roland* and *Les Confessions* of Rousseau. That first day I carried into the classroom a small attaché case containing the notes taken during the summer. The room was filled, and I began talking about the Middle Ages. I had had no experience with timing such a lesson, and did not realize that a minute can be very long under such circumstances. If the minutes moved slowly, the notes I spoke from flew by fast. I passed through generations and centuries, and before I knew it, I had come to the end of all those notes taken during the summer. I had given the entire survey course, and there were still ten minutes to go. I picked up a copy of *La Chanson de Roland* and read the battle scene of Roland's death to fill out the hour.

When the bell rang, I said to myself I must have moved this class: I had given them the high points of my summer meditations. The students all stood up and walked to the door. When one fellow turned around and came back to the desk where I was putting my notes back into the attaché case, I felt cheered that at least one soul had been touched. "Sir, how do I go about dropping this course?"

From that day forward, the problem of timing a lesson has been uppermost in my preparation. With practice and the passing of years, the opposite danger began to declare itself: that of having too much to say, garrulousness, in a word. The only hope of offsetting that steady flow of words a teacher may demonstrate is to watch reactions in a classroom, to hear the comments of the students and incorporate them without losing sight of the theme of the day's lesson.

Three sophomores in that survey course my first year at Duke showed some signs of friendliness as well as a strong interest in French literature. One of them, Bill Buck, is today a lawyer, and the other two, Frank Jacobus and John Dunaway, are French professors. They represent three very different temperaments corresponding to three recognizable approaches to a university class. Bill enjoyed the teacher's efforts to put something across and carefully measured the teacher's success or lack of it each day. He best remembered the side remarks, especially those tinged with some personal reminiscences on my part. He is a fine attorney today in Oregon.

Frank was closely attentive in class. He was eager to improve his French and to enjoy his growing facility in speaking and writing the language. I knew in a few weeks' time, by the way he watched the technique of teaching, that he would become a teacher. He is that today at Davidson. John had a much quieter approach to me and to French than Bill and Frank. I was impressed by his obvious linguistic gifts and by the way with which he related to other students in the class.

One evening mid-semester I went to the Oak Room for dinner. It is a faculty-student dining room where I ate dinner regularly for several years. I noticed John Dunaway sitting with a few fellows at a small table. I said "hello," as I passed his table, and he suggested that I take the empty seat. He was a gracious host, introducing me to his friends, and involving me in the conversation I had interrupted. When the others left, John and I had a few minutes alone, and I asked him about the future and the kind of work that attracted him. His answer came quickly, "The ministry. It has been on my mind for some time. But French is running a close second." Because of the girl he intended to marry (and did marry), John went to Emory for his last two years, and then he and Trish returned to Duke for graduate work—in French. His dissertation and his first two books were to treat religious writers.

The advanced course that first semester was on twentieth-century French poetry. I remember clearly only one student, a senior girl, Linda Orr, because of her perceptiveness of the poets. She continued the second semester with the course on Baudelaire, designed especially for graduate students. One day in April she shared a moment of jubilation with us all by telling us she had just received notice of her admission to the Yale Graduate School to work in French. An admirable student, she was also a poet, and through the years has sustained her dual vocation of teacher and poet. She must have sensed that this dilemma of a dual focus was mine also, and we freely discussed the problem in Durham or Paris or Nice whenever we met. I warned her about the young men and women who cease being young when they begin to follow the beaten track of the professions.

When in the second semester of the survey course, we came to the Baudelaire poem *L'Invitation au voyage*, which was being read and studied for the first time by the undergraduates, I seldom hesitated to tell the class a story about the poem and my effort to teach it for the first time at Yale. When that class was over, one of the fellows came up to the desk to tell me that for the first time in his life he had felt something of the beauty of a poem. Poetry had always turned him off, he said, bored him or embarrassed him, but this had been different. He repeated to me a few of the phrases that had struck him: "mon enfant," "ma soeur," and the refrain, "Là, tout n'est qu'ordre et beauté."

It was wartime. The student was drafted, went through boot camp, and eventually served in the Pacific area. On his return he came to visit me and to give me a sheet of paper which I still have and which I have shown to several classes whenever the moment was appropriate.

In the line of duty, my student had to shoot a Japanese soldier, as young as he was. In accordance with the rules, he had to go through the papers of the enemy soldier. In his wallet he found some paper money, a girl's picture, and a folded sheet of paper, on one side of which *L'Invitation* was written in beautiful handwriting, and on the other side a Japanese translation of the poem.

This precious paper is more fragile each year, but I still unfold it in class after we have studied the poem, explaining its origins and thereby telling my best antiwar story.

When students become curious about my habits of rising early to have an hour or two for writing before the university day begins, I often quote Thoreau's sentence: "Morning is when I am awake and there is a dawn in me!"

Through the years I have forced my morning to be the moment that immediately precedes the break of dawn. The sky is still dark, but it is about to change, imperceptibly at first, but with such timed precision that I am renewed with the loftiest feelings I will have throughout the long day ahead. It is indeed a long day if one rises that early when the sky is the sign of everything infallible and inevitable. The breaths I draw at that hour seem to parallel the streaks of gray that cut across the dark of the sky. Is it possible I am still breathing as the new color in the heavens lights my way into the thought I had relinquished the night before?

Dawn! The cycle is concluded and renewed at the same moment. And I know the dawn is in me, too, because even the slightest degree of hope is a rising of light that will nurture it and allow it to grow during those early hours when God's world is again visible.

A year, a lifetime, a century, yes, all centuries, all time, are in each morning dawn. When whiteness finally takes over the sky, I know then that all previous hesitations and failures, all denials and betrayals belong to the past, and the dreams of my night are then made more real. The present is hope-filled and my conscious memory of the past, even of yesterday, is already softening the blows I thought I received and camouflaging the colors and the lines of scenes no longer visible. I try then to deflect the memories in order to encourage the dawn of new thoughts and projects and to smell the fresh air of morning. So unambiguous that air! I breathe it in and my lungs fill up effortlessly, joyously. That purely physical swell of my diaphragm is both the sign of my breathing life and the promise of new words already filtering through my consciousness. But I know they come from my unconscious self so deep within me, so permanent, so faithful to the truths I tend to deflect and dilute and alter.

This play I am in, this comedy, is far along, and I often wonder in the morning stillness whether I will remember my lines. They are expected, these lines I have said so often, and yet with age a sense of truth becomes more palpable to me, more insistent. Might it be that this new sense, which is perhaps a renewed sense from childhood, will efface my memory of the old lines I have said too often? I have said too many things that were called for by the role I was playing.

Rehearsals, those studied, endless rehearsals when I was both actor and director.

The light of the morning in these advancing years shows me a possible way to a part never imagined before, to a part not learned, where lines would be answers and not questions, and where the answers would come so directly from the heart that I would learn from them some flash of truth about myself. Let me call them morning answers because they would have no dependence on the night before, on the darkness of shadings and ambiguities and approximations.

I would like thus to greet my fellowmen, all those I am to encounter throughout the day and throughout the evening that follows the day. To make this day unique because of its morning that lights up my eyes and my mind—that is my prayer, said in the first hour to Our Lord who caused this earth to revolve and seek the rays of the permanent sun.

The desire to work is of course part of the early morning uplift. I look at the sky first and then at the paper. Both sky and paper are empty. One is vast, and one infinitely small but capable of inducing a thought which, if the right words are found for it, may expand limitlessly throughout my day.

There are few words in my pen. I turn them this way and that, because no idea will be reached until there is some word for it.

I put down the pen, clean my house, and return to the paper in order to write another thought of my mind, to make visible another fable. Will anyone follow such stories? All my possible readers are inventing their own!

As I teach the legends of Proust and Dante, of Baudelaire and Nerval, I form my own, and my listeners do not always realize the strange filter, the strange amalgam a lesson in a classroom really is.

When I write, instinct leads me to the rare and precious, but my reason tells me to look for (and find) the simplest word, so threadbare that it has become diaphanous.

To start with nothing—how well that suits the early hour!—is better than to start with a copious outline or a rough draft. The mechanism of a well-written page is invisible. The page that emerges from an outline is too clearly that.

The male and the female spirits are so evenly distributed in me that when they quarrel, the result is a family squabble. I feel this competition when I write. The male is the creative impulse, arrogant and determined. The female is passivity, the part in me that wants to

47

absorb and feel and understand before any words are put on paper. One races ahead and one holds back. One manipulates and tricks my dreams. I am totally, hopelessly incestuous, one part of me chained to the other in perpetual intercourse!

Work is not the effort of writing. It is the imperious need to discard all that I want to say glibly, and this means all that I have already said. I am still analyzing the symptoms that keep me from saying what I want to say. They force me to leave my room and go outside, but the idea in its bareness and coldness returns and hurls me back to the table.

Mourning doves (1966)

By the beginning of my third year at Duke I realized that I felt at home. I had become accustomed to West Campus, to the chapel tower, to the library and the language center next to the library. I had been away from Durham for a semester, the first part of 1966, largely spent in Paris and Nice, and when I returned and the new semester began in September, I found myself welcoming the students, rather than being welcomed. I was recognized by more people as being on the staff of the university—a French teacher who came early to his classroom for possible visits with the students before the day's teaching began. On parking my car each morning, I took pleasure in looking at the trees and the shrubbery as I walked to the classroom. The squirrels and the abandoned dogs seemed glad to welcome a solitary mortal that early in the morning.

That fall of 1966, a glorious season of sunlight and warmhearted students, I knew that Duke was where I wanted to be.

The survey course, designed primarily for freshmen who had had three years of French in high school, was taken also by French majors, but by that third year I was aware that it was attracting students primarily interested in literature, in English and American literature, in the art of writing, and in what was soon to be called "comparative literature." I can think easily of at least three fellows who entered my class that fall and who had already a literary sophistication about them: Mike Grimwood, David Guy, and Harry Stokes. They wanted practice in hearing, speaking, and writing French, but more than that, they wanted a literary experience in a foreign language, because they were somewhat aware of the importance of French in the achievements of authors they admired or were beginning to admire: Eliot and Joyce, Stevens and Beckett, Yeats and Lowell.

The interest of such students made the course more stimulating for me to teach. Mike and David were only slightly apprehensive about their use of French in class. They were on the whole serene and seemed determined to enjoy the course as much as a course can be enjoyed. Harry was (or appeared to be) more worried. He sat in the back of the room, fully concentrated on what he was inscribing in his notebook. At the end of the class he was the last to leave as he waited for others to get their answers to quick questions, and then, when the scene was his, would slowly open his notebook, and in guarded speech force me to clarify this point and that point, and add a few questions of his own on points I had avoided in the lesson directed to the entire class.

Harry's face remained serious and concentrated. His dress remained stable throughout the year, and throughout the years: a pair of white ducks and a tan-colored jacket, a fairly unusual costume for Duke students. His general manner was one of shyness and his speech was contradicted by the harshness of his questions which ploughed into me. I tried to get him to smile at the end of those brief conferences when he and I looked into his notebook, into those magnificently written, orderly pages. Harry's handwriting had strength as well as beauty. As I pushed him out of the room to get ready for the next class, a slight smile might form on his face and then disappear as if he were thinking "I don't really find those answers totally satisfactory."

But Harry, as well as Mike and David, were authentic literature students, accepting the seriousness of literature and feeling something of the exaltation that can come from it.

After the two sections of the survey, I was ready at 11:20 for the advanced course which that fall was explication de textes. It was a large course of forty students, many of whom were new to me. During the first meetings I called especially on the few students I knew in order to discuss the method of explicating a text, and then gradually as we began studying some of the texts I had chosen I learned the names of the new students. The tallest one, a heavy-set fellow, seemed a bit detached from the group, although he was fully attentive in class. Before I was able to involve him in our class discussions, he had cut class on two Fridays and had done poorly on the first class paper. In giving him the corrected paper, I said as quietly as I could, "Mr.

Bodkin, this paper was not too good, and you have cut two Fridays. Are you going to come to every class from now on?"

His face was youthful and animated as he looked very directly at me. "Sir, I will have to be absent three more Fridays this semester." He spoke quietly, apologetically, but with total self-assurance.

In a flash I understood the situation. "You are on a team?" "Yes." "Football?" "Yes." "Varsity?" "Yes, sir, but I'll do my best to keep up with the work." By the end of that first semester, I was aware of the importance playing football had for Robin Bodkin, and the growing fascination that French held for him, both the linguistic knowledge and practice he enjoyed and the literary values of certain texts we worked on: *Les Pas* of Valéry, for example. To offset the tremendous muscular power of his body, Robin adopted for his own the most subtle and the most delicate of the texts we used.

In the spring semester of 1967 Harry Stokes, still a freshman, and still taking the survey course, forced me to pay attention to the *Archive*, Duke's literary magazine, sponsored by William Blackburn, whom I remembered from my first evening in Durham. Harry, whose temperament was a mixture of extreme shyness and fearless perseverance, manifested his friendliness by believing, and then telling me, that I had as much "right" to the *Archive* as his English professors. The literary event of the spring was a lecture by Stephen Spender, invited by the student staff of the magazine. Harry found out that I had not been invited to the social events connected with Spender's visit to the campus, and so he set about inviting to his room all the students on the *Archive*'s staff and the poet-visitor.

"You must come too. Promise you will come. This is really for you to meet Spender." When I asked him the size of his room, I fell into the trap he had set. His small room made the event impossible. I tried to tell him this as I felt his scheming mind working on my mind. So, I accepted the inevitable: "You want my apartment, don't you?" "Yes, we'll bring the wine."

Impresario and attentive friend, Harry organized the evening when the students, sprawled on my floor, said almost nothing, and when Spender and I talked, as I remember, mainly about southern France. A few years previously, Spender had reviewed my *Mallarmé* in the *New York Times Book Review*, and I had longed for a chance to thank him for his sympathetic article. When this detail was revealed, Harry felt justified for his scheming, and I felt grateful to Harry.

That spring semester moved on fast after Spender's departure. I had never felt, at Duke or elsewhere, that I had before me a trapped audience of students. My courses were not required. Each hour in a classroom was different from all the others because I was, at least in my own mind, trying to be not only a teacher of French literature but also a broadly educated generalist. Fundamentally I was concerned with the nature of literary expression, but I was also trying to be aware of the significance of youth and popular culture.

The larger world of students outside my classes was unquestionably that spring moving toward a kind of revolt that was to declare itself more forcibly during the next two years. I was determined to remain unanxious in the face of the rising upheaval, and in my will to continue as both general practitioner and specialist. As I became aware of the growing tenseness in the students, of the attractiveness of revolt they were either drawn to or repulsed by, I tried to relate their social and political problems to the personal and neurotic adventures of the writers we read together.

"Relevance" was the battle cry those years and it was quickly overused. When the students asked me: "Is literature relevant?" I answered them by saying, "You are really asking if literature is universal, and I try daily to teach that it is." It was always hard for students to think in terms of the distant past, even the seventeenth century. I would usually try to point out that a Racine and a Molière were writers very close to the civilization to which they belonged, whereas Baudelaire, Rimbaud, and Mallarmé were the new type of modern writer alienated from the world and deeply concerned with this alienation. Some of my students between 1967 and 1970 found in the personal journal of Baudelaire and in Rimbaud's *Une Saison en enfer* the philosophical justification of their own revolt.

I would describe the majority of the students I taught at Duke as scientifically minded and politically aware. They made up the larger part of my classes, especially in the later years when the classes were large, and I realized I was going against their fundamental belief in my stressing that in the creation of literature the irrational and the unconscious matter the most. I would try to point out, from my own convictions, that history, as it is reflected in the major literary works, is merely the recurrence of myths, archetypes, customs, and repressions. These form the stuff of life *and* of literature.

At the beginning of each class, as I looked into their faces, associating each one with a given seat, I often thought that most of these students are to become doctors, lawyers, or teachers. And then they will have sons and daughters most of whom will become doctors, lawyers, or teachers. I often yearned for a greater mixture of economic and social backgrounds, a greater freedom from the terrifying constraints of wealth and class, from the obligations that such parents demanded, from the artificial bonds of fraternities and sororities.

In at least three of my students whom I have already named, I sensed something of their liberation, and as we continued to be friends through the years, I became sensitive to the drama in each one that concerned a vocation. Linda Orr, as she moved successfully into the life of a scholar and teacher, never relinquished the time she guarded for work on her poems, for that concentration on her own words that, precisely, drew upon the unconscious and the irrational part of her spirit. In his first years at Duke, Harry Stokes developed his prowess in tennis and enjoyed exhilarating hours in tennis matches. The rest of his life was carefully divided between his own writing and his study of language and literature. Robin Bodkin during four years as a major football player encountered more hardship than Linda and Harry in salvaging time for the reading of literature, the practice of French, and for the growing awareness of what it means to be a critic.

It was easy for me in those early years at Duke to confuse my own self-education with the lessons I gave in the classroom. I was sensitive to the unusual beauty of the freshmen who, at seventeen and eighteen, boys and girls alike, combine the attractiveness of male and female, and the attractiveness comes from the development of the mind. By the time the freshmen had become juniors and seniors, I was more able to speak in class of the awareness of the unconscious, of what might be called the geography of the unconscious.

Each of us is born out of a womb—that much is perfectly clear —but we are also born out of a soul and out of the cosmos. Then as we grow into the hard prison of our social-economic-religious world, our lack of courage forces us back into the hidden darkness of the unconscious. The creative artist was my hero in every class I taught because only he has the courage to strip himself to the nakedness of light.

My students, with their excessively rational minds, were able to study a Proust and a Joyce and learn from them. They were less able, less willing, to learn from the other type of writer, a Henry Miller, for example. I never taught Henry Miller in class, and I regret it now, because he would have done them more good, with his fluid sentences, his nonstop syntax, his multiple images both obscene and anti-intellectual. They would have resisted Miller who so often denounces the rational mind that evades or ignores the demands made upon it, that contradicts its relationship with reality. But they would have learned more from Miller than from anyone else that the intellect is only one means of communication.

To the science majors I could point out that Freud was a scientist although his science deals with the sources of irrationality. The "rational" and the "moral" were always there in the minds of my students as the goals of progress. I tried in various ways through various literary texts to point out that "reason" leads to dangerously simple answers. In taking on, as I did unashamedly in class, the championship of the artist, I had to sustain, as well as I could, my belief that the artist is possessed by the forces and desires that make up the true man of power.

In my first years in North Carolina, there were a few students like Linda, Harry, and Robin, who seemed to know all this before I read with them any text, but for whom the reading of a text confirmed their secret knowledge that progress is not becoming more conscious but rather following unconscious instincts.

There I was in a new landscape never covered with snow, with no ocean nearby, with no mountain nearby. Durham is scenery on a humble scale, but I was linked again to nature as I listened very early in the morning, about four o'clock, to a pair of mourning doves outside my bedroom window. Their almost human song (their mating song, I suppose) is the saddest of sounds as they announce the coming of a new day. During the daytime I watched them often—more graceful, more refined than pigeons, so bland in color that they merged with leaves or grass or roofs. They never sing then, as they move elegantly over the grass or fly boldly from roof to tree. Always invisible when I hear them. Always silent when I see them.

If the early lament of the mourning doves was my link with nature in North Carolina, it was also my link with the day before, with the classroom thoughts I had tried to express about the poet as our safest seer, as the guardian of the temple, as the caretaker of archetypes, as the spirit closest to those ambiguities of language that teach us how to harness energy and turn it into form.

Antigone or Creon? (1967)

In the fall of 1967, on returning to Durham from summer school teaching at Brigham Young University in Utah, I found that my apartment at 17-D Valley Terrace, to which I had moved after two years in a smaller one, was home, a modest one, but my own. It was large enough to contain the pictures I wanted to keep on my walls, and the books I needed for my own study and pleasure. I could see trees outside although I lived some distance from Duke Forest, the extensive area owned by the university where members of the faculty and administration have built large and handsome houses.

I have never been conscious of forcing myself into a pattern of living. I am a part of humanity but I do not have to imitate it in a social sense. I have always been distrustful of the small social groups that form in a university world and just outside of that world. This resistance to society is related to what I have defended the most consistently throughout my life: the work of the creative spirit in man. Society is against the creators. This is true even in the best of the universities, in departments that have little to do with "creators": physical and social sciences, for example, and even in literature departments where traditional scholarship is stressed and where today literary theory is studied at the expense of literary texts.

The creative spirit when expressed in students and teachers is inevitably under suspicion. It represents for most men an abnormal pursuit, a dilettante's waste of time, an ill-defined, ill-fated vocation. Parents and teachers alike, the majority of students, are against this smallest of minorities. We are oddities, and I have grown accustomed to hearing in the social groups I attend from time to time, veiled accusations leveled against the young and the old who practice the arts and uphold the new arts as they are being created. By the beginning of my fourth year at Duke, in September 1967, I was more conscious than ever of my role of interloper in the world and more determined to play that role without a mask. The simplicity of dawn still guided me, and I was learning how to make my life comparable to that simplicity.

Into my freshman course I welcomed fewer obvious future French majors and more hesitant students doubtful about the wisdom of doing more French and yet eager to profit from their early preparation in the language. Jim Brand, from Texas, a soccer player, and Lyle Sanford, from Virginia, were typical of that type of student, curious to learn if college French had any interest for them. Jim ultimately chose psychology as his major, and Lyle, English, but both returned to my new classroom (014) their senior year, almost as friends (which they indeed became after their graduation) to see what the symbolist poets might say to them and to reassess my teaching enthusiasms. Their tentativeness was over, and I welcomed them back, remembering their freshman hesitations and shyness.

How unknowing I was, in the fall of 1967, of the friendship Jim Brand was to show me during the following years. Ten years later, in 1978, on reading my first memoir, he had reached that level of frankness and understanding that permitted him to write: "I enjoyed the book, but when are you going to give us more gristle, religion and sex?" By then, Jim had become my best critic and a fine physician. I suppose "gristle" had something to do with his medical training.

By that fourth year, I looked upon my classroom as Thoreau looked upon Walden. Students came into it, left it, and a few came back, as visitors to Thoreau used the Concord River leading them to him and then outward from him. The Concord, as sacred as the Ganges! My first encounters with students, usually in their freshman year at Duke, were always tentative, and I often asked myself: is there enough going on here to bring them back when, with the study of a single author, a Proust or a Dante, I would have greater chance to discuss with them what one major writer had made out of life. When they did return, I wondered what the various reasons might be that would explain the return. During the first week I knew they were wondering too.

My advanced course that fall of 1967 was a history of French literary criticism. It was a large group evenly divided between seniors and graduate students who seemed willing to study critical theories and achievements especially of the nineteenth and twentieth centuries.

Structuralism, and what today is called semiotics, was the announced subject of the end of the course, and the students were eager for an initiation. Each of the forty students prepared an oral report on one critic. Each performance was in French. The members of the class as well as myself assessed the use of French and the teaching skill of each critic-teacher.

As I listened to Robin Bodkin on Proust and Lawrence Greenberg on Bachelard, I remembered their apprehension of two years earlier. John Dunaway, who had been in my first class at Duke, was now back as a graduate student and gave his report on Maritain's *Art et scolastique*. As I write this, in 1978, his first book has just reached me. It is entitled *Jacques Maritain*. Jim McNab, a Scotsman who had had some experience as a teacher, spoke to the class on Charles Mauron. He explained critical theories and answered questions on them with the buoyancy, enthusiasm, and expertise of a man destined to be an excellent teacher. Betsy Colford who had come to us from Smith had a less exciting topic to expound: the criticism of Albert Thibaudet, but she did it with such fervor and such fluency that she held our attention on a critic who already seemed dated by comparison with Sartre and Lévi-Strauss. Mike Grimwood discussed the latter's *Tristes tropiques* with the aplomb of a cautious judge quietly insisting on the new brilliance of structuralism.

There they were, the younger scholars, taking over my work with that freshness and eagerness I could no longer claim. They were exploring books that had not been written when I was a graduate student and exploring theories that would have shocked my Harvard teachers. With at least twenty of those students I had established some kind of personal rapport. I knew something of their backgrounds and something of their plans and hopes for the future. They were puzzled by my celibate life, uneasy in trying to explain it. It gave them access to me, and they tended to call my feelings for them, my interest in them, "paternal." They never actually said that to me because they knew, subconsciously at least, it was not true. Had they said it, I would have corrected them by assuring them there was nothing "paternal" in my nature.

Whenever I met one of their real fathers, I usually felt a surge of jealousy for that man having such a son or such a daughter. But then I quieted my feelings with the conviction that I had the better relationship. I knew the son or the daughter during a few years of momentous change, of growth and awakening, when we came together over the mysteries of a literary text. That meeting in a classroom easily led to more private meetings when discourse on sex, religion, morality, politics, careers, basketball, could be far freer than it ever could be had I been father or father figure.

If I had ever felt that paternal possessiveness, I would have profaned my Walden. I would not have been able to look at the glaucous hue of its waters or the stony shore or the clear wild ducks.

During the late sixties, as student activism grew, modernism in the streets grew too, and our conversations touched more and more on pornography, rock music, William Burroughs, and Virginia homegrown. The mysterious identity of the student facing me in the classroom or in 17-D was comparable for me to the explication of a text. One helped to reveal the other. The teacher and the taught became interchangeable. The one who spoke the more by day became the listener by night, as my life grew into a cooperative activity.

A decade or more ago one spoke of the hapless student, the captive, pinned to his seat third row rear, forced to listen, forced even to participate in matters he kept thinking he would like to bypass if he could find a way to drop the course, or at least to change sections. But today the classroom is a changed world, so changed in fact that the teacher is the hapless prisoner, and the student is omniscient. No longer is he captive, constrained, or timorous. He is watchful, curious, attentive when he feels the lesson has been well prepared by the teacher and related directly, or indirectly, to his major preoccupations (which have not changed through the years): discovering the world, choosing a vocation, analyzing the problems of love and sports, and wondering how he can write the paper that is due and still remain fairly contented and in good health.

It is foolhardy to hope to be impersonal and objective in the classroom. After the formal pattern of the teaching is done, and even while it is being done: the study of the genre of the work, the analysis of the poem's prosody, the principal agon of the play, the possible sources of the novel's protagonist, and the other numerous aspects of literary study that are brought up in the classroom, or that are not brought up because of lack of time—after all that and during all that, there is the sacred obligation of the teacher to bear testimonial to what he is teaching.

But what kind of testimonial? moral? esthetic? archetypal or anthropological? Testimonial, I would say, to all of these, whether specific or implicit. The teacher is inevitably the man who exposes his feelings to students ten or twenty or thirty years younger than himself. To take sides with such a writer as D. H. Lawrence or Henry Miller or Sade is a spiritual striptease for a teacher. If in expounding the writings of André Gide, the teacher emphasizes the boredom and the corruption of respectability Gide speaks of, and the need to safeguard a man's freedom or *disponibilité* before all experiences, he opens himself up to criticism of a moral order.

Most university students know something about passion, but they know very little about the study of passion as it is fixed for all time in a poem or a play or a novel. In their own lives, time eventually reveals the monotony of passion and its lessening, and it is hard for them to realize that what they once felt romantically on a dark beach at night is radiantly present in Heathcliff's love for Cathy, in the young man's love for his own body in Valéry's poem on Narcissus, in Aschenbach's fervent daily cult for Tadzio. The teacher is committed to explain such episodes as these and, moreover, to give some sense of his own ambivalence toward them.

Within the space of a generation our attitude toward the literary hero has changed because our attitude toward man has changed. The tragic hero had once been canonized by artists and critics and moralists as a human figure in defeat, as a man crushed and humiliated by a force or a fate he was unable to avoid. Oedipus, Antigone, Hamlet, and Phèdre were elevated in their degradation and set apart from ordinary men and women by the simple, powerful designation of "tragic figure."

Even the word *tragedy* now seems pompous and false, almost ludicrous. The terrors and mysteries of the modern hero are not those of Electra or Prometheus or even of Hamlet. We tend to call him today the antihero because the energies he finds in himself are primal and nonethical. The classical sense of tragedy is that of a man (Oedipus) or of a woman (Antigone) in conflict with the moral code of the city. Each suffers because of the city's law. The modern hero is indifferent to the city's law because he judges it basically false and arbitrary. There is a law more just than the city's. It is the law of his body, of his conscience, of the deepest, most primitive part of his human nature. Tragedy, in the classical sense, has no meaning for the outsider, the pariah, the rebel, the hippie, the profligate, the midnight cowboy, the easy rider.

For some time now this new antihero has been collecting his credentials and leaving evidences of his nihilistic mind. *Le Neveu de Rameau* by Diderot in the eighteenth century is surely among the earliest representatives. In Stendhal's *Le Rouge et le noir* of 1830,

Julien Sorel had very little significance for readers of his day, but ever since Camus' *L'Etranger* was published in 1942, Meursault's attitude toward the society that condemned him has been compared with that of Julien's in ultimate circumstances that are similar.

Since Nietzsche's heroic figure, described as "beyond good and evil," the amoral hero has occupied the first position: Lafcadio of Gide's *Caves du Vatican*, in search of some motive for living; Thomas Mann's Aschenbach, in search of beauty; Joyce's Stephen Dedalus, in search of a father. The search for some form of self-identification we read in the novels of Henry Miller, Jean Genet, Philip Roth, far surpasses any sense of tragedy, and the search is even more striking in such films as *Pierrot le fou* of Godard, *Belle de jour* of Buñuel, *Teorema* of Pier Paolo Pasolini. A new era began about 1967 when many seemingly disparate forces or illuminations declared themselves. In time they will appear as corroborating explorations of the self and of the world. Man's first walk on the moon will not appear totally distinct from the student rebellions, or from the new forms of literary criticism, or from the relaxed laws of censorship.

The sixties will be known as the decade when man first reached the moon's surface and when students began insisting that literature must stay in relation to experience. For centuries students had been told that they must learn what is beyond them, and today, more insistently than ever, teachers are beginning to say to one another: "Teach always what is beyond you. When you think you have learned something, drop it and go learn something else." The moment of truth can come in the classroom, and when it does, it should be celebrated, it should be epiphanized. This new kind of teacher will then have the right to assume teaching what interests him also interests his students.

No literature of other centuries surpasses our own in power and magnificence. But in works of our greatest writers: Yeats, Eliot, and Stevens; Joyce, Kafka, and Proust; D. H. Lawrence, Mann, and Gide, the young readers of 1967 found elements that the young readers thirty years earlier had not found: a bitter hostility to the assumptions of civilization. The large subculture of youth today is telling us that the only possible definition of a hero is Freudian—namely the type of youth who stands up manfully against his father and vigorously overcomes him. More dramatically than ever before in the history of man, we have witnessed the defiant rebellion of the son against the sadistic, the impersonal father. Freud's lesson on the Oedipus complex, written down fifty years ago, a theory based on a myth that belongs to prehistory, was in the 1960s a widespread phenomenon reproduced in student rebellions and hippie demonstrations.

Rebellious students were reliving the ancient myth of the son bent upon denying and eliminating the father's figure. Many believed that this could be carried out only by acts of violence and in a spirit of intolerance. Even the more mild popular films of those years demonstrated this phenomenon: *The Graduate* and *Goodbye, Columbus*. A few more violent and more important films demonstrated it more forcibly: *Lord of the Flies, Easy Rider*, and Antonioni's *Zabriskie Point*.

An analogy occurred to me in 1967 concerning the war going on between the establishment and the young. The establishment was Creon, the dogged, unimaginative ruler applying the law because the law protected his reign and insured a false kind of peace. Students and other youthful dissenters (*contestataires*) were Antigone, who followed not the law of the city but the unwritten law of her heart. Those young people, either in small groups facing a dean or a judge, or congregating by the thousands at some rock festival, had such an instinctive, overwhelming conviction about what must be changed that they represented in reality one figure, one voice. They were the same Antigone, frail in their youthfulness, feminine in their long hair and beads, unarmed except for a handful of dust, strong in their moral conviction that the law of the city was erroneous and had to be changed.

So, Creon stood on the right, and Antigone on the left. But there must have been one hundred Creons to one Antigone. Creon had age on his side, and reasonable speech and promises of order. And moreover, he was always attracting to his party Antigone's sister Ismene, who, as she grew older, grew more fearful of revolution. It has never been easy to distinguish between the self-righteousness of Creon and the self-righteousness of Antigone. The spirit of Antigone, a pure, fearless spirit, lived in the young during the late sixties, as they demonstrated in the streets, in the ghettos, on the campuses, and as they were put away in Creon's prisons.

Youth and age. In the past the struggle between them has always been unfair and uneven. It still was, in the late sixties. Age has had almost everything in its favor. Creon has always won out. Since I was born in 1908, I was a contemporary of Auschwitz, Hiroshima, Vietnam, and the Watts riots. My students knew of these tragedies. Thanks to better schooling and better teachers, thanks to films and television, to hitchhiking and airplanes, the young are more learned today, they are wiser and more philosophical than the young in earlier ages. When they lose respect for their elders, it is usually with good reason. The older members of the community compromise and bargain, seal and buy the rights to freedom and to happiness, allow wars to start which they will not and cannot finish. They live under the shadow of Creon.

Rebellion and its history in film (1968–69)

When classes and examinations were over in early May of 1968, I escaped from Durham, from the tedious end-of-term duties, to visit Naples for the first time. Like all the freshmen ending their first year at the university, I yearned to get away and lead at least for a few weeks a life in a totally different setting and in, if possible, a different language.

The flight to Naples answered my basic need for change and had also a scholarly motive. I was writing a book on Stendhal and wanted to see first hand those spots he speaks of in his journal of 1811. The Vesuvio Hotel, on the bay of Naples, was large, elegant, and comfortable. I liked the noisiness of the foyer and the quiet of my room, very high up, that looked out over the bay. My breakfast arrived promptly each morning. My efforts to say a few words in Italian to the waiter as he handed me my tray was vocally and linguistically the kind of change from which I profited the most. Ten minutes before he was due to knock on my door, I would plan and rehearse a few sentences that might follow my "avanti!"

The Vesuvio roof had been converted into an admirable restaurant. Since I took both meals there each day I quickly became acquainted with the maître d'hôtel, a Tuscan who had worked in Swiss hotels and who spoke fluent French. I enjoyed the view of the bay and the coastline from that high spot and found myself on the first day reciting from a Nerval sonnet the line: "Rends-moi le Pausilippe et la mer d'Italie." Le Pausilippe—il Posilippo. In our first conversation, I asked the maître d'hôtel if it were close by, and he simply pointed it out, on our right, down the coastline, actually not very far from the hotel.

From Stendhal's *Journal* I had jotted down all the spots he mentions, and had discovered them in just a few walks. The small San Carlo theater had been his favorite opera house. It was closed for the season, but one of the guards let me in for a few minutes. The morning I visited it was warm and sunny. I enjoyed the crowds in the *galleria* as I made my way back to the hotel. All the places where one could get a late morning espresso were crowded. The hotel foyer when I reached it was unusually quiet and empty. In front of one of the two elevators stood the elevator boy, who recognized me and held the door open. I missed his smile and greeting. The expression on his face was sad, and I asked him what was wrong. I was the only guest in the elevator that trip. He burst into an explanation which was hard for me to follow because of what I supposed was the Neapolitan dialect. But I heard "Kennedy" and "morto," and what I thought was "Bobby." Was he saying "Bobby Kennedy has been shot?" I said, "You mean John Kennedy." "No, Bobby, Bobby."

I went to the roof-restaurant and to my good interpreter, the maître d'hôtel. He confirmed the tragedy. It was indeed Robert Kennedy who had been assassinated. The feelings of shock and grief were all the greater at that distance from home. He was for me, after his brother, the second American promise. There was weeping in the streets of Naples that afternoon as I walked about. How grateful I felt for those tears in the eyes of Neapolitan women, and men too, who talked together on the sidewalks and in the stores! They knew he was a Catholic like them and had a family larger than theirs. They lived through, as I did that afternoon, the swiftness and cruelty of death.

The Kennedys had been for me the Yankees reborn, with excellence of thought and excellence of language. As I passed the mourners on my Naples walk that afternoon, I thought of how the Kennedys had nurtured the spirit of my country, of how Robert Kennedy had seemed yesterday the national inevitability. From the roof of the Vesuvio that evening I watched night settle down over the bay and the city, yes, over il Posilippo, and the emotion that choked me covered the full human scale of promise and fate.

During the fall of 1968 and the spring of 1969, the students at Duke and throughout the world took over the center of attention. The revolt had been slowly prepared by the hippie phenomenon and it ended when the words hippie and flower children went out of use in the early seventies. For the students it was much more than a revolt against the "establishment" and the administration of a university. It was a courageous refusal to accept the lies of civilization, all the hollow values of money, science, and power.

The Altamont Festival of December 1969 marked for me at least the end of a movement which began in the middle sixties soon after I arrived at Durham. It began in music and poetry with a record album I bought and played so often that I knew by heart the lyrics of *Sergeant Pepper's Lonely Hearts Club Band*. The Beatles were magicians in those days. The power of their art gave power to the rebellion of all the students who were united in those haunting melodies and in such words as "A little help from my friends," as sung by Ringo. It was a code song whose secret meaning was revealed to me by my students in class on a Mallarmé sonnet I was trying to decode for them.

They were extraordinary days when the significance of youth and popular culture came to the forefront, when literature and sex, when education and violence, all seemed to be interrelated. I tried to understand the sources and influences of those Liverpool boys in Elvis Presley, Bob Dylan, and the Who, as I similarly witnessed the effect they had on the language, the dress, and the hair of my students. In their first film, *A Hard Day's Night*, I could see the impact they had on huge audiences of the young, and in their second film, *Help!* I saw the effect of a Rimbaud prose poem in the snow scene with a piano. ("Madame X établit un piano dans les Alpes.")

In esthetic domains with which I was more familiar, I could follow the changes being brought about at the same time by John Cage and Merce Cunningham in music and dance, and by Julian Beck and Judith Malina in their courageous Living Theater. But I learned more from the Beatles in listening to the jauntiness of "When I'm sixty-four," and from the unspeakable sadness of that song where "Oh boy" is sung at the end of several lines, as in "I saw a film today, oh boy." When I learned that the final line of "A Day in the Life"—"I'd love to turn you on"—was the cause for its being censored, I grew as indignant as my students.

The very cover of the Sergeant Pepper album was a course in history as well as a glorification of the four Beatles. They celebrated themselves as well as Marx, Lawrence of Arabia, Marlon Brando, Oscar Wilde, Mae West, and numerous others. It was an effort for me to move from the Beatles to the Rolling Stones, but my students helped me in this course on counterculture, when they quietly explained that "help" in "A little help from my friends" was both "love" and "pot."

In our endless discussions of films I was more at ease because I am an old cinema addict who has never suffered guilt from watching films, and who seldom uses "good" or "bad" (as his students do) in speaking of a film. If the dialogue is poor, if the story is insipid, if the acting is mediocre, I focus on other matters, on the myth behind the film or on the theme and its relationship with my own fantasies, both conscious and subconscious. I am always able to relate my familiar subconscious desires with what I see on the screen. I am hypnotized by pictures, probably because my life is spent mainly with words— foreign words predominantly.

Several new films in the late sixties were addressed especially to a youth audience. They were films on student revolt, youth scene films where rock music played an important part and where the new trend of eroticism and violence was visible.

I would place *Woodstock* at the head of such films. It was not an ordinary film, built around a scenario, but it was both an accurate document and a set of beautiful pictures on the youth movement of those days. It was the film of a "happening," and as I watched it, I felt for the first time in several years a little hope for humanity. It was a film celebrating that peace enacted by the vast hippie world, the hippie tribe. Michael Wadleigh had made his film into an overwhelming apology for rock music, for long hair, for the indomitable spirit of hope that only the young possess.

In several of the films quite specifically directed toward the younger audience, the scenes of violence and pathos often induced laughter at the same time because of the off-beat type of acting for which the young did not have a word. "Camp" is the word, once used to refer to irregular offbeat behavior, and then used by such critics as Susan Sontag, Parker Tyler, and Christopher Isherwood to designate a certain kind of acting prevalent at the time of the student revolt and related to the principal neurosis of that day: the failure in communication, and in particular the failure of one generation to communicate with another.

The style of acting I am arbitrarily calling "camp acting" is a combination of acting a role and making fun of the acting or of the role or of both. The camp actor feels superior to the role he is playing and

66

keeps telling his audience by implication that he is playing around with the role and not playing it straight. Camp, as Susan Sontag elucidated, is a love of the unnatural, an indulgence in the artificial. It is always duplicity in some form or other. It can be humorous (as with Gould, Sellers, and Carol Channing) and we may be drawn to it. We may also be repulsed by it when the humor is based upon a mockery of human ideals and ambitions, and a mockery of the art of acting.

The young, when they are among themselves in a social situation, tend to talk in what I would call a camp style. Often what is being said is of a critical nature, but camp criticism has to be humorous. So, when the young see this camp style in a film, they recognize it. It is their own style, only more biting and more deliberately played. "Campiness" is so much a part of the ordinary behavior of the young that when they encounter it in a film, they don't look upon it as any special style that should be named.

The new critical spirit in the students was fashioned in part by the new films because the best filmmakers of the past fifteen years have been critics also. The most critical filmmakers are at the same time the most creative, and they are still in Europe, men like Fellini, Antonioni, Godard, Visconti (now deceased), Losey, Buñuel, Louis Malle (*Le Souffle au coeur*), Truffaut (*Nuit américaine*). From time to time an American filmmaker, such as John Huston, in *Reflections in a Golden Eye*, and in his more recent *Wise Blood*, rivals the achievements of the foreign filmmakers. These men comprehend the need to interpret the new culture for the student who is both scientifically and humanistically trained. A comparable critical-creative movement is going on in the other arts which many students follow as closely as they follow the development of rock music and jazz. The new serious music of Varèse, Webern, and John Cage hurts the ear. The new paintings of Helen Frankenthaler and Joan Mitchell are hard to look at. The new books of William Burroughs and Beckett are hard to read. The new films of Fellini (*Roma*), of Pasolini (*Porcherie*) and Kubrick (*Clockwork Orange*), are hard to follow.

My students who followed films the closest in the late sixties and who freely discussed their relationship to films seemed always to settle on Fellini's *Satyricon* as the art film of their day, especially when they checked the film's narrative taken from Petronius: the story of the young loafer Encolpio, who hires himself out to men and women, but not too successfully, and who has lost his potency through a curse of

Priapus. When he resumes his worship of Priapus, he recovers his potency.

The young who watched this film sympathetically were quick to realize that Encolpio's adventure was theirs: the insistent drive of the young to make themselves sexually attractive and vulnerable. This drive has to be revived through a regimen of exercise and sacrifice, so that the potency can be restored and then exhibited and consequently spent again.

Given the basic theme of Encolpio's adventure, Fellini is more interested in recreating a world that is collapsing. Quite literally at the beginning of the film, we watch the collapse of buildings and an avalanche of stones. This scene of destruction is one of disintegration announcing and paralleling the moral disintegration we watch in the following scenes of vices and excesses so exaggerated as to be monstrous.

Both the Latin work of Petronius and the Italian film of Federico Fellini are about licentiousness in the society of a licentious and literate emperor. Encolpio in Petronius is a wandering scholar, one in the school of the rhetorician Agamemnon, whose students, after the lesson, spilled out into alleyways, marketplaces and brothels. When we heard the words in the film: *sono uno studente* ("I am a student"), there was inevitably a shout of glee and recognition from the students in the audience of the movie house.

Encolpio and his lover Gitone are invited to Trimalchio's banquet. This orgy scene, often referred to by the Latin words *cena Trimalchionis*, occupies one third of Petronius' book. By some historians, the entire decline and fall of the Roman Empire has been read into the orgy, as I suppose one day the decline of America will be read into such films as *Easy Rider*, *Carnal Knowledge*, and *Trash*. It is significant that these three films about the young, and directed to them as audience, are concerned with male impotence.

In the film, Encolpio is the clue to watch. He is the adolescent, like today's student, seeing ugliness, living the drama of corruption as only the young can see it and live it. Older people do not see it that clearly, or refuse to see it, except for the artist, who remembers best his childhood and adolescence.

At the opening of the film, Encolpio is standing before a wall covered with graffiti—scratches, coarse markings, words, and drawings. At the end of the film, we see the same wall, but the graffiti have changed into frescoes. They are fragmentary frescoes, as if parts are missing or have been destroyed. Time has converted graffiti messages and drawings into art. The ghetto violence we saw at the beginning of the film has been transformed into the angelic, asexual figures of a frieze. As also at the end of the film, Encolpio flees the city and goes to the seashore where the sunlight blends sea and sky, and the screen reproduces Rimbaud's word in *L'Eternité*:

> Elle est retrouvée!
> Quoi?—L'Eternité.
> C'est la mer allée
> Avec le soleil.

I saw the film *Teorema* by Pasolini three times in Nice in August 1969. It was shown in its original Itialian, with French subtitles, at the Rex Theater, on the rue Masséna, which I have always found to be the best theater in Nice for avant-garde films. It stars Silvana Mangano and Terence Stamp. (The Italian of Stamp might easily have been dubbed. He speaks very little.)

Pasolini is both author and director of *Teorema*. This title, theorem, is justified in the rigorous working out of a problem which the film reveals. It is a term used mathematically as well as mystically. The full title might well be given as "The Theorem According to Pier Paolo Pasolini" to complement the title of his earlier film, *The Gospel According to Saint Matthew*.

As the triangle was used in the Middle Ages to designate the mystery of the Trinity, so the theorem was used by the sixteenth-century French poets to represent the mystery of the Redemption: *Théorèmes sur le sacré mystère de notre rédemption*, by Jean de La Ceppède, for example.

A theorem is a vision. *Teorema* is a vision presented in the form of a demonstration. Starting with the image of a handsome young Visitor reading Rimbaud, lines extend from him that touch and alter each member of a wealthy Milanese family. At first only the cover of the book is visible, but those spectators who know the iconography of Rimbaud recognize the sketch by the poet's friend Ernest Delahaye: "Rimbaud with hair combed back, in the style of Parnassian poets." Later in the film the Visitor reads out loud to two members of the family the last two lines of Rimbaud's text, *Les Déserts de l'amour*. By this time in the scenario, the two key themes have been lucidly established as the desert and love.

There are multiple sources here, but especially the spiritual meaning of Rimbaud's desert of love, and a familiar plot in pornographic literature in which a young man, either a visitor to the family or a member of the family, seduces in one scene after another every member of the family, including servants. This is the plot of Apollinaire's *Les Exploits d'un jeune Don Juan*, and it is the general plot of *Teorema*. Although the accusation of strong eroticism has been leveled at Pasolini, the tone of his film, its beauty and its meaning, make it into a contemporary work of mysticism drawing upon sexuality and the desert of Exodus, of Jeremiah, and of Rimbaud.

This film brought together for me three or four of the major obsessions of my life: the art of films first and most obviously; religion in its aspects of angelism which became clearer to me in the writing of Rimbaud than in the work of other poets; the power of words, a scenario in this case which is Pasolini's adaptation of Rimbaud's myth; and finally the power, the mystical, liberating power of the sexual act.

Pasolini proved to me, as in a theorem, why Rimbaud has been so important for me. The subject of "angelism" is at the basis of Rimbaud's experience and writing. He uses the word "angel" to designate a presence, either animate or inanimate, that imparts strength or wisdom to man. In the deepest sense he makes of the word, it represents an obsessive drive in a man to restore himself to a pristine, angelic state.

The poet's mission and the angel's mission have so intimate a resemblance that they appear identical. What is that mission? It is to put men into a relationship with a limitless world. Poetry would then be the most powerful ascesis, the most powerful discipline at man's disposal to change his earthbound being into an angelic being.

Dante in 014 (1970)

January 1970 was an auspicious beginning for me: the opening of a new decade when the agitation of the late sixties seemed to be quieting down, a new classroom for my courses, and a new course to teach I had not previously taught at Duke.

Such changes, not one of which was minor, and whose effect on me continued through the entire year because it carried into the fall semester as the year wore itself out, marked an inner psychic change in mental attitude and satisfaction of many kinds. The first five years at Duke were behind me. They had been trial years when I had been constantly, although not always consciously, testing myself in relationships with students, colleagues, administrators, secretaries, barbers, gasoline dealers, neighbors at Valley Terrace apartments, clerks and check-out girls at Kroger's supermarket. North Carolina had been in many subtle ways a different world in which to live. I had grown accustomed to a new tempo of living, a new speech, a new climate, a suspicious watchfulness on the part of some southerners with whom I had come in contact. I had had to prove myself in many small ways acceptable, or at least not exaggeratedly different from the Americans in whose world I was now living.

So, when the new events began occurring in January, I was no longer new to the campus and to the community. I felt somewhat assimilated, somewhat recognizable by French majors but also by students interested in literature, by film buffs, by students testing themselves as writers. A small world, but it was a distinguishable world, and I was no longer on the outskirts. Premedical, prelaw, preforestry students had begun electing my courses, and the numbers made it necessary to find a larger classroom.

I had always taught in 217 in the language building (the former law school). Only one classroom in the building was larger. In the basement, 014 had sixty-three seats. I asked for it, for all three classes, held every year I taught at Duke, the first three class periods on Monday, Wednesday, and Friday. In 1970 there was no official Italian teacher. To fill the gap I was asked to give a course on Dante which in past years I had given at Bennington and the University of Chicago.

Room 014 was spacious, comfortable, cut off from the rest of the building, and became for me more than a classroom. I soon practiced the habit of arriving early, about 7:30, in order to settle down in the room and glance over the notes I had prepared for the classes. Between eight and nine o'clock one or two or more students dropped in to ask questions about the work or simply to chat. The room became a meeting place where I began three days in the week with friendly visits. Room 014: a steady and steadying center for eight years, the site of conversations, classes, and examinations at the end of each semester.

I allowed the feeling to grow in me that at last I was a member of the university and even a member of the community. This new sense of belonging encouraged me to follow more closely than I had heretofore the infant year as it began developing and the world of nature in North Carolina. Springtime in the South is a quickly passing period of beauty. It lasts only a matter of a few weeks before the trees are covered with leaves and the days have warmed to sultry levels. The freshness of the new growth is replaced, faster than in the North, by a robustness that will last it through the heat of the summer. I saw the sprigs of forsythia in January that year, but generally the daffodils blossom first, and then the redbud trees and the forsythia. The leaves are tiny and bright green on the branches. Suddenly it is summer. There is no adolescence of the year in the South.

When I began teaching the *Inferno* for the first time at Duke, I wanted to accentuate the psychic over the moral and the religious. I wanted to consider Dante's descent into Hell as a descent into his subconscious, into his past, in order to understand why he is lost, why he is estranged. To justify and understand himself, a man has to know the worst about himself. By "worst" I mean those experiences, often forgotten or concealed, that have alienated him from the order of the world. Hell is the world reinvented. It is composed of one fantasy-picture after another, and each one is a form of obsession which if allowed to remain in the form of an obsession would cause serious suffering in a man's being, would impede him from self-realization and ultimate salvation, even salvation in the purely human sense.

Dante is the fountainhead of literature for me, the source. I have never felt the need of going before him to earlier writers, to the *chansons de geste*, or Chrétien de Troyes, to the Greeks or the Latin writers. They are all there in Dante, in places where I can see them, not analyzed, but used and illuminated, assigned to some niche in a vast reproduction of the world and the apocalyptic life of the world beyond the world.

The course on the *Inferno* was the hardest for me to teach, the most complex one for me to prepare each time I gave it, and the most exciting to give. I was more at home, and therefore felt more secure, with French literature, with the three courses that seemed to be approved of by the students: symbolism, Proust, and the modern theater. I had first to study carefully each canto and then plan ways of presenting it and decide on how much time to allow the structure of the canto, the theology and the psychology behind it, and its relevance to our world today. What words would I emphasize, what lines would I read in Italian and urge the students to memorize, thus giving them some exercise in Italian sounds and grammar.

These problems became a part of my daily life each semester I taught the *Inferno*. The schedule was one lesson per canto, which meant that with each year's revisions I would subtract details and try out new details. I wanted some of those miraculous lines and some of those episodes to remain in the minds of the students for the rest of their lives.

Often, as I prepared and reprepared the lessons, I would think back to my senior year at Harvard, 1929–30, when I took Professor Grandgent's course on *The Divine Comedy* in Sever Hall. It was the last year he gave the course. We were about twenty students, and most of us had studied Italian for one year in order to be admitted to the course. We used Grandgent's edition, which gave only the Italian text with abundant notes on language, history, and mythology. This edition was not to be displaced until 1973, when Professor Singleton's edition was published.

We knew that we would be asked to translate in class, line by line, the entire *Commedia*. Most of us, in preparation, used Charles Eliot Norton's rather close translation and checked in Grandgent's notes the necessary information on syntax, grammar, and history. Usually the class began with Professor Grandgent reading about thirty lines in

Italian, taking off from the last line translated in the class before. Then he would call on us, each by name, to translate approximately twenty to thirty lines. During the year we heard the Italian of about one-third of the *Commedia*, and listened to the awkwardly phrased, slowly articulated translation of the entire work. Very infrequently, perhaps once every two weeks, a student would ask a question about the meaning of a word, or the ending of a verb, or the use of some myth. Grandgent then would raise his eyes from his text, and with a slightly surprised expression on his face, answer the question. He never once asked us a question about meaning or interpretation. The course was simply, day after day, throughout the entire year, an exercise in literal word-for-word translation.

Year after year as I moved out from Proust into Dante and then back to Proust, I realized that Dante was not obsessed with time as Proust was. Dante's power as a poet is that of seizing time and inventing for it a pulsation that beats in the present. He puts together a structure for time, for all time. Proust, on the other hand, is time's victim. The descent in *A la recherche* is not into Hell—he is there already—but a universal, impersonal descent into the void. Because of life's fluidity and ephemeral aspect, death is real for Proust. Dante, who has no dread of time, no obsession with it, would call it that force that assassinates and ironically sustains life and promotes it.

I always made the effort with my students at Duke to point out how relatively simple it is to make the transition from the dead in the underworld regions of Homer and Virgil and the damned souls in Dante's *Inferno*, to the descent into the subterranean cosmos of his personality, which a man today can achieve, especially at moments of great crisis in his life when he needs to consult the dead of his race who still live in him, and the dead figures of his own personality who desire to return to the living self and resume an interrupted existence.

The subconscious is endless in a man and as deep as Dante makes his Hell. It is filled with as many grimacing and sad and violent figures as those we encounter in the Italian poem. The speech of those lost figures is as enigmatic, as dramatic, as elliptical as the speech of Filippo Argenti and Farinata and Cavalcanti, father of Guido. In the circles of his Hell, Dante encounters ghosts of the past who have some relationship with his own moral scruples and defects, as today a man encounters in successive medical consultations and self-analyses the origins of his inner conflicts.

Each of the five springs at Duke when I taught the *Inferno*, I tried to read it for myself in accord with the new critical-linguistic perspective of semiology. I have come to see more clearly how this poem (this *poema sacro*), like every great poem, is a hesitation between sound and meaning. Each reading is a reliving of the poem as an ancient, remembered message, and a message that is being ceaselessly renewed. The example of Dante dominates that of all other poets for me. How miraculously do literary works touch one another and penetrate one another! The *Commedia* comes from Homer and Virgil, from the Bible and Aristotle and Aquinas; and it reaches forward to Eliot and Pound, to Joyce and Proust, and into the still unwritten works of my students.

Proust and *Clockwork* (1971)

Between January and May of 1971 I was on sabbatical leave from Duke and taught two courses at the University of Utah in Salt Lake City. During two summers prior to that year I had taught summer school at Brigham Young University at Provo, and there had met Robert Helbling, chairman of the Department of Foreign Languages at Utah. His invitation to come as a semester visitor was most welcome. I was anxious to live again in Utah and in a community not totally Mormon. Provo had been that: 99 percent Mormon, I imagine, a center of strong religious belief and unity of purpose. All those Latter-Day Saints I met, students and faculty, could not have been more cordial or more attentive to my needs and well-being. But from time to time I suffered from a sense of being apart from them, of holding different beliefs. They lived so strictly according to the letter of their laws that by comparison I felt floundering, unattached, almost invisible.

The atmosphere was different at the University of Utah, where I was told the percentage of Mormons was fifty. This seemed accurate in terms of my own observations and conversations that semester. My life during those few months was restricted. Without a car, I lived within walking distance of the campus and one restaurant suitable for my evening meal. The few people I met and would have liked to see more often were busy with family obligations, with study, or with devising ways of making others study.

Robert Helbling, the man in charge of my activities in Utah, was a forthright counselor and gracious in every way. One afternoon at the beginning of the semester he held a reception in his home for a long-term visitor, myself, and a week-long visitor, Jorge Luis Borges. I was delighted with this chance of seeing Borges, who was accompanied by his translator and secretary-poet, Thomas di Giovanni. A few years previously I had had some correspondence with di Giovanni over some of his translations when I worked on the staff of *Poetry*. He remembered this, and we spoke first about that epistolary-literary acquaintanceship and about his visits to Bennington to talk with my old friend Ben Belitt.

The line of guests intent upon meeting Borges was diminishing when Thomas di Giovanni led me over and introduced me. The writer's blindness was apparent. I had to take his hand and shake it. He bent toward me slightly and asked me to repeat my name. He was hearing it for the first time. "You are a Scotsman, aren't you?" he asked. I answered, "Yes, originally, but I was born in Massachusetts and consider myself an American."

There was a slight pause then as he took hold of my arm. He seemed to be trying to remember something, and I kept silent too. After a minute's recollection, Borges said, "Will you let me say an old Scottish ballad?" Then he drew himself up and began reciting words totally incomprehensible to me. His face I still remember because it appeared transfigured as his spirit overcame his blindness.

The Utah stretch away from home base did me good, and I returned to Durham in May to rediscover a world now familiar and preferred, in which I seemed to have a role to play. A few older friends and a few students greeted me. However curious my life may have seemed to them, they were allowing it to be that without admonishment, without counsel for a change of habits and manias.

It was summertime already in early May. There had been no spring in Salt Lake City, but there would have been no spring in Durham had I been there. From my years in the North, I still missed watching the spring come in. But I knew that this privation would be recompensed by a long, glowing summer season as I settled back into my life at home.

That fall semester of 1971 I attempted once again to give my course on Proust in the now customary form of two sections, one in English and one in French. Teaching had not become easier for me because with each fall and with each spring at Duke, I found in my classes a good number of students I already knew. Proust would be a new subject for those students, but I would not be new to them. They had become familiar with my speech, my habits in teaching, and my various quirks. Friendliness was in them, but also a tinge of critical friendliness. Their manner was courteous, but they had become so accustomed to me in the same classroom that courtesy had turned into a relaxed, instinctive habit of attentiveness that embraced the work which had to be done and the familiar manner in which it was to be carried out.

The class conducted in English had the larger number of students new to me. Among them was a graduate student in history, Jim Winders, destined to become through the next few years a good friend. His knowledge of many subjects struck me as unusual for one his age. He was as concentrated on the classwork as anyone in the group, but unlike most, took few notes. The reason for this was simple, and I learned the reason soon. His powers of recall were prodigious. His mind recorded everything he heard or read, and kept everything in place so that whatever he needed to use was there. Jim was an authority on popular culture and became, without fully realizing it, my teacher. His doctoral thesis was divided into three long chapters: "Dada," — "Beat," — "Rock." How I enjoyed the many conversations we had over two or three years on these and related topics!

In the same class, front row on the side next to the door, sat a graduate student in English, John Richowski. As I taught the class, he wrote steadily. I suspected he was not consigning to paper the points I was trying to make about Proust but rather writing out questions about the points. When the class was over, he usually waited until all the students had left and then fired at me, in a very courteous manner, significant questions, difficult questions, for which in many cases I must have given him unsatisfactory answers. His interest lay definitely in criticism rather than in Proust, and I soon realized that he was reading and assimilating the new books that were appearing in the structuralist-semiotic approach to criticism.

John's combined interests in linguistics and science provided a rich background for his study of the new criticism. The first time I visited his apartment in Durham—his expertise in cooking rivaled his competency in criticism—I examined his personal library of the new books on critical theory, volumes only recently published, but destined to become key books for many of us during the next few years. His thinking was clear and precise, especially when he was concerned with difficult problems. This verbal articulateness crowned his elegance in dress, his courteousness, his tenacity in exacting from friends and books and the preparation of a meal the best that was to be exacted.

In the French section of the Proust course a different kind of relationship existed between the students and myself. I greatly enjoyed this shift from one language to another. Ostensibly the subject matter was the same in the class conducted in English from 10:10 to 11, as in the class conducted in French from 11:20 to 12:10. However, the man Proust and the achievement of his novel were more intimate and more real in French than in English. A specific word in the text— *mufle*, for example, or *tilleul*—the rhythm of a sentence or part of a sentence, the sound of a place name—Lannion, Caen—were magical formulas that transported teacher and students already addicted to a love for France and things French. Since the students taking Proust in English were being cheated (without their knowing it), I had to emphasize in that class such matters as characterizations and themes and structure. For the French section, language was all: every metaphor was real, every mystery was intact and protected from any facile interpretation.

Both undergraduates and graduate students used the French language as an entrance into that most special world of memory. I tried, by reiteration and repetition, to make the characters and the situations in the novel as familiar to them as characters and situations in their own lives. But especially I tried to bring about this familiarity by means of phrases and words and metaphors that we recited as magical formulas, as a litany that would in the course of time fill a corner of their memory, to be tapped whenever Combray was mentioned, or the avenue des Acacias, or *le petit pan de mur jaune*.

In teaching the Proust course, which had become for me a biyearly renaissance, I tried to have the students feel that the primary source of literature is language—and life as it is recast into language. That goal was harder for me to reach than the easier part of the lesson: the way in which the personages of Proust bear the seal of their creator's complex and mysterious genius. Behind the scenes in Paris and Balbec and Venice, behind the passages on Elstir's paintings and the laughter of Mme Verdurin, I wanted these new readers of Proust to understand—even faintly—to what degree writing is the instrument of an ascesis and the beginning of a salvation—the privilege granted to literature. I wanted them to sense the miracle by which the artist, initially a neurotic, finds his way back to reality through art.

By the end of 1971 the students, because they had had less experience with films, were not as aware as I was of the large number of striking films that had been released during the previous twelve months: *Carnal Knowledge*, with a script by Jules Feiffer and directed by Mike Nichols; *Sunday, Bloody Sunday*, a scenario of Penelope Gilliatt; *The Last Picture Show*, directed by Peter Bogdanovich; *The French Connection*, starring Gene Hackman; and Robert Altman's *McCabe and Mrs. Miller*.

At the end of this brilliant list came, in December, *A Clockwork Orange*, and I found that the reactions of students to it were more intense, more articulated than their reactions to other films of the preceding two or three years. *Clockwork* held them and held them a second time when they returned to it. I suppose the principal reason was the shock of seeing themselves in this film—both in their real life and in their fantasy life.

It has been called a film of the future. (The novel by Anthony Burgess, of 1962, on which the film is based, throws the action into the future.) But I prefer to look upon it as a film on the fantasy life of the young, which is timeless. Every episode: the milk bar, the scenes of violence, the parental apartment, the cure, and the cure from the cure, are all recognizable as elements of our contemporary world. But the atmosphere of every scene has elements of fantasy, with phallic fantasy dominating. The phallic fantasy is realistically portrayed in the crotchguards Alex and his "droogs" wear, in the false nose Alex puts on, in the bodily movements of the rape scenes, and in the huge white phallus sculpture Alex uses to kill the cat-lady of the Health Farm.

The idea of the future is in the opening shot of the film, a close-up of Alex where we see a sinister expression on a baby face. Malcolm McDowell, who plays Alex as brilliantly as he had played the leading character in *If* a few years earlier, is the most photogenic of the new film actors. That close-up shows all the themes: the blue eyes of the teenager, the black derby of the hoodlum, the false eyelashes on one eye of the youth fully aware of his physical attractiveness and the power he can wield over older people.

No film comes closer than *Clockwork* to revealing both graphically and dramatically the youth culture today. To the obvious themes of violence, drugs, and eroticism, one should add, to account for the second part of the film, the philosophical theme of pessimism. *A Clockwork Orange* appeared to me in 1971, and still does today, the most pessimistic work of art since the days of Dada. And since dadaism demeaned or refused the production of art, we might claim *Clockwork* in its total pessimism the equal of *Les Chants de Maldoror* of Lautréamont, in 1870. Thus a century is framed by two works, equal in their graphic power, one in words and one in pictures, and equal in their revolt against society.

The first sequences are an evening with Alex and his droogs (pals), an epic evening reminiscent of Roland, the Cid, and Maldoror. It all starts in the Korova milk bar where the milk is fixed with drugs. In the traditional epics, the soldiers needed wine and prayers of the mass before setting out to destroy the enemy. First, Alex and his friends beat and stomp on an old drunk. It is a warming-up exercise in sadism. Then they mess up a rival gang of teenagers. Here they are at their best physically. It is a beautifully maneuvered romp. Next, they invade the home of a writer and gang-rape his wife. Then we see them in front of a wall covered with graffiti. And then we are in Alex's room, where he is alone, not in the least exhausted from his evening. He needs this moment of solitude which allows him to get the cassette into the stereo and play Ludvig Van's *Ninth* during which he is able to reach a sexual climax.

This first part of the film, from the milk bar to Beethoven's "Ode to Joy," establishes for us, the spectators, the strong stylization constant throughout the film and characterizing it. Malcolm McDowell, in the role of Alex, is the supreme example of antihero, of the amoral young running rampant while the older members of society live barricaded behind doors. We remember that he played in *If* the leader of a student rebellion in a boys' boarding school. At the climax of that earlier film, McDowell turns a machine gun on all his teachers, an effective way of ridding the universe of those obstacles belonging to another age.

In both *Clockwork* and *Maldoror* the violence is so highly stylized that the time of the action is not quite the present. Is it tomorrow? Or the day after tomorrow? At least we are made to feel it is closer than we think. Malcolm McDowell seems to be the star of the future, the ultimate teenager, the ultimate student whom we fear and to whom we are drawn as to a revelation. The teenager bar that legally dispenses drug-spiked milk indicates at the beginning that we are not exactly in the present, but such a bar is predictably not very far off. There is a similar timelessness in *Les Chants de Maldoror* as in most Gothic tales and in the novels of Sade.

When students, particularly female students, complain about the violence in such a film as *Clockwork*, and the sadistic scenes in

Lautréamont, I find myself suggesting that they should look upon Alex as a visual manifestation of our subconscious. This suggestion is not made just to soften the effect of some of the scenes or to reduce the horror they might generate. I make the suggestion because that is what Alex seems to me to be. Everything is extreme and provocative in the film: the visual effects, the sound, the sexuality, the music, the language (part Russian, part Cockney, part Burgess). No film needs a glossary as much as *Clockwork*. And the pessimism of the film seems as destructive and absolute as we can imagine pessimism capable of being.

I have almost forgotten the second part of the film: the Ludovico technique designed to control violence. The change in Alex is reached in two weeks. In his study of the Bible he is shown daydreaming of erotic biblical pleasures. He is considered rehabilitated when he is shown scenes of violence and is thus made ill, when the sight of a nude girl provokes nausea, when he licks the boot of his tormentor. Alex becomes a hopeless human at the mercy of every violent element in society. He is finally as strange as a mechanical orange.

Gradually the moral emerges when we begin to realize during the cure scenes that what is being done to Alex is worse than what he has done to others. We watch him being deprived of free will and would prefer to see him as a thug. When the writer appears again in the film, and, in order to be revenged, plays Beethoven and drives Alex to a suicide attempt, we are relieved that a new program of reversal to Alex's original condition is taking place. It is a program that will reinstall all his love of brutal sex and violence. A free will to do evil is better than no will at all. The novel of Anthony Burgess and the film of Stanley Kubrick helped me during the next eight years, in teaching the *Inferno*, to define free will and a man's power of choice.

How to teach a poem? (1975)

In the spring semester of 1975 I offered my course on the *Inferno* for the third time at Duke. The presence in that course of Chris Colford and Fred Zipp, both of whom were working hard on the Duke *Chronicle*, incited in me thoughts concerning the day-by-day news they gathered and explored and exploited, and complementary thoughts concerning the text before us in class and my efforts to make it appear to these new readers as an art form that originally had been related to "news" (the story of Francesca, for example) and which had been cast into poetry.

A university resembles a great newsroom. Events that are transitory—a scandal, a change of academic policy, a defeat in soccer or a victory in basketball, a visiting lecturer who aroused or bored his audience—these were inflated in the news columns written by students and then the following morning read by large numbers of students before their classes began, and even, surreptitiously, during their morning classes. When I observed their absorption in reading the *Chronicle*, I felt challenged to try to transfer that absorption to whatever canto we were reading. Their immediate world of sports and films and politics, both national and academic, had to be transcended if there was any point at all in giving this course on a text of the fourteenth century. And I urged myself, as if I were breathing deep just before a race began, to keep my thoughts and my words on the highest things, and, like Orpheus, to sing praises of the gods.

Teaching is a performance, with language as its medium. A performance, because each hour is different from all other hours. It is also, on the grimmer days, an act comparable to running the gauntlet, if I can take that image as signifying a crossfire of any kind, an ordeal that lends itself, in every word spoken, to criticism and censure. As self-protection I tried to keep the points coming so steadily on whatever canto we were considering that criticism and censure would come, if they came at all, later in the day or the next day when the notes of the class would be reviewed by the student in his room and he would see the thinness, the ambiguousness, the unsteadiness of the notes. No matter how strong the text is, any course about the text is built on sand whose form is altered by every wave that covers it.

The survey course in the spring was based on readings from the nineteenth and twentieth centuries. It began with romanticism, a movement of such complexity that I have grown weary through the years of trying to make sense of it for students who are reading for the first time Chateaubriand and such poets as Lamartine and Hugo. The human experiences expressed in these texts are closest to the youthful experiences of these students. Classicism in the fall semester was infinitely easier to teach, and the terms we would be coming to later in the spring would be clearer: realism, surrealism, existentialism, structuralism.

All the attempts to define romanticism are failures because no one definition is satisfactory. At least one could point out what it wasn't, and what it was often called: the flamboyant triumph of Hugo's *Hernani*. As we read and analyzed some of the poems, I tried to suggest that it was the meaning of a particular experience of one man. That experience usually involved his sensibility, his emotions, his aspirations, and even his madness. The young romantic in revolt against society and even against God was a fairly obvious aspect to agree on. The romantic, feeling himself unsuitable for bourgeois society, was a concept my freshmen grasped quite easily.

Far more difficult to analyze was romantic melancholy and the demonization of the romantic hero as in Lewis and Byron. *Le beau ténébreux* was a term that attracted both the young men and women in my class, but they were uncertain about the phenomena of nightmares and hallucinations. The concepts of romanticism that meant the most to me were precisely those that meant the least to the students: the youthfulness of the poet's force in his will to liberate man and his art.

My students that year at Duke had grown up at a time when the current cliché was the gap between the generation of the young and the generation of the old. They were amused in applying it to romanticism and to the rights of the young in every age. This helped me considerably as I tried to emphasize the truth that nations come and go without defiling the spirit of the young. When we neared the end of our classes devoted to romanticism, I suggested a few far-out analogies in the hope that the students would not cling too closely to the familiar definitions. Might we look upon romanticism as childhood, as that search for unity a child feels and understands? Why not call it the quest for the grail and for the pure sources of being?

William S. Hart had ridden through my childhood, and I knew that John Wayne had ridden through the childhood of my students and had helped to shape some of their dreams. And so I reminded them of those Wayne pictures, of that star (who was not an actor) riding at the end of each film toward a world that was not the world of corruption and intrigue and ambiguities. I reminded them too of Joan Baez who never trained her pure soprano voice and who sang at protest meetings during the sixties and into the seventies and who in her songs held on to the freshness and pain of adolescence.

In the fall semester of 1975, I returned to a course I had not given for a few years, on twentieth-century French poetry. I used bilingual editions of the poets, emphasizing Valéry and Apollinaire at the beginning, and then reading selected poems of Claudel and the surrealists Max Jacob, Saint-John Perse, and René Char. It was a hard course for me to make significant because of the number of poets studied, and because in the English section there were always a few students who knew no French. Part of the course touched on poetics and theory, and I counted on those lessons as being new for everyone and therefore involving everyone on an equal basis. Premedical students, prelaw students, and science majors took the course, largely (I imagine) because they had tried me out in other courses. One or two had said to me, "Your title changes, but it is always the same course!"

The French majors in the French section were able to enjoy more fully any given poem we studied, although some of the texts, especially those of Char, were among the most difficult to be found in modern poetry. I already knew quite well several of those students, and I was moved to see them explore texts close to their own age after our earlier and easier exercises on Lamartine and Vigny. They had become franker with me, and more relaxed, but I never became sufficiently relaxed to ask them what that one course was that some believed I was always teaching. I made up various answers for myself, but no one formula fitted.

When we finally made some sense out of the boat metaphor in Apollinaire's "Mai," a student asked, "How does one hit upon such an image, where does it come from?" I tried in my answer that day to relate it to romanticism and to the search for unity I had once defined in class as explaining the romantic fervor. A great metaphor, I said, may come from many different experiences, all of which are mysterious: from sleep, for example, or from love, or from the gods. It may come in a verse, or in an aphorism, or in an image. A metaphor and the words that surround it are one stage of a series of inner transformations.

Between 1970 and the spring and fall of 1975, my method of teaching became more fixed than previously, and the students learned quite quickly what the system was. A course is, for me, the plot of a book, the project of a book I would like to write. It has themes and counter-themes, predictions and echoes, many characters who make promises and who reveal, as they promise, moments of illumination and conviction in phrases so startling that they appear magical.

Those are the phrases I have the students repeat under many guises, because they are the only ones where the French (their French as they speak) is accurate. At least they have said those phrases and heard them and thought about them. When the final examination comes, they will write out those phrases in their blue books, and then gradually the phrases will sink into their subconscious minds.

Each time the exam comes, it will be an exercise in counterpoint. Many of the students will execute it impeccably, with the echoes and the resonances in the right places and at the right time. The ideas of French writers will find their place in the vicinity of a province or a city or a river. A political regime will be restored with the name of a painter or the title of a book of verse. A mosaiclike map will be the questions and answers, because ultimately this is what I want: a concert of names and places and terms that will invoke some of the ambitions and accomplishments of France.

While proctoring the final exam in a course, I enjoy the silence of room 014. From time to time I look at the heads bent down over the blue books. One of those heads lifts up now and then. The student looks first at me to see what I am doing, and then looks up at the ceiling as if that were the best spot to contemplate for a moment of meditation. They are subdued. It is the end of something.

Tomorrow will begin for these students the gradual dispersal, the falling away of this group who met with me forty times for fifty minutes each time. Forty hours of their lives spent in this same classroom with me. Not a very long time to teach such a subject as Proust or Dante or Baudelaire, and to hope that it count in some intellectual, moral way. Impossible to measure the effect now, but in a year or two or ten, there will be a few testimonials. They will come to me in strange, unexpected places and times.

And always, during the three hours, I suffer from feelings of ill-defined apprehensions. Most certainly these apprehensions come from my not knowing exactly what these young people think of me, what their reservations about me are, what their friendliness really means. How can one know the thoughts of another person?

The final examination on twentieth-century French poetry: a large class composed of many different personalities, some of whom I have come to know this year. Here, even more than with my undergraduate classes, I am at a loss to know what the students think of Duke, of life and death and love. Let me accept the premise that I will not know, never know. And let me turn to some other conundrum: who is Beatrice? what was Beatrice for Dante? was she a girl? a woman? an image? a fantasy? was she God? or was she simply the means by which Dante the poet could articulate his thoughts and compose his art?

Those last hours of 1975, spent in 014, made the room seem to me more than ever an oasis, cut off from the university, a place reserved for great subjects, where I make the effort to be a teacher, apart from the inevitable rivalries and hatreds of a department. A place for questions, because the word *question* contains the related word *quest*. When, in the sixties, I read Edmond Jabès' book *Le Livre des questions*, I pondered this relationship between *quest* and *question*. Then, in September 1979, Richard Stamelman, from Wesleyan, sent me his article on Jabès and indicated in his inscription his memory of my questions at Duke when he was writing his doctoral dissertation on Apollinaire. A question is a search for something that is often beyond the normal, the expected answer. As a teacher I have often been surprised by answers that opened up other questions more significant than my original question.

When in class contradictions rise up out of the very questions I ask, and the students smile at the growing dilemmas, I quote a sentence of Socrates that Plato uses in one of his dialogues: "I have told you that I was born many."

In the poetry class, as we moved from poem to poem, the questions of the students rose up almost always from their desire to fix the meaning of a phrase and to understand the syntax, the order of the words. The poems of Apollinaire and Char, in particular, stimulated these questions, and the questions stimulated me, too, as I tried to answer them and say over and over again, in some form or other, that the actual subject of such a poem is not of very great importance. The students were puzzled by such a claim no matter how I tried to phrase it. I once said: "When you look at a stained-glass window in the cathedral of Chartres, when sunlight is coming through it, you don't worry about what subject it is depicting. You enjoy its mysteriousness and its sheer beauty. It should be the same with the glowing phrases of Mallarmé and a René Char. Don't try to unmask such poets. Their art is far greater than their thought."

At the best moments in such a class, I was being repaid for a life work, and I knew, without the slightest regret, that the harvest of my life is as intangible as the first flash of light that dawn brings to the sky.

How to teach Beckett? (1976)

The year 1976 was my last full year of teaching at Duke. I was to teach only the spring of 1977 and enjoy a sabbatical leave that fall, and also in 1978 I taught only the spring and retired that summer.

The excitement of teaching was at a high peak for me throughout 1976, in all three courses both semesters, and in the summer course I taught that year. I had always had many gifted students in my years at Duke, but in 1976 they seemed to be more intent upon studying the actual subjects of the courses: Proust in the spring, and symbolism in the fall.

Automatically now, ever since Flash had appeared in January 1973 with the volumes of Singleton and Grandgent on his knees, I checked in the English section of Proust how many fellows from Delta Sigma Phi turned up. I counted three the first morning: Tom Gore, Kim Bauman, and Paul Honigberg, old friends to me, who had brought along with them a fourth brother, Chuck Wheeler, already, as I imagined, prepared for and documented on my habits. Through that semester Chuck was to keep me informed about new films and counseled me on which ones I should see and which ones I could let go by.

The length of the reading—all seven volumes of *Remembrance of Things Past*—discouraged many students from electing the course, but that year most of the old friends had already a love for and a knowledge of literature that were impressive.

My first course each morning was the survey—nineteenth and twentieth centuries for the spring. Nap Gary, who had already taken the first half of the course, in a quiet, unobtrusive way had shown keen interest in French, in both language and literature. He too, like

Jeff Humphries, came from Indian Springs. His attention to French almost equaled his keenness over athletics and the fraternity he was joining. The goals of the course were both linguistic and literary, and I was eager to discover which students were interested equally in the two goals and who might continue with more advanced work. Nap certainly qualified, with three others: Jonathan Banks (from Virginia), John Brooks (from North Carolina), and Bruce Metge (from Chicago).

All of these students, and so many others I could name, were on the verge of making important decisions. They were testing their abilities, their tastes and inclinations—both open and concealed inclinations. They were students trying to write in a foreign language and beginning to realize that language, both foreign and native, is inseparable from culture, inseparable from an understanding of human experience. The reading of Proust that semester, as well as the reading of the romantics and Flaubert and Stendhal in the survey course, made it easy for me, and appropriate, to point out how the art of writing reduces the chaos of experience to some sort of order.

I had to oppose from the beginning of the semester the firmly rooted belief in the minds of those students that there is one interpretation of a difficult text that had to be found at all cost. Otherwise all search for meaning was futile. I had to try to bring them around to the opposite view: that all signs in a text are open to a new reading. A new reader, as well as an old reader who is rereading, has to be liberated from the shackles of an arbitrary and sterilizing "taste." All literary language is simultaneously improvised and composed.

By the time we reached *Le Rouge et le noir* in the survey course, we were well into *Le Côté de Guermantes* in the Proust, and it had become possible for me by then to point out theories I could not have started with. By that time most of the students had become resigned to the belief that Stendhal and Proust would not provide them with a heartwarming, entertaining narrative. We had been able to agree that in all writing of such seriousness there is an obscure activity going on in which a considerable element of malice may be discovered. Most events that occur in a man's life are without notable meaning and tend to be forgotten. When a novelist of the stature of a Stendhal or a Proust revives such events in the lives of his characters, he will find in them components that are sexual and demonic and theological.

The one summer school course I gave at Duke three or four times I called Theory and Form of Tragedy, in memory of the course I gave at

Bennington several times after inheriting it from Francis Fergusson. When Francis left Bennington to go to Princeton, where he directed the seminar on criticism, he bequeathed to me his two favorite courses: on tragedy and Dante. At Bennington, the course was always referred to as Theory and Form, but at Duke it was simply called Tragedy. Each time I revived it, I changed it drastically because of new readings in anthropology and mythology, and of more careful readings of Aristotle, Nietzsche, and Artaud. In addition to students unknown to me who enrolled in the 1976 summer school I found six whom I knew from a few years back: David Guy, at ease with whatever device or theory I would try to use; and Flash, who seemed to note possible changes in theory and practice; Mary Ward, who was gradually becoming a specialist in films; Jim Raporte, who had just returned to Duke after a year in Paris; and two of the younger students, John Brooks and Jeff Humphries, the sturdiest of the literature students who were demonstrating in class and out of class a growing interest in semiotic criticism.

The daily meeting was a trial for teacher and students alike. As soon as the hour and a half were over Monday morning, I had to begin working on the Tuesday class, and thus it continued until Friday. The religious origins of tragedy held us too long that summer. Whether it was *Antigone* or *Phèdre*, the liturgical aspect of sacrifice and redemption seemed to demand our attention, and the long class hour passed faster than it might have. But when we came to the theater of the absurd, to the theories of Artaud and Genet, to the plays of Ionesco and Beckett and Pinter, there we were being constantly faced with the chaos of our own world. The religious origins were still there but more concealed under the plight of mankind, and I felt myself more and more falling back on the playwright himself, on the writer and his function, on the degree of control he demonstrated over the subject matter of his play. I often referred directly or indirectly to Freud's theory that art can stabilize neurosis without removing it.

After the preceding semester, with my efforts to teach Stendhal and Proust, when there had been, inevitably, discussion about the writer himself and the relationship between him and his work, the summer course on tragedy was a welcome change and a pleasure because there the play counted—the text and not the playwright. When we talked of *Antigone*, there was no talk of Sophocles. *Godot* received full attention, and Beckett was simply the name of the playwright. Without studying it in any systematic way, we were constantly referring to *Hamlet* and agreeing with one another that Shakespeare is the most invisible of writers.

I had planned to focus at the end of the course on Winnie in Beckett's play *Happy Days*, as a modern instance of a tragic character. The mound of earth in which she is placed reaches to her waist in act 1, and in act 2 she has sunk up to her neck. Unable to move her body, she resembles the suicides of canto 13 whose bodies are tree trunks and who have lost in Dante's Hell all power of moving. Plato asks the question: are men sheep, slaves, puppets, toys of the gods? Hasn't Winnie, in her endless chatter, moved beyond the status of a character and entered some form of madness? She is conscious, but she demonstrates a shadow-bound consciousness. She has become intimate with what is unfathomable. She lives during that hour and a half on the edge of what Baudelaire and Pascal called *le gouffre*. Perhaps only the truly tragic hero sees into the emptiness of the world, the hollowness of a man's consciousness. Winnie speaks almost uninterruptedly—although Beckett has indicated several pauses in her discourse—and she knows that nobody is listening out there. We the audience listen to Winnie the actress, but Winnie the character has no audience, not even her husband, Willie.

In 1979, a few years later, I had some illuminating conversations with my friend and former student from Bennington, Martha Dow Fehsenfeld, who that May in London had watched Samuel Beckett direct Billie Whitelaw in *Happy Days*. Somehow that play, more than *En attendant Godot* and *Fin de partie*, had stayed in my mind, haunting it, and obsessing some of my dreams. *Oh! les beaux jours* is a burial service for humanity. The poetry of paralysis, of immobility, is much more than an expression of avant-garde art. I remember Madeleine Renaud, who created the part in Paris, and especially the choreography of her arms. According to Martha, Beckett insisted more on the hopelessness of Winnie's plight when he took over the direction of his play. She already knows the extreme point she has reached when she is awakened by the bell and utters her first words: "Another heavenly day." The force that holds her is the force of tragedy: that is what I would have tried to explain or discuss, had I gotten to the play with those students in the summer of 1976.

When Winnie is buried up to her neck, and only her eyes can move, we realize how eroded her consciousness has become. It is hard not to think of Dante's suicides, of Pier della Vigna who will remain thus planted for all eternity. She is the bearer of her destiny, and here, in the full Aristotelian sense, it is an implacable destiny.

There have already been many Winnies, and there will be many more. But there have not been as many interpretations of the play as there have been of *Waiting for Godot* and *Endgame*. As is true of all of his writings, here in *Happy Days* there is no self-indulgent pathos. Man's fate, woman's fate is stern, and demands a hero, a heroine.

In trying to teach in class other texts of Samuel Beckett, I have felt that what Beckett has learned from living (and from reading Dante) coincides with a temperament that has grown in our time, a temperament that is in my students more than in me. This may be the clue to Beckett's continuing and growing success. Adamov, Genet, Ionesco are already relegated to the past of the theater, whereas Beckett is still in the avant-garde.

I sensed first in Winnie the immobility of Dante's suicides, but there is also in her the will-lessness of the vestibule, of the "neutrals" in canto 3. She is the tragic figure unable to affect her time or events or her destiny. The chronicle of her life is about petty things which we see in the assortment of objects: a toothbrush, a looking glass, a handbag, a pistol. But it is also about cosmic matters: about the death that awaits her. Her soliloquy is her last rite, her extreme unction. She is about to pass to judgment.

What a pertinent example *Happy Days* is for an illustration of Baudelaire's theory that art places a veil over the terrors of the abyss. ("L'art voile les terreurs du gouffre.") The critics and the teachers in their classrooms will continue to tell us what Beckett takes care not to tell us. When they speak or write, they rely on philosophy and metaphysics, whereas *Happy Days* is a drama, a tragedy cast in a form that could have been written only in our years. Winnie is as unique and as representative as Antigone and Phèdre.

So I add these notes to that summer course of 1976, when, at least as we were looking at *Fin de partie*, I pointed out how ideal a playwright Beckett was for a teacher who likes to have two sections of a class, one conducted in English and the other in French. Samuel Beckett: Dublin-born, but Paris-based.

I had always wanted to reach in Symbolism (fall 1976) the teaching of a subject that could be called "literature" and not "French literature" or "comparative literature." This was the course that, by its very nature, had to emphasize the incantatory power of words, the secretive power of a metaphor, the primitivism of a rhythm that we might enjoy saying and hearing over and over again.

Often the questions we were able to raise in class had no facile answer and we considered them gravely. Is writing an irrelevant act? Or is it the most relevant of all acts? The symbolists often used *Hamlet* in order to declare and celebrate the redemptive role of words in human beings. In the two courses on tragedy and symbolism, *Hamlet* became a *point de repère* in which the poet exposes himself at the pinnacle of artifice. Isn't *Une Saison en enfer* an example of self-purging in the same way that *Hamlet* is, in which the private obsessions of the writer are converted into a rhetoric for public consumption? Do the words of a poet impoverish the truth or do they create another truth scarcely suspected by the poet? We are not purely rational—I tried to say this in some form or other in each class—and we are not innocently good. These two statements were shortcuts to the central positions of symbolism and tragedy.

Whether it was an episode in Proust—Bergotte's death scene—or a single sonnet of Mallarmé—*le pitre châtié*, after we had worked on it line by line, word by word—we were then in a position to consider the leading questions about art: what it is and what it does. When Bergotte rolls off the divan in the art gallery and dies, with Proust asking the question: *mort à jamais? qui peut le dire?* and when the clown in Mallarmé's sonnet pushes his arm through the tent for his escape, we were able to see, each of us in the classroom, that art in the formal creation is the opposite of the vast, formless strength of the natural world. A few times in those classes, I used Ezra Pound's definition: "Great literature is simply language charged with meaning to the utmost degree."

My tendency has been to call upon psychoanalytic interpretation —the *Illuminations* of Rimbaud encouraged me in this—and declare that literature is nothing more or less than our primal fantasies. From the far past of a man's life there are many forms of dark debris that keep shifting about, and if the man begins to write, these debris begin to move up toward the surface of his consciousness.

But art will not cure a man of whatever illness plagues him. There is such compulsion in the writer to tell his story that he can easily believe it is the demon driving him to his desk. A shrewd writer does not revise the emotions in his work, but he reworks its language. Language which is in us and had formed us looks for the subject of the poem or the novel, and then the subject finds the language.

I have always liked Flannery O'Connor's definition of fiction as that art based on mystery and manners. "Mystery" is for her our position on earth, and "manners" those conventions which, in the hands of the artist, reveal that mystery. She was often asked in her public appearances how a young writer who has not lived very long can find enough subject matter for his books. Her answer was usually the same: anyone who has survived childhood has enough information about life to last him the rest of his life.

The words a man speaks, and especially the words a man writes, have a redemptive role. They reveal his sinful consciousness.

Proust, sexuality, and art (1977-78)

For the last two months of 1977 I was back in Durham in total contentment to be home again with the familiar objects of my apartment and the familiar routines of running it. I knew the memories of Florence where I had spent September and October would grow richer in time, but they were momentarily put aside as I reestablished myself in Durham and began preparing my course on Proust for January, which was to be my last teaching assignment at Duke. My retirement was scheduled for the summer of 1978. I determined to live in the present during the coming semester and enjoy the classes without planning and scheming on ways to live and places to live when May would come. I succeeded in doing that, largely because of the heavy schedule of three sections and the way in which the students took to Proust. Any lack of interest in the course that particular semester would have shattered me.

I began rereading *A la recherche du temps perdu* with the hope of finishing it when the students presumably would be finishing it, in late April. It was approximately the twentieth time for me through the novel, and, as always in the past, the reading absorbed me totally. The passages and episodes I enjoyed the most were still there—I read some of them out loud—and the less familiar passages I tried to scrutinize more closely, convinced as I was that every sentence in the three dense volumes of the Pléiade edition was significant. My markings from the other readings were there, in various colors, and I added to them sentences I must have read on earlier readings too fast or too inattentively.

During the two months in Florence, my mind had been nourished on what I had *seen*. It had been an experience of expansiveness when

96

my vision had concentrated on all that was outside of me: the streets and squares of the city, the stone façades of the palaces, the paintings and the architecture. My readings of Proust began pulling me back into myself where I recognized again the characters of Proust, as real to me as real friends both living and dead. And I began reliving familiar thoughts on the mysteriousness of human personality, on the gamut of sentiments that destroy us: fear of death, sadness from the passing of time, the intermittent torture of jealousy, the drive to possess another person sexually, and the stark fear that once that was accomplished the promised experience of love would be over.

Mildly formed convictions concerning sexual drives in myself and in friends I know well grew more firm in me as I read Proust that season. Some of those beliefs coincided with Proust's, and in fact had been strongly influenced by him, and others, while not Proustian, did not seem to be in contradiction with him. I encouraged in myself the rehearsal of these thoughts about sex and attempted to reconsider them during the last two months of 1977.

I have always avoided analyzing a strong emotion and a moment of happiness because they lose in any analysis. They belong to the present, and as long as they endure they are in the present. But like most men (and women) I am just as much influenced by the past as by the present, and that presence of the past inevitably erodes a strong emotion, especially a sexual emotion, and an experience of happiness, especially if that happiness is at least partly sexual.

We are all patients with repressions, and these repressions have sexual origins. Whatever neurosis dominates me at the moment, I have to say: "Let it flourish, it pays better dividends than conventions." Whenever the neurosis becomes so strong that I am perturbed by it, I fall back very deliberately on the experience of sleep in which so many problems can be resolved. Oh! the sinister adventures of sleep that always avoid the blandness of consciousness, and in which the self that sleeps stalks and finds the real self!

Love affairs? No, they are quite simply not worth it! If today I were asked, "Who is beautiful?" I think I would answer: "Children!" They in their beauty surpass most adolescents and all young men and women. But the beauty of children changes so fast that even that cannot be cherished very long. When their beauty begins to fade, then they fall in love and by definition become uninteresting. When a friend is in love, give him up, give her up, for as long as the intensity of the love endures. A man in love has lost his relationship with the world.

I doubt if original, spontaneous love exists any more. From childhood on, from books and films, from bull sessions on sex, we are taught how to love, what words to use, what acts to perform, what sentiments to feel. Women learn the rules more obediently than men. They learn to act continuously. For both sexes, being in love is existing in a form of slavery. To be in love is to be shackled. It is hard to be in love and not want the beloved endlessly at your side. That is the danger.

We are so closely allied with an inferior and brutish nature that I wonder if anyone knows what chastity is. Love, far from being a form of happiness, is a form of anxiety. It almost inevitably has its origins in the fortuitous: a chance meeting, a sudden recognition, an introduction we had hoped to avoid. Then unexpectedly we realize we love someone who is indifferent to us, whom we might never have met if we had not attended a given function. We fall in love with the mystery of a personality about whom we will never learn what we would like to learn. As long as love endures, our curiosity remains frantic, and the one loved remains safely outside our frenzy. The day comes then when we know that our frenzied feelings are far more real than the creature we love.

Our *idées reçues* on sexuality were first clearly stated by Flaubert, and then, half a century later, Proust analyzed the theory again and gave it its fullest expression. He moves the topic of sex away from morality, religion, and rationality, and gives it a more purely psychoanalytic explanation. When the year 2000 comes about, I imagine there will be no distinction made or felt between homo- and heterosexuality. I no longer know what the criteria are for so-called normal sexuality. The best I could do, in a vain effort to distinguish the sexes, would be to say that a man's speech, a man's discourse, is one of repression. A woman's speech is largely of desire. She is oppressed because she speaks (and writes) of present matters. He is repressed and thus speaks (and writes) of the past.

Woman exists as a body in the sexual act. Her pleasure is greater than that of the male. He is concentrated on two matters: erection and ejaculation, and he tends to speed them up for fear of any sign of impotence. When ejaculation occurs, it is for the male a sign of power. This is his satisfaction and this is also his denial of sexuality. To exist as a body in the sexual act, a male would have to become female. This does occur, of course, and when it does, I would say that homosexuality is present in both male and female.

At least the old polarity of male-female seems outmoded, as we are heading toward the new unisex, or, I would prefer to say, back, way back, to the beginning of time, to the original bisexuality. There are as many sexes as there are individuals: this is the only single belief I can easily accept, and I predict that the subject of androgyny will be explored during the next twenty years by literary and art critics, by psychologists and anthropologists.

A sexual affair begins because there is not only attraction but need, and the need is stronger than the attraction. Then the new dimension of love, as it grows between the two, is exalted by anguish. This is not too strong a term—of course it is Proustian—because behind the need felt by each lover there is a complex psychological drama of which he is not fully aware. In his need for his mother, each man is inexorably predestined to the experience of anguish whenever he falls in love with a woman not his mother. The character Marcel in Proust's novel, when he is suffering from jealousy over Albertine, thinks as much about his mother as he does about Albertine. In fact, Marcel never seems to think about Albertine herself, but about the effect of jealousy in himself. He looks ahead in time—to Venice perhaps—when he will feel pure tenderness rather than jealousy. But when that stage is reached, he knows that the love will be over. The ending of an "affair" is predictable, as the beginning of an "affair" is predestined.

Whereas Marcel yearned to learn everything he could about Albertine, he feared that his own personality was being invaded. We watch Marcel living in the past, and even in the distant past when he associates himself with some mythological character. The past is more present than the present. Love is a monologue. It is almost never a dialogue. In canto 5 only Francesca speaks to Dante. We never hear Paolo speak. And in Proust's novel we follow Marcel's torment of jealousy while we, like him, cannot see clearly the character of Albertine.

In love the background is more significant than the figure set against the background, the setting of the fortuitous meeting: a restaurant, a classroom, a tennis court, a bus ride, a halloween party. (It was the sea at Balbec for Marcel.) When we can't know the beloved, we fall back on the place where we first met her. Fate struck us there and made it impossible for us not to love and not to suffer.

Fantasies give us our problems, but fortunately our fantasies keep changing. The rising up in us of a new fantasy is comparable to the fortuitous meeting with a possible new partner. And then what a startling metamorphosis when the unreal becomes real and the real becomes unreal!

Our consciousness is a void we keep trying to fill. Our subconscious is overflowing. The sexual fantasies we try to stuff into our consciousness (conscience?) are pale and weak by comparison with the unsought fantasies of our dreams.

It is easy to believe that much of what happened to us during adolescence has been forgotten. Not true. Nothing has been forgotten, but much of what happened has been recast by our memory in its willful drive to reshape and reinterpret, to embellish in a form closer to fiction than to autobiography.

So, in early January 1978, I returned to classroom 014, after a semester's absence, in order to begin my last semester as a teacher at Duke. For several years two parts of the Proust course never underwent any change: the very beginning, the first five or six minutes of the first class, and the last fifteen minutes of the last lesson at the end of the course. The intervening lessons would change, either slightly or considerably, depending on many things: the use of a new passage in the text or the revised use of a familiar passage, the development of a theme, references to theories of new critics concerning Proust himself. Only the very beginning and the ending of the course had been stabilized.

That January morning in all three sections I began the course with the same thoughts: "Proust is the French literature course I enjoy giving the most." (Several of the students present that morning had taken the Dante with me and knew of my special predilection for the Italian poet in my own life and teaching.) "Yet, despite this fact, it is the course I worry about giving to young people because of the feelings of guilt it gives me. It is not the literal story of the novel I worry about, not the characters and the episodes, but it is the effect of the reading on you. If you stay with me through the semester and do the reading and come to class, you will be changed by the end of the course. When May comes, you will not see humanity in the same way you see it now. In learning more about mankind through Proust, you will lose your innocence. I will continue to feel guilty about this. Do I have the right to teach such an author and thus alter your lives and your attitudes? It is not too late to drop the course."

The ending of the course was to be in 1978, as it had always been previously, the story of my chance encounter in Paris, in 1930, with the character in Proust called Jupien, whose real-life name was Albert Le Cuziat. That story I have told in *Journal of Rehearsals*. It could not be told before the end of the course when the character Jupien would be instantly recalled, and his various scenes instantly remembered by those who had just finished reading *A la recherche du temps perdu.*

Section one, at nine o'clock, was always the quietest section. It was the smallest, with thirty-five students, and with fewer students whom I already knew. With that first class I had to work a bit harder to stir up responses, but that effort gave me clues which I could use for the second section at 10:10 that filled the room—sixty students who had slept an hour longer and were more boisterously ready to respond. Section one was my rehearsal for section two.

To my left, as I stood facing the class, the entire second row was filled with a group of friends, surrounding in its center Bill Brown, whom I remembered from the symbolism course but whom I had not known well during that semester. He had then distinguished himself to me in two ways: by wearing throughout every class a golf hat, or rather, golf hats, of varied colors. I had never seen him bareheaded until that first meeting of section two, and throughout *Proust* he remained bareheaded, as if the shift from adolescent Rimbaud to starkly solemn Proust demanded his changed appearance. His other distinction in the symbolism course had been his friendship with Ted Weiss, the poet at Princeton, whom I had known at Yale. Ted and Renée Weiss had brilliantly sustained publication of the *Quarterly Review of Literature* through the years. Since Yale, we had corresponded, met once at Nice and La Napoule, and planned reunions without ever bringing them off. Because his family lived in Princeton, Bill Brown brought me news from time to time from Ted Weiss.

Almost every class had a "mystery" student for me, who, although not unapproachable, made no approach, who performed impeccably, but who revealed neither clear enthusiasm nor clear distaste. In section two his name was David Gombac, who the first day arrived just at the beginning of the class, entered the room quietly looking at no one, and took a middle seat in the last row. This entrance, as if it were timed, occurred the next spring when I taught Dante in my new role of "emeritus." David Gombac and I exchanged just a few words in those two semesters—about Chicago, which was his home. I could never tell his reaction to the classes. I associated his beautiful handwriting with the mysteriousness of his character. Then, on the last page on the last blue book of the Dante final examination, he wrote out in two lines a personal appreciation of the two courses, words that resembled engravings on granite for me.

Section three, conducted in French, filled all sixty-three seats, and was, as always, the group with the largest number of students who had worked with me before. Apprehensive about the length of the reading but also proud that they had reached this level of competency in French, they launched into the new work.

When the course began in January, I was well into my rereading of the novel, and I had begun a very slow rereading of one of the smallest studies ever written about Proust, which had become for me one of the most stimulating critical studies on *A la recherche*. I had read it when it first appeared in 1964, my first year at Duke, because I had been struck by its title: *Marcel Proust et les signes* by Gilles Deleuze. A prophetic title containing the word *signe* destined to play the central role in literary criticism for the next ten years.

I had grown tired of stressing in earlier years the psychological aspects of the novel. Deleuze confirmed my feelings that Proust was basically a Platonist. In the action of the novel Marcel never looked for "signs"; they were encountered by him accidentally, and then in the course of the encounter they were deciphered in their relationship with earlier signs. This was applicable in the early part of the novel to *la petite madeleine*, a fortuitous signal that Marcel had to interpret. And likewise at the end of the novel, the episode of *les deux pavés de la cour* happened in a similar fashion and was deciphered in a similar fashion.

Proust: an exercise in hieroglyphics. This guided me in my new preparation of old lessons in the spring of 1978 and helped to renew for me the power and the beauty of the entire novel. As the students read it for the first time and became involved in the story, in the behavior of the many characters, in the metaphors on memory and jealousy, on the writer's vocation, on the duchesse de Guermantes' red slippers, I tried suggesting, without undue insistence, a search for signs and a way of interpreting them by allying them with earlier signs. This approach, more than any I had previously attempted, helped to prepare the grandiose conclusions that Proust makes about the reality of art in *Le Temps retrouvé*.

A first sermon (1978)

Before the beginning of the Proust course in January 1978, my feelings had been mixed: half excited expectancy at going through the novel again with new students, and half concealed sadness at knowing it to be my last course at Duke and the literal ending of my teaching career. (I did not know at that time or throughout the semester that I would be invited, as an "emeritus," to teach Dante at Duke the following spring.)

And yet, once the class meetings began, and the work resumed full force, I was not disturbed in the least, and seldom thought about the crucial moment I had reached in my life. I thoroughly enjoyed those classes as the students became involved with the text and were gradually building up familiarity with it. Never once did I remind them of my prediction—spoken not too solemnly—that they would be changed by the course. And they, too, as far as I could tell, forgot the prediction—until the course was over.

Two events marked for me the ending of the course and of my teaching at Duke. A few of the students who were editing the *Archive*, especially its chief editor, Haun Saussy, and who were in the Proust course, asked permission to hold a public meeting to honor me. It was announced as open to my students and friends, on a late Sunday afternoon, in one of the Divinity School lounges, the same room in which a few years earlier we had celebrated Proust with a slide lecture by Harry Stokes and madeleines (cooked by Yvonne Rollins) and tea. I kept to myself those sentimental memories, but they were very much in my thoughts and I felt sufficiently self-indulgent to cherish them.

As the date approached for the *Archive* meeting, and as nothing had been said to me about what was to happen, I felt somewhat apprehensive and decided to ask Haun what I should be prepared for. He replied, a bit surprised that I had not intuitively known about the program, "You are to read to us. We thought you should choose a few of your favorite French poems you have taught here at Duke and read from your own writings anything you would like to read."

So, I was to be the one performer in a program which I thought had been designed to honor me. It was too late to modify such plans, which were really no plans at all. The friends who attended that Sunday afternoon in April, and the students, made the occasion seem a natural one: a reading for the *Archive* by a faculty member rather than by a visiting writer. I read as the students had suggested, a series of French poems that had always been a part of my yearly teaching, and then a few passages from this very memoir, especially pages on dawn and early morning work. I ended by reading a few poems I had been writing that semester on characters from Proust.

The second event had been scheduled six months earlier. The Duke Chapel ministers had asked me to give the sermon at the eleven o'clock service on the last Sunday in April, which was two days after my last meetings with the Proust classes. I felt honored by this invitation but fearful that I would be inadequate. The chapel staff knew that I attended mass every Sunday at York Chapel. This request to give the sermon in Duke Chapel was a gesture of graciousness. It was to mark the end of my formal teaching at the university. I worked on the brief sermon in an effort to speak as directly as possible to the students by giving a few references to moments some would remember from the classroom.

When Helen Crotwell, the associate minister of the chapel, invited me during a telephone conversation, my first answer was: "Helen, I have never given a sermon in my life." "Well," she answered, "that is not what your students say." Those words gave me pause, and I decided not to prod any further, and simply to accept this first and final pulpit appearance. As soon as I began speaking from that elevated spot, my apprehension stopped. I print the sermon here on these pages, because I had made one request: not to have it printed as is the custom in the chapel for sermons given by ordained ministers.

Sermon

*It is a privilege for me to present to you this morning what is to be
called a "sermon," but which I prefer to think of as a sharing with
you of some thoughts about a passage from the Gospels.*

*I am not following the church calendar because Easter was a few
weeks ago, and for my text I am going back to a moment before the
resurrection. Such a liberty should be granted a man who is giving his
first sermon which in all likelihood will be his only sermon. It is
appropriate that the sermon be given here in this chapel of Duke
University.*

*The title of this sermon, if I gave it one, would be quite simply
"Belief." And to approach a possible meaning of belief, I am taking
one of the last seven words spoken by our Lord on the cross. One of
the two thieves crucified with Christ, the one usually called "the good
thief," has just said to him: "Lord, remember me when thou comest
into thy kingdom." (Luke 23) Jesus answers him—and this is my
sermon text—"Today thou shalt be with me in Paradise."*

*A personal reason is behind my choice of this particular text.
Throughout a large part of my life, I had hoped to hear a sermon on
this text, and I never have. It has always seemed to me the most
dramatic of all the statements made by Jesus that have been recorded.
Even more than dramatic, it is a sentence charged with meanings that
proliferate as we think about them, and that quickly go beyond our
powers of comprehension.*

*Let me take a minute to review what had immediately preceded
this central moment in the history of the world. It came at the end of
eight days when Israel had been darkened, when the Gentile world
had been blinded, and when the Son of Man had been handed over.*

*But the time had come for the prophecies to be fulfilled. The events
took place swiftly: he was betrayed, he was taken over by the authorities, imprisoned, reviled, forced to carry his cross, nailed to the cross
and then elevated on the cross—the French poet Claudel has described in an admirable metaphor Christ during those last days of his
life: "a great stag at bay, stumbling in the midst of the dogs." ("ce
grand cerf aux abois, et trébuchant au milieu des chiens.")*

*It is the picture of the final scandal. We should not forget that
everything he did or said during the three years of his ministry had
seemed scandalous to many, to the majority, perhaps. He upset the
Chosen People on the seventh day of the week, and we might say he
upset the Gentiles on all the other days of the week.*

This moment on the cross is one of supreme clarification. It reminds us of that moment in the life of Adam, Christ's great ancestor, when he was expelled from the garden. It reminds us of that atoning animal we read of in Leviticus (chapter 16), the scapegoat loaded with the sins of the people and sent out into the desert. Now it is the Son of Man expelled from the city, and, more than the city, expelled from the world. The final picture we have of our Lord as a man is Christ raised on the stocks above the earth.

From that last stopping place, we can hear Christ saying seven words. The first is a general word of pardon of those who had participated in the crucifixion: "Father, forgive them, they do not know what it is they are doing." The second word is often interpreted as the founding of his church when he says to his mother and to his disciple John: "Woman, this is the son. This is thy mother."

The third is the simple yet overwhelming sentence our Lord says to one of the thieves: "Today thou shalt be with me in Paradise."

On his level, at his right and at his left were two thieves undergoing the same fate, spread out, exposed, forming with him one group, and thus fulfilling Isaiah's prophecy: "He would be counted among the wrong-doers" (chapter 53). These, then are the two companions our Lord chose from all mankind for the last hours of his life. With his third word, he establishes in relationship to himself a right and a left.

Who were these so-called thieves, one of whom is impenitent and who says ironically to Jesus: "Save thyself and save us," and the other, the penitent thief who suddenly believed and said, "Remember me." These men were two prisoners from the jail in Jerusalem. They were probably not literal or petty thieves, but political prisoners, men who had belonged to the Jewish underground, who had participated in what we would call today guerrilla warfare against the Romans. Men of violence, revolutionists, strong personalities.

One of them remains unbelieving, but the other, on the right hand, is stirred by the sight of Jesus enduring his punishment, and abruptly, unexpectedly, knows himself to be in the presence of God. And Jesus, sensitive as he always had been to the slightest movement of the spirit in others, knows that he is not dying alone and unloved.

This story of the two thieves, which is almost a parable, has a counterpart in contemporary literature in the two tramps of Samuel Beckett's play Waiting for Godot. At the beginning of the play, Vladimir, the more optimistic, the more hopeful tramp, is meditating on the Gospel story, and says: "One of the thieves was saved." There is a pause then while Estragon, the pessimist, pulls off his boot that is

paining his foot. And Vladimir continues: "It's a reasonable percent-
age." With these words he is saying that salvation is a 50–50 chance.

A bit later Vladimir resumes the dialogue with the question: "How's
your foot?"

> Es. Swelling visibly.
> Vl. Ah yes, the two thieves. Do you remember the story?
> Es. No.
> Vl. Shall I tell it to you?
> Es. No.
> Vl. It'll pass the time.

And then, like many Bible exegetes, Vladimir wonders why only
one of the Evangelists, Saint Luke, speaks of one thief being saved.
He grumbles a bit as he says: "The four of them were there—or
thereabouts."

The effect of this dialogue is to make us, the spectators, identify the
glib Vladimir and the resentful Estragon with the two thieves, and to
see both sets, theives and tramps, as dividing all humanity into two
groups, believers and nonbelievers.

Beckett knew the famous use that Saint Augustine made of the
story when he advised: "Do not presume; one thief was damned. Do
not despair; one thief was saved."

The hardest question to answer concerning this episode is: how did
the good thief come to believe that Christ would be king after his
death? The only possible answer involves the power of grace, and the
best we can say is: the spirit of truth touched him. He must have
realized that we come into existence through God's love. We are
called into this world because of love.

The thief uses a messianic term: "when thou comest into thy king-
dom." And Jesus, in his answer, uses a word he never used in his
teaching, another messianic term that appears only three times in the
Old Testament, and only three times in the New Testament: the Per-
sian word "paradise," meaning "orchard" or "royal park."

"Today thou shalt be with me in Paradise." The word "today" is in
this context the future, the immediate future after death. Human
experience, human wisdom, human history have not given us an
explanation of what Paradise is. Grace in one instant came to the
thief. Not only was he absolved by Christ, he was sanctified, he was
canonized. In one moment he moved from alienation to redemption.

It is the most spectacular story of belief in the Bible, even more
spectacular than the story of Saul of Tarsus who became Paul. I say

more spectacular because Paul had always been a highly moral and good man. The scene itself was not one to inspire hope. Everything around the dying thief seemed God-forsaken. Yet he knew by his proximity to Jesus that he was on the edge of the Kingdom of God. When he said: "Remember me," he knew that this man was the king, on his way to his kingdom.

The astronomer Copernicus is buried in the cathedral of Frauenburg in Germany (now Poland). On his tomb is an epitaph in Latin, said to be composed by Copernicus himself. In English it would read:

> *I ask not the faith St. Paul received nor the grace St. Peter obtained but what you gave to the thief on the cross, grant me!*

These verbs in the epitaph: receive, obtain, grant—lead me to conclude with this thought: that by converting an action that had placed him in jail, the thief, in turning to our Lord, quite literally stole Paradise.

When the evening of that sermon-Sunday came and the strong emotions of the day had quieted down, I knew an ending had taken place and felt determined to turn it into a new beginning. I had first to resist the fear that teaching and writing were over. They had always gone hand in hand, and although I was fully involved in writing, I had no plans at that time for further teaching.

So I set about resisting the fear of an ending that might not be a beginning. Resistance to something was the law of the New England nature. I questioned that thought and smiled at it as countless New England pictures flashed through my mind in a confused but heart-consoling vision of my past. There was no sequence in the scenes that moved in and out of my mind: minnows I had tried to catch as a boy in the pond at the bottom of my street; the granite quarries of Vermont I had seen as a young teacher at Bennington; my favorite walk in Boston along Commonwealth Avenue to Beacon Hill.

Pictures of my family in Brookline, more an atmosphere than an influence, held me then and gave me a sense of sorrow. I had been the first in my family to attend Harvard, the first to teach, the first to attempt a commitment to a career of writer, the first to study the civilization of France and Italy. Could I now defend the activities of such a life against the more practical and more humble careers of those generations I knew something about who preceded me? From the point at which I stood in my own generation and watched the generation of my students, I was still appalled by the horror of specialization where we learn too much and are uncertain about everything we learn.

I had lived fourteen years in the South where I had become accustomed to its gentleness and friendliness. I had been invited to visit and speak at several colleges and universities, and each of these visits had added to my experience of the South: the University of North Carolina at Chapel Hill and Greensboro and Raleigh, Virginia Polytechnic Institute in Blacksburg, Virginia Military Institute in Lexington, Saint Andrews Presbyterian College in Laurinburg, Georgia State and Emory in Atlanta, the University of South Carolina, Campbell, Mars Hill, Wake Forest, Davidson.

Here I was, having reached almost the age of seventy, a Brookline-Bostonian, educated at Harvard, who had remained a collegian, and who was still trying to educate himself, mainly by means of books, both old and new, published in France. My intellectual ambitions had always taken care of my lack of social ambitions. Early in life I had taken to the pen, and yet I have no wit in my writings and no scope.

When I first went to France, I found it a civilization barely tolerant of the outside world. This was not a surprise to me because Boston, the first city in my life, is quite similar to Paris in its insularity. The insolence I found in French banks, post offices, restaurants, and *bureaux de location* in the theaters was a bit sharper than comparable Bostonian insolence. French insolence is self-confessed in the aphorisms of Vauvenargues and La Rochefoucauld, in *L'Amour-Médecin*, and even in *Le Grand Testament*. So, I read exclusively French books when I lived in Paris and became my own teacher.

The hauteur of French professors is unparalleled, and I learned quite early that universities teach badly. Professors are interested only in their own writing and research. As a professor writes his book, he worries constantly about the attacks that will be made against it, and he has to relax in the classroom, tell stories, ingratiate himself with students who will never read his book when it is completed. High schools teach much better than universities because of the arbitrary training they give to memory. Education is the training of one's memory.

There was no pain in me during that early fall, but there was a numbness in my body as I looked into the months ahead without a program of classes. I took longer walks past creeping juniper and magnolia trees, and I felt for the first time what a long way I was from the cold of Vermont, what a long way from the past. I was missing the harshness of contrasts in New England, and I was missing too the plotting and planning of future courses. Within myself I argued daily that it was enough to educate myself and to rewrite some of my poorly written pages.

During my first nine years at Duke, Jack Fein had been my chairman, and, much more than that, had been a friend who had helped me in countless ways. I refrained from speaking of my strange anxiety to anyone, but if anyone might have sensed this anxiety in me, it would have been Jack. He was at that time dean of Trinity College and in that capacity had the right to invite me to give, as an emeritus and without salary, a course not classified in the usual curriculum. He invited me to offer in the spring of 1979 a course of my own choosing, and given in whatever form I wished. It would be, once again, the normal time for Dante, and I had it announced in two sections, after struggling to win back classroom 014. Such were my sentimental ties with that room that it was impossible to imagine giving the *Inferno* elsewhere. That blackboard, those walls, those seats, that podium —they formed the mise-en-scène I needed and wanted and finally won.

The principal lesson about living that I had assimilated in my long life was the lesson that we learn best from the accidental, the unintended, the unforeseen. History going on outside of us is always colliding with our personal history and making us seem totally insignificant. I would come home from my daily jogging—a mere half mile —and read about the oil spill along the coast of Brittany, or about the entre-chats of Baryshnikov, or about I. M. Pei's addition to the National Gallery of Art in Washington.

I read about contemporary history as it unfolds each week in *Time*, *Newsweek*, and *L'Express*, and then I watch the version of that history which the new films provide. A reincarnation of the god Pan had appeared on the disco floor. Pan's new name was John Travolta. With his seeming strength and innocence, reviewers placed him immediately in the center of pop culture, providing us with the newest version of the idealized American street kid. I saw the film twice, and with my more generous interpretation of history, I would claim that *Saturday Night Fever* is a Dionysiac dance performed with macho grace. Disco means both music and an environment for the music. It is successful only when it moves our sexual desires into a dance. The Bee Gees' music for *Saturday Night Fever* was an American tribal ritual.

From Pan Travolta presiding over a Brooklyn disco community we moved, thanks to the big screen, to another film on a community, in Pennsylvania, clustered about a steel mill, where a very subtle film director, Michael Cimino, showed us the pathos of friendship and love set against the fatal Vietnam War. *The Deer Hunter* began with the dance celebration of a marriage. Robert De Niro was not Pan, but an omniscient god to be sacrificed as he witnessed other sacrifices and refrained from sacrificing the huge stag on the mountain pass.

We watched the forces of evil and the forces of good in *The Deer Hunter*, and we read the lines spoken by Solzhenitsyn at the Harvard commencement about those same forces of evil beginning their decisive offensive against our planet. How the Russian writer scolded his adopted West for our overabundant hope in political and social reform!

When Isaac Singer was interviewed on the occasion of receiving the Nobel Prize in literature, he insisted on referring not to the stories for which he had received the prize, but to his books for children. His favorite readers are children who don't pay attention to critics or to psychology or to sociology. Children do not try to understand Kafka or *Finnegans Wake*. They believe in angels, devils, witches, goblins, logic, clarity, punctuation, and other such obsolete stuff. Children do not expect their favorite writer to redeem humanity.

I have never enjoyed watching Woody Allen on the screen. Here my students give up on me, and, without clearly saying "you're hopeless," classify me in some remote category. I tried again, with *Manhattan*, to comprehend the wide appeal he has. That film has the familiar eclectic list of recommendations: Groucho Marx, Mozart's *Jupiter Symphony*, Flaubert's *Sentimental Education*. Diane Keaton, in the role of a magazine writer, telephones at one point to an invisible character she calls "Harvey." Might he be, I wondered, Harvey Shapiro, editor of *The New York Times Book Review*? That Harvey was my student and friend at Yale some years back. I still have some of his earliest poems, which I admire, and I intend some day to ask him if he did play unwittingly that invisible part in *Manhattan*.

I feel put in my place—squarely so—when students sensing my lack of enthusiasm for Woody Allen, point out that he is for them what Chaplin was for me. *Playboy* called him one of the ten sexiest males in the world! And *L'Express* used one of my favorite words that I have always associated with Villon: *un philosophe chétif* (a *weakling* philosopher) and another favorite word I keep in my mind for Molière:

un pâle bateleur (a pale *clown*). So be it: he is a *chétif* and a *bateleur* who quotes Camus and Kierkegaard, who refers to Fellini and Mahler, and who wanted to name one of his films *Anhedonism*. Since his company refused to allow such a title, he forged out of the sound of the word *Annie Hall*.

I want to see *Manhattan* again. It was Allen's eighth film, built especially on gags. I concentrated on the gags, but now I would like to concentrate on the conventions, cruelties, and chance encounters that celebrate New York. I want to see again how he uses galleries, restaurants, and streets as he shows us his picture of a dehumanized society, a world desensitized by drugs and fast food. I want to see again the view from the twentieth-floor balcony of Woody Allen's penthouse apartment on Fifth Avenue.

If we were able to draw up a creed that would account for the success of Chaplin and Woody Allen, it would certainly involve their most generous belief that says: every way of life is curious, every way of life is worthy of being used in a film. The world we look at in a film has to be connected with our past, even if the past returns to us as a bundle of disconnected memories. This allows us to tolerate our mind's oddities as we watch the oddities of Chaplin's movements and listen to the oddities of Woody Allen's gags.

My students during the last years of the seventies belonged to a very special generation: post-Vietnam, warless, causeless. They were not escapists although some of them had made themselves into masochistic drug abusers. They saw more clearly than my students of earlier years into the barriers of race, language, birth, habits; and I was able, thanks to them, to see more clearly than ever before that history is the history of education.

Dante in 1979;
Renoir as "quad flick"

After the fall semester of 1978, spent in retirement from teaching, I
returned to classroom 014 in January 1979 to teach my course on the
Inferno. At each of the first meetings, one of the students would
speak to me before or after the class, and relate himself or herself to
someone of the past. David Cecelski, when I asked about his name,
indeed assured me that Liz Cecelski was his sister and that she had
told him to take Dante. Ed Cassady explained that he was a French
major and had come to Duke from Indian Springs School in Alabama.
I told him about his two predecessors: Jeff Humphries and Nap Gary.
Joe Devlin, the lacrosse player and brother of Karen, was in the class,
having taken Proust the year before. Because of an injury, he was not
playing lacrosse that semester, but he introduced me to David Hill, an
active lacrosse player, a new student in Dante. I attended two games
to watch David play and sat beside Joe who explained to me some of
the more subtle points of the action on the field.

In one of the early classes, in speaking of the religious orders in the
Middle Ages, I mentioned Monte Cassino. That class was hardly over
when a new student, Jim Scott, bounded up to the desk to ask if that
Monte Cassino was the same place that had figured in the Second
World War. I assured him it was. Jim was an avid student of World
War II and confessed that with the words Monte Cassino my course
took on some meaning for him. He had wondered why he found
himself studying such an outlandish subject as Dante.

As soon as the course got under way, and for both sections, Dante
became again for me, and for the first time for the students, a bewil-
dering complex of ideas, experiments, ambitions, energies, and espe-

cially pictures. I tried to warn the students, both old and new friends, that Dantean knowledge, as we became familiar with it, would absorb us, and that we would have to be, at least at the beginning of the course, principally passive. We were in the process of meeting a genius, I told them, whose ideas they would slowly absorb. We must never forget Dante's compound nature of patriot, moralist, and poet. Moreover—and this I had to repeat to everyone of my classes every year—every standard in America is different from the standards in Europe.

Throughout that semester, the Dante course and the students taking it occupied much of my time spent outside my apartment. At home each day I wrote or rewrote a page or a passage in the manuscript of what I hoped would be a small book: *A Reading of the Inferno*. I expected that my thoughts otherwise would be overcast by the ending of my teaching at Duke and by the preoccupation with what my life would turn into with the coming of summer and the latter half of the year.

That was not the case. My thoughts did take a nostalgic turn—but in terms of weather and landscape. I imagine that this train of thought was an instinctive self-protection against a possible wave of self-pity. I found myself contrasting the very mild, almost imperceptible changes in climate of North Carolina with the more dramatic changes in the North, and particularly in Vermont where one has to pay attention to weather in order to survive. This particular motif in my thoughts was in reality a return to the past at a moment when the present gave every evidence of drawing to a close.

Would age force me into a drastic change in my manner of living? Could I continue living in Durham without having a specified university role to play? Would it be embarrassing for my colleagues and students and myself to stay on when the reason for staying at Duke was no longer valid? I veered away from facing such questions and thought of winter and spring coming to Bennington as I remembered their advent during the decade of the fifties, twenty years earlier.

As I looked outside of my apartment at the bare trees lining Chapel Hill Boulevard, and as I walked outside or jogged around Valley Terrace, I remembered romantically the dark time in December in Bennington when one day the Walloomsac was open water and the next day solid ice. January was the month of snow and rabbits, and even deer, small and big animals standing out clear against the snow.

By this time Bennington had become a set of pictures, fixed in my mind. Was there time ahead for me when Duke was to be condensed into a similar set of pictures?

This was not a morbid questioning of fate, but a measuring of time and space, of apartments and fields, of roads along which I had walked in Boston and Chicago, in Paris and Bennington, in Nice where la promenade des Anglais seemed to extend as far as Cannes. These were diverse lands, with or without snow in February and March. Wherever I had lived, in February the days became longer and the sun rose higher. April was always the miraculous month in Vermont when pussy willows appeared and when deer came close, looking for grass. Then came the first robins when fields began to turn green. With the first signs of farming, the woodchucks turned out in good numbers.

In the middle of that Durham spring, two very different kinds of invitations came that concerned the immediate future and that helped dissolve the worry of where to live. Ella Fountain Pratt, a good friend who for several years had been in charge of music and entertainment programs at Duke, asked me to speak briefly about Jean Renoir at a showing of his film *La Grande Illusion*, on June 13. Thus I had good reason to continue living at Duke for the first part of the summer. The second invitation, of major importance for me, came from the University of the South, in Sewanee, Tennessee—a request to teach the fall semester of 1979 and the spring semester of 1980.

Thanks to the goodwill and efficiency of George Core, editor of the *Sewanee Review*, I found myself scheduled for a year at Sewanee which I knew of largely because of the quarterly to which I had contributed often during the course of twenty-five years. One day in Boston, in his apartment on Garden Street, Austin Warren had shown me a copy of the *Sewanee Review* and told me about its editor, William Knickerbocker. I was a graduate student at Harvard, and Austin felt it was high time I began to pay attention to literary quarterlies not solely French. This was about 1934. I remember Austin saying that the Anglican Church had founded the university, with a theological school attached to it, and with a bishop as chancellor.

I had published articles or reviews under each of the editors who succeeded Knickerbocker: Allen Tate, John Palmer, Monroe Spears, Andrew Lytle, and George Core. In fact, when John Palmer was giving up his editorship, he wrote me to say I was one of the candidates from whom his successor was to be chosen. I was not the lucky candidate, but I remember the excitement I felt at the possibility of a radical change in my career. So, the radical change was to come about many years later—but not so radical since I was to teach French at Sewanee and see with my own eyes that place to which I had written so often. Sewanee was to be more than a blue-covered quarterly.

About this same time a letter from John Cheever announced to me that the Academy-Institute of Arts and Letters was giving me an award for *Journal of Rehearsals*. This "Vursell Memorial Award" pleased and gratified me. The long award event itself, a very crowded gathering, with cocktails and luncheon, followed by the ceremony where one hundred and fifty people sat on the stage, members of the Academy-Institute and those receiving awards, interested me from beginning to end. As I was leaving the stage after the ceremony, a man approached me I did not recognize at first. He extended his hand with a word of congratulation, and then said, "I am James Dickey." I replied, "Now I recognize you from having seen you in your film *Deliverance*." "That is the way I usually look," he replied. "I wanted to tell you that I have never forgotten your story about Jupien in *Pantomime*." Of all the brief exchanges on that memorable day, Dickey's words meant the most to me.

On the following day I took the train to New Haven to spend a few hours with Catherine Coffin. After the many superficial encounters with the great and the less-great literary figures gathered in New York, I needed another kind of reunion where the past would be invoked but always in terms of the present. I needed to talk with Catherine, who had never ceased being a friend since that distant day in the spring of 1943 when I first met her. It was a meeting of the Alliance Française in New Haven where I had given a talk on Apollinaire. At the end of the talk, a lady rose and gave in fluent French various notices to the other members of the alliance.

At dinner the next week—I remember the yellow plates from Quimper—she introduced me to her young son Bill, a pianist and student of Nadia Boulanger in Paris. Catherine's husband, William Sloane Coffin, had recently died. That first evening I learned a bit about her family and a great deal about her attachment to France and her love for twelfth-century French architecture and sculpture. Her daughter Margot was a student at Wellesley, and her oldest son, Ned, had graduated from Yale and was entering the business world. Bill was about to study at Yale. His goodwill and good humor, his remarkable linguistic skills, his warm graciousness equaled his mother's, but neither she nor I could have imagined that evening that he would eventually serve Yale as chaplain for eighteen years, during which time he became a well-known, eloquent public figure, and now serves as chief minister at Riverside Church in New York.

France was the immediate reason for my friendship with Catherine. It remained constant through the years, but other bonds of affinity in temperament and interests in many subjects grew quickly: art, literature, music, films, mutual friends. It was very much a Yale world she created around her, and she graciously allowed me to be a part of it. With the ending of the war, Catherine moved next door into a large house that became the scene of memorable dinner parties with friends in New Haven: Henri and Marguerite Peyre, Thornton Wilder and his sister Isabel, Bill and Margaret Wimsatt. Conversation was quite deliberately directed by Catherine. Presiding at the table, she proposed topics by asking a few leading questions. The three men I have just named were all eloquent and even controversial speakers. With the first sparks of controversy, Catherine fanned them and urged her guests to make bolder and bolder points of theory.

More than the dinner parties, I enjoyed a lunch or dinner at the Faculty Club later, where, alone, Catherine and I reviewed the previous dinner party. At such moments Catherine's broad interests became clear and especially her desire to learn of human attainments and to understand human motives. She has been a very privileged person and has always been eager to share those privileges. One day we drove to a nearby town in Connecticut so that I might meet her famous brother-in-law, Henry Sloane Coffin. On another occasion we went by train to Washington where I saw the National Gallery for the first time.

In preparing for that trip Catherine had asked me to do a favor which I was anxious to carry out. Since her husband had been president of the Metropolitan Art Museum in New York, her name was known in museum circles, and she had not dared seek permission to see the Barnes Collection in Philadelphia. She asked me to write to Mr. Barnes to ask for the privilege of seeing the collection, and to add to the request the information that "my elderly aunt" (that was her phrase) would accompany me. Catherine thought the formula would fit. I was a French teacher interested in art but not a specialist. I composed a most servile letter. A week later a slip came to me from Philadelphia, a rejection slip, with the printed words "You are not allowed to visit the Barnes Collection." As if that were not sufficient reproof, Barnes had taken the trouble to add in his own handwriting on the bottom of the card: "Nothing doing for you and your aunt." We did not stop at Philadelphia on the way to Washington, and during the morning at the National Gallery we pretended to forget about the Barnes Collection.

I returned from my trip to New York to an engagement in Gross Chemistry Auditorium on June 13, 1979. (Here in the summertime the Duke "quad flicks" are shown.) I had prepared a ten-minute talk on Renoir and *La Grande Illusion*, and gave it that evening to a filled auditorium where I saw many friends and students. I doubt if any one of them realized that brief talk was in a way my farewell to the Duke community. I wanted it to be a homage to Jean Renoir, who had died in February at the age of eighty-four, in his home in Beverly Hills, California. He had been buried in France, after a state funeral.

I began my remarks by pointing out that to speak of Jean Renoir at all was to speak of history because of the role he had played in filmmaking. Chaplin had called him the greatest film director in the world. At least four French directors whose films the students were beginning to appreciate had acknowledged their debt to Renoir and the degree to which his films had inspired them: Truffaut, Godard, Louis Malle, Eric Rohmer. Twice in Woody Allen's film *Manhattan*, he refers to Renoir.

I wanted that evening at Gross especially to point out how, in a truly iconoclastic way, Renoir devoted his life to undermining the canons of so-called good taste. He believed the public is stuffed with lies—clichés—and has been trained to cling to its conventions.

Les Règles du jeu, his film of 1939, produced two years after *La Grande Illusion*, is considered by most film critics his masterpiece. I proposed as a possible reason for this preference the theory that *Rules of the Game*, more than any other single film, interrupted the incessant flow of cinema clichés. For us today it is a dissection of French high society on the verge of extinction, a film both farcical and tragic. This theme connects it with *La Grande Illusion* and carries out in cinema art what Proust did in a much more elaborate way in the art of the novel.

I decided that the best way to speak directly about the film was to consider the meaning of the title since it seems to refer to a precise theme on the subject of World War I, as well as to a generalized theme. Specifically, in the light of the film's action, it refers to the illusion of hatred that divides men, that divides countries one from another. Both Hitler and Mussolini denounced *La Grande Illusion* and forbade its being shown in their countries, whereas President Roosevelt urged every American to see it. Again, specifically, it refers to the illusion that there exists a strict opposition between the proletariat and the aristocracy. This would accentuate the belief that there is a true aristocracy (*une vraie noblesse*) and a false aristocracy (*une fausse noblesse*).

In a more general sense, *les grandes illusions* (if I made the word plural) could be those dreams that help us to live. Since the film is both an escape story and an antiwar tract, we might see it as the picture of man pursuing an illusory sense of freedom.

When the film was over, I made my way to the back of Gross Auditorium, to the long stairway leading down to the parking lot. It was dark there and I moved cautiously step by step. Halfway down I saw at the bottom two figures emerging from the dark of the parking space. Flash and Ed Harrison were waiting for me. I had noticed them in the back of the auditorium when I began to talk, but had imagined they had left, as everyone else had, by the front entrance. They had surmised I would be parked in that particular spot, where in fact they had seen my Pinto. They gave me a hand down the last steps. The slowness of my descent was due mainly to fear of falling, but it was also due to the feeling that the very small service I had just performed for the "quad flicks" that evening marked the true ending of my work at Duke. Perhaps Flash had sensed this too, and in his usual quiet way he settled me into my car and drove his Rabbit in my wake until we separated on the highway.

Other places

Brookline

The story of a life is the story of an education, the story of how one is reared and prepared, led forth to one's universe. It is the finding of one leader or leaders who will point the way to the new universe that is our own. Old universes are constantly being discarded for new ones. We have to be led away from old universes that have served their purpose, and be guided toward a new goal, a new universe. This occurs each time we change teachers or habitations or cities. It occurs imperceptibly with each new dawn when the past of a single night or a single day appears useless and worthy of being cast aside.

The principle or law which I came to feel more clearly in the last years of my sixties was always present in my New England background, in that belief I seem to have been born with that the world is something that has to be changed or at least reformed. What is behind this instinct to reform that seems to be a permanent part of the New England temperament? I would explain it in this way. It is a belief that when left alone, a house, a town, a street, a school, a human being allows to grow within it forces of evil. These have to be resisted. Otherwise corruption will set in, bringing with it stagnation and death. Resistance to this evil, so mysterious that it cannot be named, is a major trait of the inhabitants of that region of the world where extremes of heat and cold sharpen the feelings and almost victimize both men and women, both girls and boys.

New England houses are never cool enough or warm enough. Except for the houses that have just been built and that are occupied by non-New Englanders. I learned early in life that exterior nature is either too boiling or too freezing. My temperament seemed to be governed by temperature. I lived only in winter or summer and yearned for some brief span of time that would separate the two harsh seasons, that would lead away from one and help prepare the other. The milder intervals were so brief that they had no reality for me.

Winter and school: discipline and law within the building, and snow outside. At the few moments when the discipline slackened, I would look out the window to watch the snow falling and wonder how long it would take me to make it home on foot, and indeed wonder whether this time I would make it through the drifts. And what might happen if I didn't make it!

Summer was escape from school. But that did not mean an escape from discipline. The discipline was in the constant need to resist any summerlike indulgence. Before the sun became a course of punishment, it might—briefly—suggest warmth, indolence, relaxation. Lilacs bloomed at that moment, white and mauve-colored lilacs, and we marveled for a week or so at their resistance to the winter cold.

The earliest form of summer discipline that I can remember had a very definite connection with elementary school. The building I attended—Edward Devotion School—was closed. The yellow bricks of its walls seemed yellower under the full light of the summer sun. Aunt Polly, the oldest of four children, of whom my mother was the second oldest, was secretary to the superintendent of the Brookline schools. That position, my aunt Miss Mary Adams held between the ages of twenty and seventy, with full authority and distinction, in an office at the back of the Town Hall. During the span of the part of those fifty years when I was alive, she was a loving, attentive, generous, and possessive aunt.

School had hardly closed for the summer when Aunt Polly invited me to visit her in her office. I always went there with great interest and avidity because of a ceremony repeated each time. After a brief conversation in her office—Superintendent Aldrich was on his vacation, and Miss Polly Adams was in full control—a conversation about the year's work and the health of the various members of the family, she led me into the stockroom. From the bulging shelves, she picked supplies she thought would excite me the most: a block of paper, a few pencils, a notebook, a ruler, and even a textbook or two. With these gifts Aunt Polly made it clear to me, without having to put it in words, that I was to continue on my own with schoolwork during the summer.

The format of the various notebooks, the sharpness of the pencils, the whiteness of the pages did inspire me to work during the summer:

to write, to study, to memorize. I collected all the booty from that stockroom as one might collect treasures, arranged them in my desk at home, and, moreover, used them. But one matter worried me, from the first to the last of those visits to the stockroom. My aunt was as upright and highly moral in her conduct as she was tall, dignified in bearing, and stalwartly erect in her walk. Weren't these gifts stolen goods? I never expressed this thought audibly, but it was in me because it contradicted all I had observed in Aunt Polly's behavior. Years later, when she was in her seventies (she lived until the age of ninety-two), after retiring from the School Department, one day I did mention this worry of mine as a kind of joke. But she realized the joke was a worry. Her aging features tightened as she pressed herself against the back of her chair in her tiny apartment on Commonwealth Avenue.

"Did you think I was stealing from the School Department? Of course not! I would never do that! Those were samples I gave you. Mr. Aldrich told me to get rid of them as best I could."

Relief settled on me then! The integrity of my aunt was intact. If only she had explained "the samples" when I was a boy, my summer study would have been more serene.

I believe my aunt saw in me what she had hoped to become herself, a good student and a lover of literature. The shadow of the School Department fell over me early in life. The world of the school became familiar to me through my aunt's office in the back of the Town Hall, the stockroom, and the talk about my teachers, whom she knew personally. By rights she should have been one of them, but she took, as fate willed it, the next best position, that of their friend, adviser, defender. Through the years of her reign, she argued as an attorney might in defending the cause of the teachers whenever they were attacked by principals, superintendents, or parents. The respect I developed early for teachers came to me from their performance and also from Aunt Polly's praise of them. She identified with them, and I identified to some degree with her.

As soon as I reached an age when I was capable of taking care of myself after school let out in the afternoon, my mother resumed her work, interrupted by my birth, at the other end of the Town Hall, in the large office at the front entrance, as assistant town clerk. The pattern never seemed strange to me as I was growing up, but today it appears to me significant in my understanding of New England family life, of moral structures, of resistance to minor infractions against the law.

Consider the pattern: two sisters, who were for me aunt and mother, one occupying the back of Town Hall, sturdily efficient in running the Brookline schools and sensitive to any examples of injustice on the part of teachers, pupils, or administrators; and the other, occupying the front of Town Hall, more jovial in manner, more liked by her co-workers, but equally alert and hostile to any political maneuvering. My mother would defend the town clerk when he was attacked, but privately she attacked him in his office when she felt he had gone too far in favoritism, in granting privileges, or quite simply in the indolence of a man who believed the real work of the office should be done by women.

After the passing of so many years I am now able to estimate the strength of those two sisters: their industry, their high morality, their gracious cordiality extended to all except those (not few in number) in whom they sensed or found deceit, affectation, dishonesty. Fundamentally alike, save in manner, guardians of the Town Hall, front door and back door, my aunt and my mother showed no liking for one another. I am certain there was affection deep in their hearts, because at any moment of crisis in the life of one, the other would help immediately and generously. A family fidelity united them at intervals, but day by day, year by year, they behaved like disapproving enemies.

The proof of their unacknowledged love for one another was me. There was no trace of jealousy in my mother when my aunt favored me with gifts and attention, when she invited me for the month of August to a hotel at Popham Beach, Maine, and paid for my expenses there out of her modest salary. She took me to my first concerts, to my first museums, and she started me reading Dickens at the age of eleven. I don't remember asking her for anything because she always foresaw my needs and predicted my desires.

My mother's love was so permanent, so steadfast that she never contradicted or criticized my aunt's giving nature. But between the two sisters, fairly close in age, there was a lifelong feud of which I became increasingly aware each year. I learned to keep them separate in my heart and in my gratitude. A few times, near the end of my mother's life (she died at the age of eighty-five), I was able to bring them together for a reconciliation that lasted briefly. The source of hostilities was certainly in their childhood. My aunt's character was based on a sense of authority. My mother's character could not tolerate any forced domination. When together, they expressed total lack of agreement over everything. Except over me. I was to be favored.

As far back as I can remember, I was aware that such favoritism was dangerous. I profited from it but did not like it. And I would give myself onerous duties, extra labors and discipline in order to offset the favors. My mother was proud to have an offspring who behaved himself. My aunt was proud to have a nephew into whom she was able to project herself, on whom she might bestow privileges she would never bestow on herself. I was an investment for her because I became through the years what she would have liked to have been.

As I was being educated in the usual sense of attending school and prolonging, during the summer, work related to school: reading books more advanced than those in the curriculum, doing bits of writing more creative than expositional, exploring areas not referred to in a school program—opera, Havelock Ellis, films, the Fenway—I was at all times aware of the difficult role of playing simultaneously son and nephew. I could easily have been the victim of a struggle of sisterly wills. But I wasn't. I never heard malevolent criticism directed at me or at either sister. I never heard a speech about obeying the law and thus disobeying one relative in order to obey the other.

My mother attended church on Sunday. My aunt did not. I regularly accompanied my mother and retained during the first few days of the week phrases and thoughts from the sermon that had impressed me. As I remember, they were phrases on a moral issue but memorable because of their context in some Bible story. I knew then in childhood, as I know now in my seventieth year, that the Bible is the great educator.

I know now that as a child I yearned for ancestral religion, for a power of belief that would attach me to the past, that would provide a radiance to the quiet, totally insignificant existence I was leading in Brookline, Massachusetts. My mind tried to stretch beyond New England to Europe, to my ancestors there, and to ancestors beyond them.

The paradox troubled me for several years. On the one hand I wanted to discover and attach myself to my religious ancestry, and on the other hand I wanted change. I sensed that some of the narrow morality I heard was depraved. That must be changed, and yet the old puritan side of my nature rebelled against change.

Although I have spoken very little about religion with friends and students, I believe I can truthfully say at the end of my life that religion has been my occupation. I almost wrote "theology," but theology is always on debatable ground. Religion means contact with

God, and theology is speech about God, the minds of various men trying to understand the experience of religion. I would rather reflect than talk.

Early in my secondary school years, when I first began reading Emerson, I copied a phrase of his into my journal and read it often until it became a part of me: "In Divinity I hope to thrive."

Such a sentence as that helped me to face what was becoming more and more apparent to me, and what I suppose might be called "our terrible freedom." We are not attached. The freedom that each of us has inherited brings with it a realization of our aloneness. Not loneliness—that, I have never known. But aloneness, separation, isolation, individuality. The synonyms are numerous by which we try to disguise that fundamental experience each of us knows more profoundly than other experiences. We are fated in every possible way to do this and that, to appear and disappear, to cry without reason and to laugh stupidly. And yet, we are free to choose not to do what we do. The dilemma is there at all times.

I believe I have come to accept this dilemma and live with it. Each thinker I have read, or reread because he speaks forcibly to me, has given voice to the dilemma of freedom and fate: Socrates (in Plato), Saint Paul, Plotinus, Montaigne. Each has spoken in his own way about man's need for expansion despite the fact that he is cast in such a narrow mold. Each thinker of this stature knows the conflicting drives in all of us toward what is lawful and anarchic, toward what is conventional and wild.

Let me summarize the thousands and thousands of words on this subject that have come before my eyes and write quite simply on this page in four words: the now is eternal.

So, as I grew up, I felt on both sides of me the strength, the determination, and the moral uprightness of those two enemy sisters. My mother's love was the pride in having a son who could be depended upon, who was there or thereabouts when he was needed. My aunt's love was for the sight of her nephew growing into someone she might have become, had she been male and favored with less sentimentality in her nature and more learning.

There was a third figure near to me at all times as I grew into boyhood and then into adolescence, more a shadow than a figure, more taciturn than the two sisters, and whose love for me was deeper than theirs because it was all-consuming. My father's love for me was uncritical and absolute. Instinctively, from the beginning of my time on this earth, I was wary of his love because I knew I could never learn from it. I could bask in it, sink in it, but would I ever emerge from it if I allowed myself to submit? Every thought in my father's mind seemed to be for my comfort and my well-being. I had to force myself, train myself, educate myself to exist away from his strong, embracing arms.

My father, whose first names were Wallace Bruce, was certainly aware, with the passing of time, of my determination, and he too tried to train himself to express his paternal love less effusively, less overwhelmingly. This training in restraint was never articulated in words between us. But it continued until his sudden death the day before Pearl Harbor. It had to continue although it often made me feel like a culprit, like an ungrateful son refusing to accept what was being offered.

The most giving and the most loving of fathers, he made no demands on me. It would have been easier on my conscience if he had. Only one request, perhaps, although never stated—not a request even, but a hope that I would be there at suppertime when he returned each night from his railroad-office work in Boston. In those days men worked Saturday mornings, and my father would return late in the afternoon with the *Saturday Evening Transcript* under his arm. It was for me alone, and it was the kind of offering he enjoyed giving me. For several years when I was growing into the world of the arts, he would always remember to bring from the city that newspaper which opened up to me those very worlds that took me away from the world of my parents, the world of Brookline and the Town Hall.

The *Transcript* was an adjunct to my education in grammar and high school. The special sections of the Saturday editions were treasures of the mind for me. As my father pulled it out from under his arm, I always sensed the pleasure it gave him to give me the pleasure of my avid Saturday-night reading, when my mind expanded to embrace the worlds of art, literature, music, travel. With that selflessness that characterized him, he provided me with the means by which I became different from him. All my father wanted was my presence in my room each night, even if the door was closed and there was no communication between us after supper. He was the keeper of my mother and me. The joy of serving us, especially in countless minor ways, was his life.

My mother, who had a pleasant but plain face, had chosen a very handsome man for her husband. But she made up for her plainness by running the house, keeping my father and me in our respective roles, continuing her career as assistant town clerk and running that office during the day. I have seen photographs of my father at twenty: black hair, black eyes, strong, stalwart body, a striking-looking young fellow destined to find early in his life a wife and a son whom he was to worship. Other people, relatives and friends, would count for him only in terms of my mother and me. Our needs filled his activities, and our fidelity to him filled his heart.

During the last seven years of his life, I lived first at Bennington and then at Yale. He managed that separation by writing to me five days of every week. His handwriting was so magnificent that it mattered very little to me that his sentences were the same formulas in letter after letter. They were not letters really but reaffirmations of love and protectiveness. They were the reaching out—through that space between Brookline and Bennington or between Brookline and New Haven—of my father's spirit expressing happiness that I was engaged in work I felt called upon to do, and unhappiness that he was no longer able to shower on me the many daily attentions he had forced me to accept in Brookline.

I never succeeded in teaching my father that education is, in its fullest sense, emancipation. As I moved into the activities of a teacher at Bennington first, and then at Yale, I was determined to succeed better with the students enrolled in my classes than I had succeeded with my father. I was never able to speak to him as I might with students and say, for example, that the elevation of the mind is birdlike. It is a soaring upward to understand an achievement of man, a flight away from the heaviness of matter, from the weight of one's body which literally is left behind in any daring adventure of the intellect and the spirit. The drama of each man's destiny is the effort to separate himself, that mysterious part of himself that dreams, from the weight of his body, and from its willful allegiance to the earth. The myth of Icarus is the clue to man's spirit which relives a daily drama of hope and defeat. The heavens are always there far above us, the implacable *azur* of Mallarmé, tormenting not only the poet in search of his poem, but every man who thinks and reads and looks up when the fatigue of reading and understanding overcomes him.

Thoreau has always been for me a father figure without a son, and in my mind he is often joined with the remembered figure of my own father. If I am reading his text correctly, reading perhaps between the lines, Thoreau seems to conceive of the Almighty as God immanent in man. On this point we would differ because God is for me transcendental. I have felt the immanence of God, also, but the image of the absolute I am trying to describe is that need of my spirit to rise up, to attempt a flight toward a goal that is permanent, toward a God who is far beyond his creation.

The two strong, valiant natures of those sisters, mother and aunt, taught me, when I first began looking at people outside my family, that the mass of men are discontented. And that other loving nature of my father taught me, long before I read Thoreau, something about the ethic of nonviolence. Then deep within myself I learned the most important lesson of my life: how to anticipate the dawn when those two eternities, the past and the future, come together in that extraordinary meeting place we call the present.

Taormina

My childhood solitude spent in New England and my adult solitude spent in North Carolina never appeared to me as something wrong or penitential. They were means by which I hoped—often subconsciously —to be a law to myself. In order to protect my independence, I accepted the fate of being in the eyes of most an oddity. I have always wanted to live in a city, in the midst of a population, but not to be a part of the city in the social sense.

An obvious interpretation of my various ascetic habits is avarice. And yet, to protect a basic simplicity in one's way of living is not necessarily avarice. Or if it is avarice in some devious way, it is also the means to avoid garishness and display, to renounce all nonessentials in order to have more time for my primary activities, all of which are related to the great books of the past and to the possible slim books of my own that may be written in the future.

I willingly confess that this general pattern of what I call simplicity would not have grown by itself if I had not found a very special kind of pleasure in saving money. Whereas the spending of money has always been hard for me to justify, the saving of money for the time when retirement from work would be forced on me, and for the usefulness it might provide eventually to others after me, appears to me justifiable.

Relatively speaking, my habit of saving, which means economizing, is inconsequential and insignificant. The result is not a fortune, as the world estimates fortunes, but the estimate for me has never been in terms of sums. It is the pleasure I derive from accumulating and the belief that this is a useful habit. It is consistent with all my other habits, the important and the unimportant ones, which, taken together, form my particular pattern of life. The accumulating of prayers and of written words would head in my ledger book the important items of hoarding.

My morning exercises and daily jogging are clearly related to this general design of accumulating. The hours set aside for reading, as well as those for writing, have the same goal of strengthening one's powers, no matter how weak these powers are. It may seem curious to group together such disparate habits as prayer, writing, collecting savings certificates, jogging, sexual activities, but they are indeed interrelated in this self of mine which is body, mind, and soul.

Prayer is the least vulnerable of all these habits of accumulating. The others are affected by Wall Street vacillations, by hurricanes and rainstorms, or by a yearly attack of a virus. The power of prayer in the history of the world accounts for most of the accomplishments that endure the longest. It is closely related to the thoughts of men assigned to paper and to the arts created by men. Whatever act of accumulating is being carried out, it is slow, daily, or almost daily, and a principal means of giving structure to one's day. It is the teacher of patience and the art of waiting. Whether one is waiting for twilight or dawn, I would call it the most discreet of all the arts.

A young child learns in the most natural way this habit, this art of accumulating, as he learns new words and adds them one after the other to his meager vocabulary. And most adults continue this same habit with harder, newer words, or words from foreign languages. Since I am a teacher of a foreign language, I carry on this habit more deliberately, more consciously than a child does. The pleasure of this acquisition grows with the years as it becomes one of the goals of life. To learn to express oneself in two ways, in an Anglo-Saxon language and in a Latin language, implies the patient drill of acquisition. A new word, practiced twenty times, is not unlike the morning exercise of twenty pushups, or twenty dollars put aside for the next purchase of a savings certificate. The moment does come when the new word is a familiar element of one's vocabulary, when the arm muscles are sufficiently strong so that no exhaustion is felt after twenty pushups, when the new certificate is bought, put into the safe-deposit box, and forgotten.

Such acquisitive habits are the safest way of preserving and holding in check a man's neuroses, which, when all is said, make him into what he is. I agree wholeheartedly with Freud when he claims that our essence is repression. We are all neurotic. All those headings that usually go under the term *culture*: the development of the sciences, the study of the arts and the new creations of the arts, religious studies and the practice of religious faith, and finally the use and development of language so indispensable to all of the foregoing—yes, all of those activities are the result of neurosis. But our neurotic traits are steadied and fertilized and exploited by the indispensable habit of accumulating, by all those antlike habits of man that fill the hours of his days and the dreams of his nights. What a Freudian analyst calls sublimation, or what I am calling here the control of neurosis, leads to culture, or, if one prefers the term, to civilization.

The infant's need to be loved is a very moving phenomenon to observe. The need on the part of the infant to be loved by parent or nurse is encouraged by hourly and daily manifestations. A place of warmth is necessary at the beginning of an infant's life if he is to survive. And then very soon in his growth, warmth of the affections is needed. These earliest needs color all of our subsequent relationships in life. Man is a continuous infancy. As we grow older, we learn to tell ourselves what we want. As so-called maturity sets in, we usually fail to realize the gap that grows deeper and deeper between what we tell ourselves we want and what our unconscious self really wants. This is the fundamental falseness of what the leading of a "civilized" life becomes: a turning away from the most basic drives of our nature. We become alienated from ourselves as we become obsessed with the history of society, with the history of the past.

I have been engaged in very few activities. Four principal ones have filled my life: reading, writing, teaching, acting. In that order. Each of the four is interlocked with the other three. As my past becomes heavier and fuller each day I live, it grows, as I look back at it, into something unthinkable. As I look ahead of me into the future, I see now not goals reached, not projects completed, but the consummation of the centuries, my total insignificance merged with everything that has been and everything that will be. My unthinkable past is an abyss, and my unthinkable future is the steadying light from the Godhead.

The dawn of each day is the assurance of eternity.

The slow accumulation of funds (avarice?) was vindicated one May when it permitted me to take off abruptly, when courses were ended, for Sicily, for the town of Taormina that had obsessed my thoughts for some time. To live briefly in Taormina would represent a break from those parts of Europe I knew and to which I inevitably returned.

I had heard of the San Domenico, the Dominican monastery turned into a luxury hotel and centrally located in the town. There I could continue to work in the early morning and, if luck was with me, and my room (cell) faced the Mediterranean, watch the dawn come over sky and sea.

The crowded social ending of every semester, when I saw too many people, friends, students, colleagues, parents, old students returning to Durham, forced me into the need to escape into the anonymity of a large hotel. The unknown of Taormina, the elegance of the San Domenico, the island that Sicily is—all of that was the goal of an elaborately planned escape for the clarifying of my mind and the renewal of my spirit. Recklessness characterized this voyage into the Sicilian past that I had come upon only in books, in the *Journal* of Gide, and in a travel book of Lawrence Durrell.

The voyage from my apartment in North Carolina to my hotel room in Sicily took place in not so much more than twenty-four hours—tedious hours as traveling always is for me—and yet so swift when the change was accomplished and I found myself in my hotel room on the second floor, a room, as had been promised in my reservation letter, overlooking the Mediterranean. I was in two different worlds at the beginning and the end of the flight. The new world that was so familiar to me on Chapel Hill Road where the yellow cab picked me up at noon, and the old world I looked at for the first time from the automobile the hotel had sent to get me at Catania the following day at approximately three o'clock. Inwardly I was excited from beginning to end because of what this first trip to Sicily promised, and outwardly I wondered, with as much aplomb as I could muster, whether all the connections would be made and I would finally reach the unknown, fabulous island.

The first part of the escape was conventional and familiar: the taxi to Raleigh-Durham airport, the flight to La Guardia, another taxi to Kennedy, the night flight from New York to Rome. Then the change was dramatic from the familiar to the unfamiliar: the smaller airport in Rome I had to find by walking, and there the search for the gate that would lead to the plane for Catania. Various strikes were on, and no one knew what my chances were for the afternoon flight. But others wanted to take that flight—Italians who knew the ways of their airports, and I joined myself with them and, like them, kept my bags with me because all luggage service had stopped. When the gates were opened, I continued to follow the Italian passengers and, like them, pushed my bags up into the hold of the plane. No ground worker was allowed to help with luggage.

Even after I found a seat and strapped myself into it, I wondered if the plane might not be grounded after all. As I looked around me in the Alitalia plane my companions seemed more relaxed than I was, more used to strikes that were called and then called off. I was not discontented or complaining, because I was concerned with bigger problems. Was I in the right plane? Would it reach Catania? And there would I find the auto sent by the San Domenico? And how would I ever find it? How would the chauffeur find me and find my bags? Would I, a few hours hence, be inscribed in the guest book of the hotel in Taormina, and would I that very night sleep in a monk's cell remodeled and furnished for a modern tourist?

The moment the plane took off was a meeting of two eternities: of the past when I had been rooted firmly in the earth with no need to rise into the heavens, and of the future when I would look freshly at nature on an island of flowers and at remains of the distant past where Greeks had once watched performances of their plays.

Despite the day's incessant anxiety which plagued me like some incurable disease, at the very moment of takeoff I thought of a letter I had received from David Miller a few days before leaving home. In the spring of 1973 David took my Dante course. He was a senior and a new student I did not know well, although he had taken the Proust course in 1971. But very early in the semester I became aware of his knowledge of the classics, of Homer and mythology. I was grateful to him for the skill with which he explained allusions to Greek culture in Dante's text. He called on me only once. We were both a bit shy with one another that evening. There hadn't been the chance to get to know each other better, and I was pleased when he wrote to me from Europe. In my answer I announced to him, because all plans had been made, my intention of living in Taormina a few weeks in May 1974. The letter I had just received was his second one. He had been in Taormina in the spring and wanted to congratulate me on my choice of a site for my brief vacation. He wrote of his climbing to the top of the hill above the town and of running down the goat path in the pure joy of all that he could see from such a high point. It was a pastoral letter in the Greek sense, with Virgilian overtones and with regrets that we would not meet unexpectedly if I chose to climb that goat path he had taken. In the Dante course we often heard him speak from the back of the classroom, but in the Proust class he had taken two years earlier, where he sat in the middle of the room, he had said very little. Now I was to track down the athletic-humanistic spirit of David Miller in Taormina, if my plane put down in Catania, and if a car were waiting for me there.

High over the Mediterranean I chided myself for my decision to come to Taormina. Phrases from Thoreau rose up in my mind in a more natural way than the airplane rose over the sea. Like a loon, I should have retired to some solitary pond and there recovered from the end-of-semester fatigue. My conscience was not at ease. I was more used to cornfields than to precipitous goat paths leading down from volcanoes. Why did I need such an elaborate shelter as the San Domenico when my New England past and Bible readings called forth images of caves, cottages, and even wigwams? Like Thoreau I once could have said: "My neighbors are the farmers of Concord." Once I was proud in saying and in believing that I could live with few clothes and few books. Hadn't I been brought up on such a phrase as: "The birds of the air have their nests?" and hadn't I once applauded such a sentence as: "I would rather ride on earth in an ox cart, than go to heaven in the fancy car of an excursion train?"

The airport in Catania—I quickly ascertained that it was Catania —was small and crowded and chaotic. On getting off the plane, I was told my bags would turn up at the customs desk inside the airport. No strikes in Sicily, at least that afternoon. I was making my way slowly to the building when I heard my name over the loudspeaker: "Signor Fowlie's chauffeur is at the customs office." It was hard to believe that everything had suddenly become simple. A proud-looking young man introduced himself to me as Mario and then introduced me with obvious pride to his Mercedes. We took off without incident after he suggested that I sit with him in the front of the auto in order to see as much as possible of the landscape between Catania and Taormina.

After passing through a drab section of the city of Catania, I of course looked with appreciation at parts of the view pointed out to me by the driver of the Mercedes, proud of his native Sicily. He was obviously rehearsing an account he was accustomed to giving, and I followed what he said but with less attention than I was paying to the gradual diminishing of anxiety in me and the increasing fatigue from the long journey. The goal was in sight, a luxury goal under a Sicilian volcano, and at least I had stopped saying to myself: "Why was I leaving the shores of Walden Pond for the shore of the Mediterranean? Why was I denying my basic belief that luxury hotels should be dispensed with because they are hindrances to mankind?" Such thoughts were interrupted when, at a turn of the road, Mario pointed out a spot high up ahead of us: "Etna!" and I saw the volcano that guarded the aerial splendor of the little town of Taormina.

From that moment on through the rest of the day, my introduction to the San Domenico was swift. The beauty of the hotel, more museum than hotel, delighted me: its spaciousness, its good taste, its almost religious sedateness. Each day I was to enjoy the wideness of the corridor on the second floor leading to my room. I had expected a cell-like room, but it was more than that: two cells at least must have been converted into my unit. A bowl of flowers and a bowl of fruit awaited me in the darkened room. The draperies were drawn over the French window. The fellow carrying my bags enjoyed revealing everything to me. He watched me as he pulled the drapes and opened the French window leading to the balcony.

"Signor, vuole venir qui per veder il mar!" He ushered me onto the balcony. To the right, high up against the sky Etna was clearly visible with a whitish smoke emerging from the volcano. To the left, and far below, I could make out the ruins of the Greek amphitheater. Immediately below, an extensive, blooming garden spread out. Bougainvillea covered the balcony itself. And finally—each of these sights had been proudly explained by the porter—in direct vision ahead of me, over the top of the garden, the gleaming blue of the Mediterranean. The biggest elements of what I had come to see in Taormina were visible from my balcony. Then my bag-carrying guide turned back into the room to explain practical matters in my luxurious bathroom and the method of ordering my breakfast for the time I wanted it. He left me then, but only when he felt certain I was duly impressed by the view from my balcony and the promised efficiency of the San Domenico.

It was late afternoon when the porter left me and I collapsed on the bed, to sleep, if possible, or, if not possible, to review the jumbled scenes of the past twenty-four hours spent in airports and planes, and finally in a Mercedes that had dropped me in front of the San Domenico Hotel in a Sicilian town whose beautiful name and history had attracted me for years. I looked at the ceiling of my room rather than at the sky outside and thought of the many ways in which this visit contradicted general principles of my behavior and travel habits. I had often declared the uselessness of brief visits, and this was to be two weeks only. I had always been proud of not being anchored to a home—to a house and a garden, for example—but was I anchored to a desire for the exotic? Taormina was not the Europe I had returned to so assiduously for study and carefully planned periods of work.

Why had I felt the need for such a trip and indulged myself in undertaking it? Wouldn't the winter of my discontent have thawed just as effectively in Durham or in Paris? Wasn't I well into the latter part of my life when I was trying to round out two lines of continuing interest since my twenties: the writing of a book on Dante and the writing of a personal memoir I planned to call *Journal of Rehearsals*? Where I was then, in 1973, and now today, in the aspect of eternity, such attempts seemed almost frivolous. Yet, in terms of personal integrity, somehow, for some reason, I had to try to complete them. I determined to make these days and nights in Taormina a source of renewal and the site of continuing efforts. I would adapt to the climate here and the circumstances, to what I had already seen from the swift Mercedes: the stony harshness of the landscape, white-hot under the sun; the softly rounded slopes; and the jagged edges that tore the sky.

"Mi chiamo Giuseppe," were the first words I heard the next morning when, at the earliest moment I had been allowed to order it, my breakfast tray was carefully placed over my writing pad as I sat up in bed. My day had begun as usual in an effort to assemble thoughts and write them down. I had unlocked my cell door an hour earlier. The knock had come at exactly the hour I had designated on the card attached the night before to the doorknob outside. "Prompt, efficient service," I said in my slow Italian to the young fellow who named himself as he bent over my bed. This was the first time in any hotel in Europe where the bearer of my breakfast tray had offered his name with the first café-au-lait (*caffè e latte*).

The Italian which Giuseppe spoke was not the Sicilian dialect, but he was Sicilian, he assured me, and had never been off the island in his twenty years. Mine was his first breakfast delivery that morning, and he seemed curious about why I was writing so early in the day. My Italian quickly slowed down and I tried French on him. He replied in French. I was surprised by his fluency and good accent. A native of Taormina, he explained that all boys attending school there studied French from an early age. The main industry in the town was hotels and tourism. French had always seemed indispensable or at least useful in finding jobs, especially at the San Domenico. He liked speaking French and was happy to keep up the practice. "I will be here each morning," he assured me, "at exactly this early hour."

Thus began my first day. With Giuseppe's French, I felt I might have been at the Paris-Dinard in Paris or the Atlantic in Nice. As I returned to the writing after an excellent breakfast, I knew the familiar pattern was established, that the morning would be for me in Taormina also the memorable season of the day. I would remain, like the Greeks to whom I was now close, a worshiper of Aurora, and renew myself each morning. Morning was dawn, and dawn was life. Such equations were truthful for me.

When the writing stint was done (I was trying to write a commentary on cantos 5 and 6 of the *Inferno*) and my shower taken, I stood for several minutes on my balcony where I watched a few lizards sliding for shelter under the bougainvillea flowers, and then looked at the sea glowing and sparkling in the bland May sunshine. It was golden at that time in the morning, speckled with white points of light, under a pale green sky. I was glad to be above it and at some distance. On the Riviera in France where I lived close to the Mediterranean and walked beside it, I was too aware of its difference from the Atlantic, the ocean of my childhood and my life in America. At Nice, for example, I missed the tides, the agitated water, the fog, the strong smell of brine and salt. Wherever I went in Taormina, I would be always in view of the sea, very high above it. On this first morning the water seemed full of lights and reflections, a lower heaven itself. Was the earth floating? It was true: the earth I was now on was insular. It was not a continent. I had begun to live for a few days of my life on the largest island of the Mediterranean. I was to be neighbor to the sea and Mount Etna.

Here I was to experience something of the permanent and absolute existence of the sea. And it was Homer's sea, the very sea of the poet who, not far from where I stood, had created the wrath of the *Iliad* and the wanderings of the *Odyssey*. But I had already established and confirmed my daily life of routine and habit. The infinite expectation of the dawn had already been in me, in my soundest sleep that always comes between four and five. After that sleep I had already lived through, on that first morning, the elevated, the critical hours of labor with words.

By midmorning, as I was to do each day of my Sicilian visit, I started out for a long walk from one end of the town to the other. To reach the main street from the San Domenico, which was in the center of Taormina, I had to climb some short stairways and pass private

140

homes, some of which were framed with flowering oleander that can grow on bare rock, and bougainvillea and flowering bushes of hibiscus. On the main street I turned left first, to the part that gradually led me out of the town to the bare countryside and that goat path going up the hill, described to me in David Miller's letter. There were olive trees on that part of the walk. The gray-silver leaves glistened in the morning sunlight. This was the olive tree held sacred in Greece, prized for the hardness of its wood, so hard that it can easily be carved. I knew from mythology that Pan sleeps under an olive tree, and I had read that it was brought from Greece to Sicily and planted first in the thoroughly Greek cities of Syracuse and Agrigente.

When I started back from the beginning of the goat path, my map, which I used only that first morning, indicated I would reach, at the other end of the main street, the Greek theater. Lawrence Durrell had once compared the length of this main street to the bridge of a zeppelin. The effect of the street was indeed that of being in midheaven. Taormina was far above the beach at Naxos. I had never any desire to go down to Naxos and break the spell of living midheaven. And the highest spot I climbed on the hill was to see the modest villa D. H. Lawrence had once occupied for three years.

When I saw ahead of me the entrance to the ruins of the Greek theater, I slowed down my walking and deliberately, in order to put off the excitement, focused my attention on the handmade jewelry spread out on rough, brown cloth on the ground on the left-hand side of the path I was following. Very few tourists had as yet come to Taormina that morning. I talked with only one of the sellers, a fellow who turned out to be a law student from Rome and the creator of the crosses and bracelets he was showing. He explained that the iron he used came from horseshoes and that his father had taught him how to bend and shape the metal. The designs were simple, and the next day or two I purchased some of his pieces for students at Duke who were leaving their "hippie" years but were still eager to wear such jewelry as signs of their liberation. My conversation with the Roman law student began in Italian and ended in French.

As I entered the Greek theater the reddish color of the stone threw the sky into a deeper blue than I had noticed thus far on my walk. That blue of the sky as well as the ruins of the amphitheater denied the possibility of change. A Greek theater of the fifth century B.C., built on the heights of Taormina! Etna loomed over it to the right, and the

Mediterranean stretched out beyond it. The ruins under the sunlit quiet guarded their secret.

The very distant past came into my consciousness as I sat down at various spots, some near the stage or altar, and others far up on one of the higher tiers. The theater had always been for me a place of obsessions. I had often felt stagestruck, and Shakespeare had been my god when I had played at Bennington scenes from *Measure for Measure* and *Lear*. The stage, more than other forms, had taught me the trickery and the magic of art. I tried to imagine on that morning in Taormina, and on all the subsequent mornings, the hemicycle filled with an audience watching a Greek tragedy and being victimized by the poetry of the text and the performances of the actors. This place was the goal of my travels rather than my comfortable room at the San Domenico Hotel with its extraordinary view.

The past was here, and I was here in the present. It was the very past that had controlled some of my life as actor and teacher. Such thoughts filled my mind as I watched a hawk or a vulture high in the air circling over the town. It was forming the same circle that other vultures had made when this theater had been filled with an audience. A race of people worthy of inhabiting the earth had once sat here and listened and watched.

After following with my eyes the bird's flight, I looked then at the sea—a compact, radiant, complacent sort of sea. A line from Racine's *Phèdre* came to my mind, and I said it out loud because it coincided exactly with the experience I was living:

Le ciel, tout l'univers est plein de mes aïeux.

At the end of act 4, when Phèdre learns that Hippolyte is in love with someone else, jealousy is added to her other suffering. She is queen and descended from the gods, from the sun itself, and she is justified in crying out: "The heavens, the entire universe is full of my ancestors." That is what I felt in the Greek theater in Taormina: everything there was full of the gods.

I felt the air to be full of invisible bolts. The path of my life had led me here, the path of my fate—out from the great snows of New England, out from the university in North Carolina where I teach *Phèdre* each year. I almost believed I could hear the muffled tone of Greek voices reciting the *Hippolytus* of Euripides, because I thought I heard the French voices at the Comédie-Française reciting Racine. I heard them above my own voice repeating:

Le ciel, tout l'univers est plein de mes aïeux.

In this place, a theater made for poetry and ritual, on the confines of the town, I constructed my fate, an *Atropos* that never turns aside. The fate of my life in its Greek terms was here with me: snowstorms and hawks, nests of field mice I had come upon walking around Walden Pond, the Seine, the alexandrine line I was repeating with its accents on syllables two, six, and twelve, the chaotic airport of Catania, Francesca and Paolo in their wind storm of canto 5. I was reliving the history of the storms that have weathered me as I listened to Sicilian voices (Mario's and Giuseppe's) speaking Italian and French, simple words that Racine had used in writing verses that came from ancient Greek.

Plays, with the exception of twenty or thirty, are ephemeral in the history of the theater extending from Aeschylus to Beckett. In order to be, the theater has to be popular. An audience has to be deceived, drugged, incarcerated. Yes, even here in this vast, open theater of Taormina, the audience was incarcerated as it listened to a chorus of mourning women or watched the antics of a Dionysian clown. Once it may have watched the body of Hippolytus carried in and knew the death of a god was being celebrated.

I have been told—and I certainly believe it—that Greek plays are untranslatable. But I can believe that Aeschylus, in the fifth century before Christ, when this theater was built, celebrated in his poetry mysterious forces in the cosmos: gods and heroes, belief and faith in the unknown. I imagined an actor-priest, or an actor-clown, leaping up onto the bench or altar or elevated structure and saying: "I am the god," and then being sacrificed or playing at being sacrificed—and thus enacting the destiny of us all. The *saltimbanque* (*saltare in banco*), the acrobat-clown dancing to attract the attention of his audience, performed the capers of a dancer as he wore the skin of a goat (*capra, chèvre*). He danced his sacrificial death, half-god, half-animal.

I knew that first morning in Taormina, and on all the subsequent mornings, that it began here, in such a place as this Greek theater, the charismatic power of priest or actor, the year-god figure in an ancient ritual dance, or two gravediggers in Elsinore, or a tramp munching a piece of carrot on our modern stage. The theater has to be this: the reincarnation of man and god, of despair and hope, of earth and heaven. The plot has to be the same: a dithyrambic goat-song, the dismemberment of the god, the scattering of seeds in the earth that will appear in the new body of wheat and wine.

Here in this place, encircled in stone, live the deeper secrets of the universe. I could see no bird, save one vulture, and no animal. But my eyes beheld the sea, the sky, and the hemicycle of stone imitating the circle of sea and sky, and containing the air that once heard Greek voices reciting poetry of life and death.

The repose of Walden Pond is never complete, nor is the repose of the Mediterranean. Nature, like the theater which imitates it, is made up of harshness and hope. From a distance, high up in the last tier, I looked down at the spot where the festal altar table would have been, and I thought of the mass, in the Roman, Anglican, and Orthodox communions, because it remains the supreme example of drama today, of what might be called the tragedy of redemption. It will remain that, as long as those present at its celebration in a church are not solely spectators, as long as they feel themselves participants in a drama which is their own. The mass can be followed and "lived" as if it were the personal drama of each one present, and indicating to each one his destiny and his salvation. The communion in bread and wine, or only in bread, taken at the end of the mass is literally the dividing and distributing of the god throughout the world, the hope offered to the world when the god returns from his death and absence. The sacredness of bread and wine, and not merely a symbolic sacredness, has remained intact throughout history. The body of the dead hero at the end of a tragedy, Antigone, Hamlet, Violaine (*L'Annonce faite à Marie*), is the symbolic representation of the dead god for the ultimate good of the community.

As once the frenzied dance of the god-figure Dionysus stirred and animated the chorus of the Bacchantes, so today at the mass the drama of Christ's death and resurrection moves the faithful in the nave of a church when they are able to transcend their individuality and merge the spiritual part of their being with the Christian tragedy of redemption. Thanks to the daily and weekly reenactment of the mass, the drama of Christ becomes as familiar to a believer as the unfolding of his own life. Dionysus and Christ are similar in the sense that each story combines passion with serenity. The suffering of the god (the dance of drunkenness and the agony in the garden), the slaying of the god (the dismemberment by the Bacchantes and the crucifixion by the Roman soldiers), and the final resurrection (the spring revival of the land and the apparition of Christ on the road to Emmaus and the ascension) merge the two principal elements of tragedy: the dithyrambic expression and the final cult—the worship of the community.

That theater was a point in space. But the earth we inhabit is also a point in space. My eyes turned easily to the cool, liquid image of the sea. Blue angels and blue devils were in that water: I knew I was in the midst of a new eternity. As Dante reports it in canto 26, that sea had been for Ulysses the image of an inaccessible freedom. Speaking to Virgil and Dante from his flame of an evil counselor, Ulysses explained how out of their oars he and his men had made wings for the foolish flight: "de' remi facemmo ali al folle volo."

The memorized lines from *Phèdre* and the *Inferno* kept me company on this first visit to the sacred spot in Taormina, and I was to recall them to mind and say them on the subsequent visits, but that first day had suddenly a luminous, gauzy blandness, and I felt eager to leave the outside spectacle of theater and sea and return to my room in the San Domenico. Theater people are nomads and teachers also. I knew I would soon be leaving this enchanted spot high above sea level and would see almost nothing else of Sicily. But from my room overlooking the sea, I could easily imagine: Palermo (and the Sicilian school of poets Dante writes of); the fields of wheat on the plateau; Naxos, down below me, which was the oldest Greek colony. I could imagine the invasions and occupations of Greeks, Phoenicians, Carthaginians, Romans, Saracens, and Normans. And then from a much later time, in the eighteenth century, that powerful secret society known as the Mafia, organized first to protect the interests of landowners, and then growing into political terrorism. I had already seen growing along my morning walk olives, oranges, grapes, lemons, and almonds, and I knew that in the countryside there would be groves of these fruits. So I walked back fast in order to lie down in my room before lunch and sort my thoughts (like seeds) and concentrate on what they might yield.

On that first day and in the next ten days with whom did I speak? After the hour of fast (and writing) each morning, Giuseppe arrived with my breakfast and spent a few minutes of conversation in French with me. There I was each morning, the mortal man needing, wanting breakfast, and the part of me I would call immortal—that part that tried in a modest way to deal with truth, to discover in words some slight aspect of truth concerning myself and the world. During the morning walk and visit to the theater, I would often have no talk or simply an exchange of a few sentences with shopkeepers. At lunch and dinner, my waiter spoke in Italian with me. The subject was food: advice on the dishes I might enjoy the most. At the table next to mine in the dining room, a retired English army officer living in Malta spoke to me quite often about Malta. The hour before dinner I spent in the garden, the largest and most spectacular garden in all of Sicily, I was told. There were a few encounters there with hotel guests, but I was often alone and enjoyed being neighbor to the sea and Mount Etna. At that time of the day the water was the same color as the sky, a very pale, luminous gray blue, shifting with a quick, dancing movement. After dinner each evening I talked, for an hour or so, with a couple from Brussels, an attorney and his wife. They were well read, especially Madame, and our talk was about French literature. We corresponded for a year after my visit to Taormina.

The days were very much the same. I took long walks morning and afternoon. A landscape radiated from me wherever I walked, wherever I sat. I felt I was watching the poem of creation. Olympus was everywhere. The Roman and the Greek worlds were set side by side, not only in Taormina, but throughout all of Sicily. One evening the lady from Brussels handed me a crumpled leaf and said, "You asked me about the eucalyptus tree. Smell this leaf." Thus I smelled for the first time the sweet odor of eucalyptus oil.

By that time in my life I knew I would never read Greek, but, thanks to Dante, I had lived close to some of the heroic writers of antiquity. Taormina was only a tourist center now, and a mere margin to my life. At night the town became a tower of silence. From my balcony, each night before turning in, I watched the smoke curling above Etna and reviewed the small events of the day that had delighted me. At that moment I was more conscious of the smells of earth and growth and flowers than I had been during the day when I was more held by the charmed circle of sun and sea, and by the ancient theater of stone. They were my introductions to Greek blue and the ocher of Egypt.

The only book I had with me in Taormina was Dante, but Thoreau was often in my thoughts because of the contrast between the Mediterranean and Walden, between ancient culture and New England, between the student of the past and the Yankee that I was. I felt Thoreau reproachful when I remembered a sentence I had never known how to interpret: "Deliver me from a city built on the site of a more ancient city." But didn't Thoreau contradict himself when a few pages later he wrote: "The pure Walden water is mingled with the sacred water of the Ganges."

On one of my morning walks late in the first week, I noticed a Greek head in stone—almost a monument—at the gate of a rather sumptuous villa. On examining it more closely the next day, I made out the name of the old herb-doctor Aesculapius. Mistletoe, that parasite of oak trees, which the Druid priests used to lop with a golden sickle, is the name of Aesculapius. Aeneas held mistletoe as he visited the underworld and thus held the power of returning to upper air. Such words as eucalyptus and Aesculapius, foreign to my early, simple vocabulary in New England, enlarged my spirit. All my life I have been a student of language, and all my teaching life I have tried to tell my students, or at least to suggest to them, that a serious study of language is comparable to the training of athletes.

During my last day the sea appeared more agitated, with white crests. That night, as I stood on my balcony, I saw for the first time since my arrival a red glow above Etna. It was a sign. I left the next morning.

Florence

Rarely has a year in my life been so uniformly centered around the study of one author as the year 1977. Only once before did it happen, thirty years earlier, when I spent nine months in Paris, a Guggenheim year, fully concentrating on Mallarmé. Dante was my obsession throughout 1977, and in fact only the *Inferno* preoccupied my thoughts, only one-third of his poem. In the spring semester, January to May, Dante was the object of all my pedagogical efforts in teaching a course in two sections on the *Inferno* for the fourth time at Duke. And then in the second semester, thanks to a sabbatical leave, I spent September and October in Florence, where I tried to convert all my practice with pedagogical devices into a book, a study guide for Dante's journey through Hell.

Beyond any doubt it was one of the richest years of my life when the classroom work gave me unusual satisfaction, and when during the two fall months in Florence I worked daily on the writing of a book I had already carefully planned, and when I lived in Dante's own city, learning its streets and museums, its churches and its river.

In the two halves of the year I was living both in the past and the present. In the spring I was trying to teach a fourteenth-century poem to young men and women of today who came to the poem with their own contemporary thoughts and opinions and ambitions. In the autumn I was trying to write my own contemporary thoughts about the fourteenth century in Florence itself that had figured so strongly in the Hell created by the imagination of Dante Alighieri.

During the writing semester in Florence, I asked myself each morning: Will I blush tomorrow at what I am writing today? (In the teaching semester I often wondered: Will I blush tomorrow over what I am

148

saying today?) In my efforts at writing, I had before me the example of a master-writer who reminded me each day that a writer comes from a tradition and shatters it. His obligation is that of being divisive and disruptive. Poets were prophets and sages long before philosophers.

Basketball was a favorite sport at Duke, and during the first semester of 1977 the Dante course provided me a chance to learn about it and observe it. Two years earlier, an episode had initiated me to the game. One morning, just before the class was to begin, David Taylor, a student in the first row close to the desk, leaned over and handed me two tickets. I saw in a glance they were for the Maryland-Duke game that Saturday. I was puzzled, and David explained patiently, "These tickets came to me for you from one of the Maryland players. He and I were friends at high school in Chicago."

"But I don't know any Maryland player. Why should he send them to me?"

"He's a French major at Maryland and has used some of your books. He knows you are here at Duke and wants you to come to the game."

I was moved by this, and made immediate plans to go that Saturday afternoon. Even if I was ignorant of the game, I would be there to watch number 44 play. During the remaining days of that week I looked forward to the event that would be a novel experience for me.

On my way to the entrance of Cameron Indoor Stadium, my student David Schmit came up to me with total surprise on his face: "What are *you* doing here?" (And I thought of Dante speaking to Brunetto Latini: "siete voi qui, ser Brunetto?") I explained the circumstances and asked him if he wouldn't sit with me in the reserved section for Maryland and help me with a few explanations. Dave recognized the name of the Maryland player and assured me he was well known.

When the game began, number 44 was the tallest black player on the floor. I kept my eyes steadily on him through the game, while Dave, in a firm, pedagogical fashion explained the moves. Maryland won the game. That evening I wrote a short note to number 44 to thank him for the tickets and to ask him about the French courses he was taking. He did not reply. The following year, in *Time*, I read of his sudden death during a practice game. His name, Owen Brown, is fixed in my mind as the athlete who sent me a greeting because of his interest in French and whose tragic death grieved me.

In the new Dante course of 1977, two students I had had in several courses, Fred Zipp and Jonathan Banks, introduced me to Mark Crow, a senior player on Duke's basketball team. In signing up for the Dante, Mark explained that he wanted to learn something about the Middle Ages, having taken courses in ancient history. Because of his height, I suppose, he sat in the back of the classroom, and we were a few weeks into the term when he first spoke to me after class one day. "I understand you want to come to one of the games."

Actually I did not remember saying that to anyone. Fred and Jonathan doubtless thought I should have said it. I replied affirmatively, and Mark answered in laconic fashion: "There'll be a ticket for you Saturday at the box office. You'll be sitting beside my mother and father."

My seat was high up, as it had been for the game in which I had watched Owen Brown, and this time I had another excellent teacher in Mrs. Crow. She pointed out especially the good and the less-good moments of her son's play. For the second time I was following a game by following one player. I paid attention also to the excitement of the crowd and marveled at its vociferous reaction to every move. Mark received his part of the applause and the shouts. How hard it must be, I thought, for Mark Crow to leave that center of adulation he occupied on Saturday afternoon and settle down into his seat in classroom 014 on Monday morning, when we would be looking at canto 5 with Francesca's story and making side comments on Francesca's Ravenna and Paolo's Rimini!

Once again, before the course was over, Mark invited me to a game, *the* game with our biggest rival, the University of North Carolina. He was the only senior on the team, and this was the last game of the season. When he appeared on the floor, I too participated in the ovation he received. Far down below me I could see Fred and Jonathan waving their arms in honor of their friend they had introduced to me. It was they who told me the following year that Mark had joined a city team in Italy and was playing the season there.

"Which city?" I asked.

"Rimini!" they answered.

After three weeks in the Tornabuoni-Beacci pensione, and daily morning and afternoon expeditions in the incomparable city, I entered the church of Santa Maria Maggiore. Somewhere I had read that the tomb of Brunetto Latini was there. A pleasant-faced janitor was dusting the benches in the back of the church, and I asked him about the tomb. "Sì, sì, Latini, a destra!" he said and pointed the way. I found it easily: a plaque honoring *Brunetto Latini poeta*, with a strange, thin column in front of it. The inscription was all praise, and I remembered from some edition of the *Divine Comedy* that canto 15 of the *Inferno* is the only known reference to Latini as sodomite.

Each morning that third week I had been working on canto 15 for my little book on the *Inferno*, as well as for a lecture I was trying to write on epiphanies in Proust and Dante. The lecture was to be given in May at Winthrop College in South Carolina. So, only high praise for that good man on his inscription in Santa Maria Maggiore, and some important praise for him in canto 15! Since my first reading of Dante, at the age of twenty, in the class of Grandgent at Harvard, I have felt close to Brunetto Latini. He is the figure of the teacher whose pupils go far beyond him and who delights in their achievements. He had been a model for me, and I was happy to pause at his tomb in Florence.

What was the city becoming for me? Sculptures, paintings, architecture, the Arno, the bridges, the shops, the two large squares, Reppublica and Signoria, La Posta, La Banca nazionale del lavoro, the handsome faces in the streets, the bodies of the agile Italians walking or riding motorcycles. I lived in a maze of great art and living beauty. What superlatives can I use? The city is incomparable.

Dante, Michelangelo, and the sensuous beauty of the Florentines I saw in the streets: these were my centers. For the first time—it was the morning of October 2—cousin Pauline and I explored the Bargello. There on the first floor, three more works of Michelangelo: *Bacco*, *Brute*, and *David-Apollo*. Cellini's *Narcise* is a worthy companion for them. They are the very Italians I see on the Via Calzaiuolo, but naked and in marble! In the chapel on the second floor we discovered the Giotto fresco with the supposed profile painting of Dante. I was pleased to learn that the profile of the man beside Dante is Brunetto Latini according to some authorities. So be it for me! I have now seen his face after visiting his tomb.

Rather than going forward and examining more and different treasures, I kept wanting to return to the Michelangelos: to the *David*, the *Four Prisoners*, *Saint Matthew*, and the *Pietà* in the Academia; to the tombs of Lorenzo and Juliano dei Medici at San Lorenzo; to the *Victory* in the Palazzo Vecchio, to the *David-Apollo* in the Bargello; to the *Pietà* in the Duomo. Nowhere else in the world, not even in the parts of Greece that Pauline and I had seen a few years earlier, has the male body been so exalted. Florence is the city of the male nude and of garbed Dominicans and Franciscans. The monks, when they are not celebrating mass, are guarding the statues and the paintings of the naked Christ on the cross, or the naked Christ being taken down from the cross (*la deposizione*). The blue-jeaned fellows in the street strut with pride in their virility. Even the deep voices of the Italian men have tones of demanding, insistent virility.

Every two or three days I went into the baptistery, not only to see it again, but to recite over to myself Dante's phrase "nel mio bel San Giovanni" of canto 19. I try to imagine the many baptismal fonts that are no longer there. San Giovanni, where Dante himself was baptized in 1265, took over for the city of Florence the role of pagan Mars. Paganism and Christianity are both in Michelangelo's sculptures. Mars has not been deposed or thrown into the Arno as efficaciously as the Christian spirit in the city believes.

Each morning I waited for the ringing of the bells in the bell tower of Santa Trinità before getting up to look at the sky. Names associated with Florence filled my sleep as well as all my waking hours. The most persistent were: Orcagna's Loggia, Savonarola (Fra Girolamo), Lorenzo dei Medici, Andrea del Sarto, Via Tornabuoni, Frati Predicatori—or Dominicans—whose name would seem to be *Domini canes*, "hounds of the Lord."

I first read the name of the painter Gozzoli in Proust—in the early passage where Marcel's father is mounting the stairs after the dinner where Swann had been a guest. To young Marcel the father resembled Gozzoli's Abraham which Swann had once shown to the boy in a reproduction. On three different mornings Pauline and I spent some time looking at Gozzoli's *Adoration of the Magi* frescoes in the Medici-Riccardi Palace. Three walls of the small, ancient Medici Chapel on the second floor show a full Renaissance procession (Benozzo Gozzoli was a true Florentine, born in the city in 1420) winding on horseback through rocky country on the way to Bethlehem. Everything is magnificent in the painting: landscape, horses, dogs, birds, the postures of the riders, attendants, and footmen, and the three kings of whom the youngest is supposed to be Lorenzo dei Medici, and the oldest, Lorenzo il Magnifico.

Dominating all of Florence is the gigantic white marble *David* of Michelangelo. He is in every shop and kiosk, in reproductions of all sizes: statuettes, cards, enlarged pictures, posters. The full-sized reproduction where the real *David* once was, before the Palazzo Vecchio, is good preparation for approaching the original, now so carefully, so monumentally placed at the end of the long gallery of the Academia.

There, under the light from the sky, and illuminated from the side walls by electricity, he is the central focus for all eyes, the biggest reason of all for coming to Florence. Let's say it: *David* is the most breathtaking reproduction in marble of the human body. The gentle power of the young hero is there in his gaze of confidence. The expression of victory is there as you realize that over his shoulder and held by one hand is the slingshot. Nothing else, save the absolute nudity of the body.

Cousin Pauline joined me in Florence for one month. Four years earlier we had taken together a Swann cruise beginning in Athens and ending in Naples, during which we stopped at various Greek islands. Learned lectures were given each morning on the boat and further lectures on the various spots on land: Rhodes, Patmos, Crete, and even Troy, Istanbul, Siracusa, Palermo. The Florence vacation spent together was different: one month in one city, in one pensione—the Beacci, at 3, Via Tornabuoni, close to the Arno and to Santa Trinità whose bells each morning at seven reassured me of the new day.

Pauline, who is called Polly by many friends, accepted on her arrival my strange regimen (I had already been two weeks at the Beacci) and seemed to prefer it to any of her own devising. I took breakfast in my room at eight and she preferred to leave her room and go to the dining room, where she sat at our table and talked with a few of the guests. I stopped my morning work about half past ten and met Pauline in the parlor of the pensione. We spent the next two hours in museums: the Uffizi, the Pitti, the Academia, the Bargello, the Medici-Riccardi. We invariably started out each morning on the Via Porta Rosa opposite the pensione which led us into the heart of the city, past the bank we used and the post office. Back at the Beacci for lunch at one, with considerable appetite, we enjoyed the meal, especially the pasta dish at the beginning and the fruit at the end. The pears were delicious that year, and the bel paese cheese. We separated between two and four, for a short rest and a brief period of letter writing and reading. Then for approximately an hour and a half we visited a church or revisited one of our favorite churches: Santa Maria Novella, Santa Croce, the Duomo (Santa Maria del Fiore), San Lorenzo. The churches were open in the afternoon when the museums were closed.

Between half past five and six each day we reached, on our way home to the Beacci, the Café Donini on the Piazza della Republica and took almost always the same table under the sky where the same waiter recognized us and took the same order of *due cappucini*. As we waited for the coffee to come, we rested our weary bodies on the comfortable chairs and enjoyed the darkening light over the piazza, which in the morning, as we passed through it, was full of sunlight. With the first sips of the hot coffee, Pauline usually said: "What a pick-up this gives you!" It was a relaxed, restful moment when we often spoke of home and family, in terms of the past and the future.

Pauline Hanson had retired in 1975, after twenty-five years at Yaddo where she had worked as assistant to the foundation director, Elizabeth Ames. I had spent a few work periods at Yaddo (Saratoga Springs, New York) before Pauline went there in 1950, and during her twenty-five years I had gone three times to spend a month: once in summer, and twice in winter. I had watched her direct a large group of twenty-five to thirty writers and artists in the summer, and a much smaller group of eight to ten in the winter. She had assumed naturally and easily all the varied duties of knowing the writers and artists, of making their work period as efficient and as comfortable as possible, and of helping to run a large estate. On arrival at Yaddo in 1950 she was innocent of the ways and habits of writers, especially when they come together under the admirable schedule and order of Yaddo, organized for creative work. She quietly recorded to herself her amazement and discoveries, and learned to adjust her powers of help and advice to those who wanted it and deserved it.

Pauline was the center of dependability and kindness at Yaddo: directors of the Yaddo Corporation, guests, groundsmen, cooks, maids—all seemed devoted to her, appreciative of her, as I have been throughout my life. If I was at all esteemed at Yaddo during my work periods there, it was because I was her cousin and she seemed to approve of me. She had inherited and developed in herself the stamina of the women of the Adams family. All the best traits of our grandmother and her four daughters are in Pauline. At Yaddo she lived in a world they could not have imagined, but she practiced there the human qualities of uprightness and a sense of duty and loyalty and efficiency that her forebears would have approved.

The poems she wrote and the astrological charts she kept of family and close friends (whether they knew it or not) are important aspects of her giving nature. Being with her daily in Florence, where her physical strength surpassed mine and where her love of Renaissance painting was deeper than mine, was an experience for me. Whatever we did together: a walk along the Arno, a return visit to the battle

154

scene of Uccello in the Uffizi; the *dolce* at the end of every evening meal we marveled at; our talks about the classical ballet she knows so well—during all that she was the perfect companion.

Pauline is the great respecter of other people's rights and habits and achievements. I wish I could record here what others have said to me about her: Malcolm Cowley, Morton Zabel, Violette Verdy, Ben Belitt, Elizabeth Bishop, Leslie Katz, Austin Warren (who was Pauline's teacher at Boston University), Jane Mayhall, Ben Weber, Ned Rorem, David Diamond, Nancy Sullivan, Galway Kinnell.

Soon after her arrival in Florence, we read one morning in the *Herald-Tribune* of Robert Lowell's death. During the following weeks thoughts about him kept crossing my mind: thoughts about him personally, of course, but perhaps more about the poet in a general sense, the writing of poetry, and then the abandoning of poetry at the poet's death. In the back of my mind, in my memory, the "tomb" sonnets of Mallarmé gradually came into focus, and, curiously enough, not the two famous ones on Poe and Baudelaire, but the less well-known sonnet on Verlaine. Lowell, like Mallarmé, wrote about the death of other poets, and with the event of death he associated suicide and madness. He had been affected by the deaths of Roethke, Berryman, and Jarrell, as we on those days in Florence were affected by his going. A strong voice, one of the strongest, was now silent.

We had just read reviews of his latest book, *Day by Day*, when the simple newspaper account of his death replaced them. It was a heart attack, in a taxi, in New York City, at the age of sixty. A swift, almost gracious leave-taking of a private world that was depicted in the poems as grim, dark, harrowing. This was the thought in me that brought back the opening line of the Mallarmé sonnet, about the black rock angered because the wind rolls it: "Le noir roc courroucé que la bise le roule."

The first time I met Cal Lowell there was no indication of that. I was teaching at Yale. A telephone invitation came from Jean Stafford, Lowell's first wife, to come to dinner in a nearby Connecticut town where they were spending the winter. It was in 1943, after he had spent some time in jail as a conscientious objector. I had read one novel by Jean Stafford and several poems by Lowell.

They both appeared shy, he more than she, but they were charmingly hospitable. During the dinner, the talk was on some religious topics—Lowell was at that time a recent convert to Catholicism—and he told me, much to my delight, that he and Jean were readers at Sheed and Ward. They had successfully recommended to Mr. Sheed that he publish my second book, *Clowns and Angels*.

After dinner—Jean seemed to disappear into the kitchen—Cal sat down beside me on a sofa and produced the manuscript of a poem he was working on. He wanted to read some of it to me and ask me my impressions about this line and that line. The poem was difficult and long, and I found it awkward and embarrassing to make comments on a text I was hearing for the first time. I remembered so well Lowell's ardor in the reading, and how he took to heart the slightest —and I fear, feeblest—remarks I made.

My other encounters with Robert Lowell were brief, in different places, and they spanned several years. At Yaddo we had some talk about Racine's *Phèdre*, because he was working on his poem on Phaedra at that time. At Brandeis University we sat together at a large formal luncheon. I remember from that meeting only one remark he made in what was almost a whisper: "Please tell Austin Warren that I am now an Episcopalian." Then, at the University of Iowa one winter I gave a single lecture on a topic the English Department had proposed: new developments in French literature. The hall was crowded and halfway through my talk I recognized Lowell standing at the back. He was a visiting professor there that term. When we shook hands afterward, I told him that was not the type of lecture he would be interested in, and explained that the topic had been requested. Elizabeth Hardwick, Lowell's second wife, I met that evening for the first time. In 1970, he came to Duke, invited by the students, to speak to them at the time of the student unrest. I attended his talk, which I greatly admired. When it was over, he was swept away by a group of students, eager to have further discussion with him, and I was unable to speak with him alone.

Those were the only meetings I can remember with Robert Lowell, whose spirit always seemed to me molded on the ills of our day. "Sa ressemblance avec les maux humains," Mallarmé writes in the Verlaine sonnet. It is the ending of the sonnet that flashed into my mind when I read in the *Herald-Tribune* of Lowell's death. Mallarmé imagines the poet Verlaine hidden in the grass through which flows a shallow stream of water. This stream, which is death, is slandered by men. The poet puts his lips to the water but does not drink, and his breath does not stop:

> La lèvre sans y boire ou tarir son haleine
> Un peu profond ruisseau calomnié la mort.

Lowell often wrote of this closeness he felt to death, and of how slight the event of death seemed to him. He was humbled before the thought of death, before its reality. But before accepting death, he wanted, as if he were an Old Testament prophet, to help bring some change to the evil ways of the world. Doom was the final moment, but before that came, there was much to be done.

I have only read about his imperiousness and never witnessed any attitude in him that could be called that. I have been interested to learn that the name Cal was first used by his classmates at Saint Marks because he resembled in his behavior the despotic Roman emperor Caligula.

The events of Lowell's life that the world knows, and rehearsed at the time of his death, are all in his poems: his conversion to Catholicism that lasted briefly, his imprisonment, his protest concerning the Vietnam War, his three marriages. The poems formalize all that, and the poet used it to reach a deeper understanding of himself and the world.

It seems to me that Lowell is as metaphysical a poet as we have had in America. He attempted, as courageously as anyone, to reconcile the opposites in us that most men fail to see as opposites. Parents, for example, who create in us a sense of gratitude, loyalty, and reverence, but who also force us into states of rebellion and a determination to lead a life different from theirs, to defend causes that are not theirs.

Lowell felt the opposites in the Supreme Parent, in God, who in the Christian tradition is our Redeemer, and who is also the great Repressor in us of desires, longings, acts, words.

The Muse is a collaborator for the poet who helps him to plot out his life. In that daily plotting, the Muse condones him, urges him to bring injury to others, and even allows him to injure himself. In all ages the poet has listened to that strange voice that does not seem to come from himself and that leads him into a poem which may be a confession of weakness, of guilt, of ruthless strategy. But like other poets whom Lowell has read carefully—Baudelaire, Valéry, Hart Crane, John Crowe Ransom—he pleads for compassion.

The year of which I spent two months in Florence celebrated the 600th anniversary of the birth of Filippo Brunelleschi, born in Florence in 1377. At his death, in 1446, the fifteenth century was almost half over, and he had demonstrated by then to all of Italy and Europe that he counted among the very greatest of his day. As I walked through the city, his name and his face flashed everywhere on a huge poster. It was very much his year, and I tried, as my cousin did, to visit and revisit the best of his work.

The cupola of the cathedral of Santa Maria del Fiore has immortalized his name. We could see it from wherever we were in the city. Brunelleschi had raised it to such a height that one sees it first on approaching Florence. Significantly his ashes were buried under that dome as if it were judged the scene of his greatest triumph.

Brunelleschi was the architect of the handsome portico in the Piazza dell'Annunziata. In that work especially I could see him as the pioneer-architect substituting ancient forms for Gothic forms and adapting them to modern requirements. He let in floods of light through the spacious porticoes that form the façade of the Foundling Hospital (called in his day the *Ricovero dei Gettatelli*.)

That particular square, the Piazza della Santissima Annunziata, became one of our favorites, with its arcades and busts of Medicean Grand Dukes, a sunlit piazza with its church dedicated to the Madonna Annunziata, flanked on its right by the hospital and on its left by a convent (the Order of the Servants of Mary). Frescoes of Andrea del Sarto are everywhere: under the porch, in the nave, and over the door of the cloister (la Madonna del Sacco.)

On a return visit to the Casa di Dante, the guardian who sat at a desk near the second-floor entrance recognized me and seemed approving that I had come back for a second look at the editions of pictures on exhibit. When I was saying good-bye to him on leaving, he stood up and said: "Let me reward you for returning. Here is a copy of the Brunelleschi poster. Would you like to have it?" It is still tacked up on my kitchen wall in Durham. The 1377–1977 celebration continues for me.

To the right of the church of San Marco is the museum of San Marco, a convent rebuilt by Michelozzo in the fifteenth century for the Dominican fathers of Fiesole. It was for Pauline and me the most peaceful spot in all of Florence. We learned that Fra Angelico (or Beato Angelico) lived there between 1435 and 1445, and during the last years of the century (he was burned in 1498) Fra Girolamo Savonarola lived there.

As we went up the steep staircase to the upper floor, we kept our eyes on the fresco of the *Annunziàta* painted by Fra Angelico. At the top of the climb we paused before it, as if it were the goal of our morning exploration. And it was that. The atmosphere of peace was everywhere in that building. At the sides of the corridors we entered each of the small cells of the Dominican fathers to look at the frescoes painted by Angelico or by one of his pupils. In the quarters of the prior we visited three cells where Savonarola had lived, and we paused before his portrait, before the picture of his execution, before his wooden crucifix, his writing desk, his two Bibles, and his sacerdotal ornaments.

It was from this convent he was taken for his death on April 8, 1498. Soon after my arrival in Florence, I had begun reading each night a chapter or two of George Eliot's *Romola* and from that novel I was adding to my very sketchy knowledge of the reformer-priest. Although born in Ferrara, he belonged to Florence where he sought to weaken the influence of the Medici and maintain the republican form of government. What a somber genius he was, whose death in the flames brought the fifteenth century to a close! Thanks to my reading of George Eliot, I began associating him with many parts of Florence: with the church of San Lorenzo, for example, where he made his début as preacher during one Lent. He preached also in the Duomo at the time of his greatest popularity when the city was at his feet. He was tried on the square in front of the Palazzo Vecchio, and that square, the Piazza della Signoria, which I crossed more often than any other square, constantly reminded me of how Fra Girolamo Savonarola of the Dominican order was hanged and burned.

When Pauline left in late October, I spent my last days alone in Florence visiting the art we had enjoyed the most: the Gozzoli *Voyage of the Three Kings*, the baptistery of San Giovanni, Michelangelo's *Pietà* in the Duomo, the loggia of the Signoria with Cellini's *Perseus*, Uccello's *Battle Scene* in the Uffizi, Andrea del Sarto's *John the Baptist* in the Pitti, the cells of San Marco, Michelangelo's *David* and the unfinished *Saint Matthew* in the Academia. I paid my last visits to Giotto's *Dante* in the Bargello and to the tomb of Brunetto Latini in Santa Maria Maggiore on the Via dei Cerretani.

On my last day in Firenze, I listened as usual to the ringing of the Santa Trinità bells at seven A.M. and read a chapter in *Romola* before going to bed that night. During the morning and afternoon walks through that Renaissance world, the wonderment uppermost in my mind was the number of personal agonies that had been transformed into art in this city, which in 1977 we could see and enjoy. A few of the great names had become daily names for me: Brunelleschi, Dante, Michelangelo, Savonarola, and I knew from the lessons they had given me that the mystery of personality remains a holy thing. Florence had taught me that the crown of life is not ecstasy, but wisdom. I had lived so steadily in the past—in the fifteenth century—during my sojourn of two months that I found myself in a state of disbelief at my own survival.

Homages

To Montaigne, Eliot,
Saint-John Perse

Without following any particular order, stocktaking became during the summer of 1979 an intermittent mental activity. It was accompanied by a weeding out of books in my library, of dishes and pans in my kitchen, of clothes in my closets. When I left in late August for Sewanee, I would leave behind me a neater, emptier apartment. Was I preparing a more definitive departure? I have had no fear of death ever in my life, but I have had a fear of not tidying everything before that event might occur. I was still more concerned with How shall I live? than with How shall I die? still concerned with my own cosmology, which begins, as every cosmology does, with self-knowledge.

We blunder through a life of continual mistakes. The writing of these pages has proved that to me, if nothing else, and in this self-study I have been fully aware of each line composing my self-portrait and denouncing me. I have read in Heraclitus how the elements of our world are in continual flux and transformation. And I have read in Montaigne, who probably took it from Heraclitus, that men too are in a similar flux and transformation. Our knowledge also is variable, that of Heraclitus and Montaigne and of a French teacher like myself who reads Montaigne and at the same time many of the ancients whom Montaigne read in his effort to point out to his reader that he never is but is always becoming.

I have never wondered why Montaigne wrote his *Essays*—he was explicit about that—but I have wondered about why I read him. And that wonderment is behind all my writing and teaching. What criteria guide us in choosing this author to read and teach, and not some other author? Are the strong critical voices of each generation those that choose for us? Are books and films that are fundamentally critical among those that last the longest? Heraclitus and Montaigne, for example? *Day for Night* (*Nuit américaine*) by Truffaut, the best movie about moviemaking ever made? *Amarcord*, that return to Fellini's small town and to his youth?

I read everywhere in the superficial writing that is turned out regularly in newspapers and weeklies that our age is scientific and that metaphysical dogmas have lost their power. But I am not convinced. In *Of Experience*, Montaigne says: "I study myself: that is my metaphysics, that is my physics." Those writers who, like Montaigne, write about the self: Plato, Plotinus, Saint Augustine, Pascal, Thoreau, Henry Adams, Gide, Jung, Eliot have taught me that each man makes his own cosmos and lives through a variability or flux that is internal as well as external. Each of these writers has written what Montaigne calls his own essays: "a book consubstantial with its author." Each of these writers, from whom I have learned so much, has acknowledged in some form or other that his book has made him. One subject for all of these writers: the self, the ever-changing self. They are the men who never repented. They are the writers who never deleted (especially Montaigne), but who, when they wrote, added on to what they had already written. Each wrote one book that spun out in endless, ever-widening circles. No revisions, no corrections, but simply extensions so that whatever they wrote at the beginning might appear in larger perspective at the end.

Montaigne and Thoreau are brilliant examples of writers who tell us how they know, how they learn, and neglect telling us what they know and what they have learned. Montaigne and Thoreau, so far apart in time and in style, in temperament and behavior, are key figures in my natural life (my New England way of living and feeling) and my life spent in French literature (an acquired life in a foreign tongue). Thoreau is not as timeless as Montaigne, but I needed to recognize myself in places familiar to me, to Thoreau, in Concord and Walden, and in such familiar controversies as that over a poll tax. The unfamiliar settings of Montaigne attracted me as experiences in exoticism, but they always led me to ideas and concepts that I read in Thoreau in far simpler terms, in expressions that were less learned and less destructive. Both writers taught me to consider seriously the phenomenon of consciousness. *Que sais-je?* And both taught me—a lesson I will always be grateful for—to live cheerfully as I seek out some mode of living.

It has often occurred to me that the subjectivism of much of modern thought begins with Montaigne, begins with the record of the essays of his life. Whenever I find myself in error—through my reason which is variable, or through some sensory impression which has tricked me, or through some illness, after thinking my body was strong and invulnerable, or through some fickleness of behavior, after believing my soul to be steadfast—I remember the training and the advice that Michel de Montaigne has given me. To recover from such confusions, no therapy is better than deliberately to write them out.

The simplest form of writing therapy would be the personal essay, such as Montaigne himself attempted. There are more difficult forms for the writer-creator where the therapeutic exercise ends in a sonnet of Mallarmé or the long-sustained exploration of Joyce's *Ulysses*. When Gérard de Nerval was suffering from mental confusion in 1853, the young Doctor Blanche advised him to write out his dreams, and Nerval began the first draft of his prose masterpiece *Aurélia*. In such a work, a man's confusions become more real and more revealing than the products of his so-called rational mind.

And yet I know—and it saddens me to know—that the skepticism of Montaigne can be a trap from which we have to learn to escape. It is true that we watch many things flash by with each new sunrise and with each new moon, and are unable to grasp them or even judge them. But we have been conscious of them, and we know that we ourselves are in that consciousness. I try to observe myself as much as I observe others. I can see them passing, things and beings, and I know that I too am passing, that I too will not stay. When some specific change is forced upon my consciousness, an illness, for example, or a sudden lapse in memory, I realize that I do not yet know my natural laws.

At such moments, I tend to take up again my copy of the *Essais* or my worn, heavily marked copy of *Walden*. Either one helps me to find myself, to discover how to live, and to ask myself all over again the problems of the timeless subjects that Montaigne airs for us as he quotes speeches made by Socrates or lines from Plutarch. Over and over he tells us that he can never see the whole of anything, of any problem, but at the same time he tells us to see nature as a whole.

No part of life is too high or too low for our observation. On this valuable point Montaigne has done me more good than Thoreau because Montaigne is the opposite of a puritan and all my life I have been plagued by irritating traces of puritanism within me. Whatever openness, whatever flexibility I have been able to develop in my nature, I owe in part to the lessons of Montaigne. The body and the soul are not separate. They are joined. The pleasures we find in books and in study, in meditation and prayer, are not unrelated to the pleasures of eating and drinking and sex.

When I read for the first time in the essay "On Ancient Customs" ("des coustumes anciennes") the passage about Diogenes, I remember my surprise at seeing such words printed on the page of so venerable a writer as Montaigne, and then my delight at such a striking example. It seems that Diogenes practiced masturbation in public, and when bystanders gathered to watch him, he said to them that he wished he could satisfy his stomach by rubbing it.

In another passage, illuminating for me in its frankness, he speaks of the ineffectiveness of his will and illustrates the point by his penis rising up when he has no use for it and remaining limp when he has most use for it. Such healthy good humor is not to be found in Henry Thoreau who steadfastly remains the puritan. I was reconciled to life by Thoreau, and my understanding of life was broadened by Montaigne.

I suppose it is the puritan in me that sends me back again and again to the essay "On Repentance" ("du repentir"). "I rarely repent," writes Montaigne. Ever since teaching Proust, that sentence returns to my mind when we read of Elstir's admonition to Marcel (in *A l'ombre des jeunes filles en fleur*) never to regret actions in his past, never to be ashamed of what he had once said or done. From Montaigne's view, repentance is impossible because our sins change with the years. As soon as we articulate them, they already belong to a younger self. I am not sure of this point, and might put it differently. They are the same sins, in my case, but my attitude toward them changes, my sense of guilt diminishes with the years. Or rather, a feeling of guilt in me changes with the seasons. One season I see the flower, and the next season I am eating the fruit. In the season after that, or during the next two seasons, I tell myself almost in the words of Montaigne that it is enough just to have lived. Living is our most illustrious occupation.

At various periods in my life, I have deliberately refrained from reading the *Essais* because of a fear that I was identifying with Montaigne, that I was tending to live his experiences. Today that seems a groundless fear. It is clear to me now that I have not identified with him, but in small happenings and coincidences in my life I am reminded of details, and usually not important ones, that I have come across in the *Essais*. I seldom drink beer, for example, but every time I do I remember that Montaigne tells us he could not tolerate beer. Whenever I forget a name, I am reminded of the passage where Montaigne claims that if he lives long enough he will forget his own name. Whenever I hear the word *virginity*, I recall the confidential remark Montaigne makes about having lost his virginity so early in life that he can't remember the event. Often in reading in the newspapers of some sadistic crime, I remember that Montaigne hated cruelty above all vices.

It would be hard for me to choose from the luxury-loving Renaissance man or from the ascetic New Englander what thoughts have meant the most to me. From both of them, from the wild, eccentric plan of the *Essais*, and from the steady, determined form of *Walden*, I learned that I am of the human race. I am one with the whole body of mankind living and dead. Perhaps more than their thoughts, I continue to enjoy their questing spirits, the verve of their writing, their magnificent self-consciousness.

Metaphysicians, psychologists, and physicians derive most of their training and their knowledge from direct or primary experience. At times I find myself questioning and avoiding the knowledge that they propose, and turning to myself as a source when I am skeptical about such matters. I suppose it is because a literary man derives his knowledge essentially from books, from a page of Pascal or a poem of Baudelaire, whereas a psychoanalyst learns from his patients. A writer is both reader and writer. A doctor is both patient and doctor. I willingly agree that the life of Freud and Lacan is their books, the record of what they learned from patients, and especially from the world of fantasies their patients have recounted. But I would propose that *in the same way* the teacher learns from his students, from listening to questions asked in class, and from the franker conversations outside of class.

How often have my own thoughts been corrected and illuminated by listening to the thoughts of students! The teacher easily becomes the student, as I suppose the analyst inevitably becomes the patient. The one in authority and the one seeking the knowledge about a book or about himself are both mirrors demonstrating a psychic process. Two beings, two psychic miracles confronting one another. I imagine that the patient observes and, in his own way, records phenomena as lucidly as the doctor. Here I am back again with Montaigne, when I thought I had left him, back with what he called the shared nature in all men: "chaque homme porte la forme entière de l'humaine condition." Wiser than most psychologists, Montaigne draws his observations as much from physical human activities as from non-physical activities. How often he tells us what a good horseman he is!

He knows that when people see him on a horse, they easily forget his short stature.

Montaigne makes life more concrete than Jung or Freud or Lacan, but he never avoids those matters that transcend the rational faculty. He knew as clearly as any analyst knows that the psyche is a transcendent phenomenon, and he is as familiar with it as he is with physical phenomena.

We are our psychic life, and I doubt if we can ever know it. Our reason keeps us within narrow limits of knowledge. To begin with, our human language is forever inadequate in any expression of our conscious and unconscious life. We simply learn to live with the psyche's complexity and renounce trying to understand it. It is exciting for me to know there is something within me, within the narrow limits of my own body, that I will never comprehend. Life is best defined by all that extends beyond us that we will never understand and never reach. Death will merely interrupt that search which never comes to an end. Our heritage? All is there—the experiences not ours that are recorded in us that we dimly feel and imperfectly understand. No one is totally responsible for anything! Let us follow what we do rather than what we think. There lies the truth.

Poetry too is about the life of a man, about all of his life: his physical and psychic being. The metaphors of a poet are about the truth he has found in living, those aspects of truth that engage him, that help him to illuminate his experience. Every poem, considered successful according to the canon of its day, is autobiographical, even a sonnet of Mallarmé and a quartet of Eliot from which the man himself seems to have disappeared. He is there, universal and private, for the reader trained to read such verses. The autobiography of Mallarmé and the autobiography of every man is in *le pitre châtié*. The psyche of mankind is in *Prufrock* and in Nerval's *El Desdichado*. In literary art autobiography is inescapable. It cannot be relegated to any significant distance from the center of the work in question: poem or novel, essay or play. To write means to recall, and there in the heart of what is recalled the writer begins to make extraordinary discoveries. At its genesis writing is one man's autobiography, and then it becomes every man's autobiography. Literature is that art in which a reader rediscovers his own life and understands it more lucidly.

The past is recorded in the shape of a tree. The past of every woman is recorded in *Antigone* and *Madame Bovary*. The past of every man is recorded in *Oedipus* and *Le Rouge et le noir*. Every life is a recapitulation of former lives, in the sense that the present moment we are living through is made up of memories of past moments. No demarcation is visible between past and present. Our mind draws from the past in the same way that our body continues to function thanks to the food we have consumed since childhood, since before childhood.

What the scientist would call objective truth is of little consequence for our minds, because the mind delights in the proliferation that crowds around any recall of an incident from the past, or around a phrase of some half-forgotten song, or around the flash of a color in one of our dreams that leads us to a meaning we had never consciously held before. It is impossible for us to cease existing in the past since we exist in the present. Proust has taught us once and for all that a remembered experience is far truer than the experience when it was first lived.

A man can never know what it is to be someone else. And yet a man, if he is a writer, tries to communicate to others what it is to be himself, what an experience he has undergone means to him. The mystery of art in its most humble and in its most elevated forms is the result of an instinctive need to communicate. What do the Beatles mean by *A Day in the Life*? What does Hopkins mean by the soaring of a windhover? What does Dante mean by Gerione taking off like an arrow into the air? What does Eliot mean by the laughter of children hidden in the leaves of a tree? What does Baudelaire mean by the poet being the architect of his fantasies? Are all such examples communications without any stable meaning? Quite possibly. A metaphor has never one meaning. It is recreated in the consciousness of each reader who is an individual different from all other readers.

Those poems I have looked at the most steadily throughout a large part of my life, a *dizain* of Scève, a sonnet of Mallarmé, a canto of Dante, an *illumination* of Rimbaud, are transformed experiences (the experience itself is incommunicable). We have to learn to experience the poem and not the experience behind it. That word we call a metaphor or an image or an example of metonomy is the significance of the poem, the concrete element which for the mind of the reader translates an idea.

Most of the experiences in a man's life are lived without an effort on his part to discover their meaning. That is the function of the artist: poet, painter, or composer—to reveal a meaning. Such meaning can be achieved only in the realization of some pattern: a musical motif, a metaphor, the façade of a church. The prolixity of nature has to be chastened and reduced to the pattern of a garden, or to the straight line of a highway. In the same way, the verboseness of man's speech has to be stricken and decimated and sacrificed if he has any hope of communicating anything to his fellowmen.

Writing is a strange alchemy. Out of something that is very personal and disordered comes a product whose words have been chastened and purified. A narrative has become a motif. A sprawling incident has been reduced to a design imposed upon the sequence of words that form a unity. The ultimate unity is always, if we use Baudelaire's word he found in Swedenborg, a "correspondence." It must be there, whether it is a novel or sonnet—a correspondence between a concrete object that leads upward toward infinity: a whale, a scarlet letter, a cup of linden tea, a woman's hair so golden it seems like metal, the bank of a river lined with marsh marigolds.

"And the time of death is every moment," Eliot writes in the third movement of "The Dry Salvages." This is the "stillness" the poet speaks of at the end of *Four Quartets*, the voice that speaks to us "between two waves of the sea." That state of stillness is both death and life in its deepest sense, when we realize that eternity is the most simple concept we have learned—by living. Even the beautiful, simplified pattern of a poem—"Little Gidding," for example—is far too complicated for the simplicity of death, which we know every moment in our life. Yes, stillness is all: that brief moment of time when we can hear "the children in the apple tree," and accept, if ever so briefly, the condition of simplicity, the state of stillness when "the fire and the rose are one."

Ever since I first read the final line of *Four Quartets*, I knew, and have been questioning the knowing, that the line is the perfect synthesis of the long poem in its four parts, as triumphant in its full meaning as the word "stelle" at the end of each of the three *cantiche* of Dante's *Commedia*. Fire, rose, stars: temporal objects (yes, even stars are temporal and will in time be extinguished), simple, familiar objects, and yet they lead us, through the art of the poet, to an understanding of eternity.

In my reading of *Four Quartets*, I find myself returning to the passage on *love* in "Burnt Norton" (in its fifth movement), "Love is itself unmoving," and trying to see if Eliot accepts all forms of love in that word: love for woman, for man, for a child; love for God the Father and Christ the Redeemer. Our first love in life is certainly our first appreciation of something timeless. And when our first love dies, we move to such concepts that come from "the children in the apple tree" and the time "between two waves of the sea." We move to an enjoyment of the sounds of such a line as well as to the concept it embodies. The ear apprehends as well as the mind. Thanks to poetry we can see what is not visible.

Eliot in his *Quartets* and Saint-John Perse in *Seamarks* (*Amers*) provide us with circular patterns of history and civilization, and we find ourselves throughout those two poems of ancestry back in our beginning. As I read aloud any passage I choose in *Quartets* and *Seamarks*, I feel myself propelled from birth or dawn to the end of silence, to midnight, and then back to the beginning where I prepare for another day. Realms of consciousness and history. Timeless and timed. Present and future. By their involvement with history and with one man's history, they rehearse for me all human possibilities and all human dreams. It is hard for me to tell whether I am moving into the heart of history or moving to a realm outside of history when I read of *les tragédiennes* descending to the edge of the sea, and when I read of the tongues of flame at the end of "Little Gidding" and realize that tongues and flames are the same thing: the power of speech recording what we know and what we do not know.

The "narrow vessels" of *Seamarks* ("Etroits sont les vaisseaux"), in their movement in and out of history, are just as paradoxical as purgation is paradoxical in the *Quartets* where fire is simultaneously suffering and love. "The dove descending" in the fourth movement of "Little Gidding" is both peace in its traditional symbolism, and destruction, if the dove is a fire-dealing airplane of history. The *tragédiennes* of the French poem enact in their gestures and movements at the edge of the sea both the desolation of the city and its renewal. Baptism may be given us by either fire or water. How easily we mythologize the Holy Spirit in the numberless ways by which it touches and transforms the human heart!

In Gérard de Nerval's first line of *Artémis*, he writes: "La Treizième revient . . . c'est encor la première." This is the most explicit statement in poetry of the circular and continuous aspect of each single human life and of all history. The "thirteenth" is the hour of death, but it is also the hour that follows life and precedes it, the hour of the moon and woman. A number—thirteen—that is both the riddle of life and the circle of life, that follows twelve on the face of the clock and that comes before one as the hand ends and begins the circle.

Time in nature builds up only to break down. It is the experience of mortality which the poetic form of the sestina (in the second part of "The Dry Salvages") suggests when Eliot evokes the time of the seasons. The "sea" in *Seamarks* and "The Dry Salvages" is both the source of life and its ending. The "rose" in *Four Quartets* is both eros and agape, and the "fire" in the poem punishes and purifies. But in both of these symbols, man is seen as being joined with eternity.

There are only four place-names in *Four Quartets*, and otherwise total autobiographical reticence. And there is not even that in *Seamarks* (where the title, *Amers*, stands for those manmade or natural signs that guide a navigator as he approaches land: a church steeple, a cliff), only the sea and the land, a ship on the sea, plenipotentiaries arriving by ship, and *tragédiennes* moving down to the edge of the sea. But the conscious life of each poet fills the poems and reaches out to fill the conscious life of each reader.

Metaphors are deeply personal data. (An elaborate and illuminating study of what I am saying has been written by James Olney, *Metaphors of Self*, Princeton University Press, 1972.) I imagine that whenever an identifiable autobiographical element might have been used (beyond the place-names of the titles), Eliot recast it into something unidentifiable. Consider the "familiar compound ghost" of "Little Gidding" (part 3) whom he calls unidentifiable. The reader is free to see that ghost as Brunetto Latini or Yeats or Joyce or Mallarmé or Eliot himself. In that passage, when a voice cries out: "What! are *you* here?" we are in a London street in World War II, and we are also in a fire-filled scene of the *Inferno* (canto 15).

Eliot is the poet speaking in *Four Quartets*, as Saint-John Perse is the speaker in *Amers*, as Mallarmé is at times a swan or a clown or an empress-child. No one of these poems forces any doctrine or philosophy on the reader, but readers tend to draw what might be called philosophical conclusions from them because of the symbols they enshrine and which seem to tease the reader into formulating themes concerning the place of man in the universe.

These three poets, one of whom was the exemplary master of symbolism, and the other two who derived much of their belief about poetry from him, never claimed to be philosophical poets. For them, history is recorded, not in books, but in the surface of the earth, in the sea and deserts, in trees and in the wind that carries pollen of flowers. For them, their autobiography is recorded in the metaphors they created: a narrow vessel, an apple tree, a toast offered at a banquet of poets.

Such are the metaphors, or possible symbols, drawn from the personal memory of the poet, which he does not fully comprehend, and which later may be more fully comprehended by the reader-critic, as he considers all the metaphors in the poems bequeathed by one poet to the generations of readers that follow him and are able to see more clearly than he did what the mind, the memory, and the creative imagination of a single man is able to put into the words of our everyday speech.

To J. Morrison,
A. Rimbaud, H. Miller

Ten years ago Jim Morrison died mysteriously in Paris, at the age of twenty-nine, and was buried in Père Lachaise, which he had visited a few days earlier in order to see the graves of Edith Piaf, Chopin, Wilde, and Balzac. I don't remember ever hearing his name during the sixties when he was a famous rock star, lead singer of The Doors. A week ago (December 1980), as I was leaving Holy Cross where I had been teaching for four months, one of my students, the basketball player Charlie Browne, handed me a large book as a going-away Christmas present—the biography of Jim Morrison—without checking with me on whether I recognized the name.

Charlie had befriended me and had helped to make my last two months at Holy Cross more pleasant than the first two months had been. I watched him play a few games, listened to some of his ideas—he was a philosophy major—and observed his friendliness with other players and students. All his life he had played basketball, and now, standing six feet ten, he dominated the courts physically and his warm spirit dominated the campus.

One evening in his room at 80 College Street (I lived at 34 College, lower on the hill that framed the campus on one side), he played for me and a few friends his favorite records of Bob Dylan and Neil Young. That evening I recalled that in September, at the end of my first class, Charlie Browne had stopped at the desk on his way out and asked me where Bob Dylan had mentioned Rimbaud. I forget now why I had referred to such a detail during the lesson. I told him it was in an interview in *Rolling Stone*. That allusion and that reference formed the beginning of our friendship.

It was indeed Rimbaud. His biography confirmed that the singer-performer-poet-philosopher of The Doors studied the life and poetry of Rimbaud and spoke of him on countless occasions between the age of eighteen and his death, eleven years later. The legendary Jim Morrison followed the legendary Arthur Rimbaud as he turned his back on the conventions of his day, as he spit on his huge, raving publics in places like Madison Square Garden, as he defied police, girlfriends, parents, and groupies.

Since Charlie was a senior, I asked him one day what he planned to do next year. "I'd like to shoot a few baskets in some northern country in Europe, where I'd be close to an empty countryside, mountains and snow and quiet." Charlie had come from the Bronx to Worcester and was already speaking of a wedding trip in July when he would take his bride to the wilds of Ontario. The contrast was there: the basketball star, accustomed to the frenzied yelling of college crowds, and the idealist, as gentle and compassionate a man as I have ever known, finding in a camping trip far from cities and crowds the setting his spirit wanted.

A similar but more histrionic contrast was in Jim Morrison: defiant in his attitude, often obscene in his gestures on the stage, recklessly singing his heart out because the poems were his own, Jim Morrison concealed under such masks the thinker who meditated on Nietzsche and Rimbaud, who searched for his true self and endlessly confused the search with alcohol and drug abuse. Preoccupied with death far more than Rimbaud, he moved closer at times to Villon and to Baudelaire. He wondered if his fate was to be found in the unconscious or in the stars. And before he was able to decide, his fate reached him in a Paris hotel in 1971.

Are all of us tracked down and tormented by such dualism? Am I also two beings in one, and often more than two? I was ready for Rimbaud when I first read him, ready for a break with more conventional books, ready to feel if not to understand such a sentence as "real life is absent" ("la vraie vie est absente"). My students today, faster than I did at their age, understand that *Une Saison en enfer* is a creation a young fellow had built out of his own guts. In the writing of such a work, Rimbaud reached the state of being beyond damage, and achieved a hard immunity to life.

Morrison had marveled that Rimbaud ended his career as poet at nineteen or twenty, and he had sensed, because of his preoccupations with death, that the ending of his own career would come not much later. He accepted very early in life, with no hesitation whatever, the belief that the driving force behind the authentic artist is his self-isolation and self-immolation. He has to assume and grow accustomed to a dislocation of the societal instinct. Finding oneself is a lifelong struggle. The struggle is evident in those artists essentially rebels: Cézanne, Van Gogh, Gauguin, and in the comparable writers D. H. Lawrence, T. E. Lawrence, Rimbaud, Henry Miller, Lawrence Durrell.

Durrell and Miller, in their early correspondence, wrote to one another about *Hamlet*, about that figure who haunts our dreams, as Mallarmé said, and who illustrated, better than most comparable figures, an outer and an inner reality. Hamlet the prince and Hamlet the inner man: these two beings in one move along separate planes in the tragedy and seldom meet. The critics try in vain to find their meeting place. They do not join. Rimbaud the docile pupil in Charleville is not the same as Rimbaud the poet in Paris, or Rimbaud the coffee merchant in Abyssinia. Jim Morrison the rock star exposing himself on the stage was not the same as Morrison the self-seeking poet.

Each of us is hopelessly disorganized in this separation of our social and our psychic lives. I have often thought that Henry Miller is an exception. Henry Miller writing *Tropic of Cancer* remained Henry Miller. It is a purely American book that could have been written only in Paris. When a few years later we began our correspondence, I was struck dumb by Henry's generosity. He set me about my business, by being friend and impressario. How I valued his golden opinion of me, and how often I wanted to say to him: "Go easy on me." Now it is too late to tell him that my best pages, all the rejected manuscripts, are festering on my shelf.

During those years when we wrote back and forth, Henry was having a hard time finding a publisher for his books, and when he found one, he had further problems with the laws of censorship. But he never ceased advising me and many other friends what to write and how to find the right publisher for our books. The tone of his letters counted more than the advice. In one form or other, he included some expression of a hope that we would reach a place on a distant planet where the dream ends and the spirit comes into its own.

It was, for a few years, a prodigal correspondence, a professing of extravagant admiration, which helped me in an almost medical sense. At that time I read Henry's books carefully, especially the first three novels, the two *Tropics* and *Black Spring*, novels that were in reality autobiography. They induced me to believe that autobiography is a revision of a life, not a straight reminiscence of it. They led me to a review of some of my favorite books illustrating various forms of autobiography: Saint Augustine and Henry Adams, Thoreau and Montaigne. They forced me to reconsider such novels I have reread at intervals in my life and that bear closeness to autobiography: *Le Rouge et le noir, A la recherche du temps perdu, Aurélia*. In my rereading of *Les Fleurs du mal, Une Saison en enfer, Alcools*, I found myself following the poet's life as it shone through those pages.

It was while reading Miller, the small books as well as the big ones, I began to realize that it is more possible today for a man to put himself on paper than in any other age. The European world of the seventeenth century, with so many brilliant writers in England and France, would not have tolerated such narratives of the self as those on sale in our bookstores today: Mailer, Rechy, Céline, James Baldwin, etc.

I can hear someone say: isn't Shakespeare in *Hamlet*? Yes, he is, but it is an invisible Shakespeare. Each of these books mentioned is the story of a critical pass in the life of a character. That pass is the subject of the book, and it creates a new mythology of the character. Miller's books have no one critical pass. They are the narrative of day-by-day activities, critical passes often of a trivial nature. The narrator (Henry Miller himself) becomes less the hero-protagonist than the familiar friend we talk to each day or write to each week.

In those earlier years when I read Henry Miller, I often wished he had fewer friends and depended on them less. I often wished he spent the time writing letters on the new books he was writing that might have permitted him to discover the critical pass in his hero's life. Such a discovery would have buttressed the structure of his book. His greatness often seemed to me a reflection of his friends: Fraenkel, Anaïs Nin, Durrell, etc. What would his greatness have become, had he remained more alone?

Letters are usually about obsolete battles. In a book of fiction the battle becomes present and active. Despair and megalomania as depicted in letters are embarrassing to the reader, but in a novel, whether it be Balzac or Iris Murdoch, such experiences can be dramatic and significant. They can be related to what Jung called "guilt-responsibility." This sentiment, if I understand it correctly, I find little trace of in Henry Miller and in his characters.

One of the world's expatriates, Henry Miller was cut off from his race as he tried to reach in his *Tropics* a non-American, a non-English dimension. He had talent enough to write another *Gargantua* or another *Satyricon*. But he never paused long enough to do it. He was always working toward the great book, always predicting, like an astrologer. If he had gone further into his autobiography, an ancestral horde would have been released. The chaos of his books, attracting during his lifetime eleven million readers, would then have found an order—and fewer readers.

How can his greatness be estimated today? I would guess by the action of such a book as *Tropic of Cancer* on so many readers in providing them freedom from guilt. A therapeutic book. A book that helped the times to change. A book that performed on countless readers a rite of absolution. Of course, to some degree all art is curative. Miller's art is overwhelmingly curative.

As Henry Miller analyzed the curative effect of Rimbaud or D. H. Lawrence on him, he described in a veritable river of language the drives and the obsessions in his own nature. He thus set himself up as breaking the boundaries of books, as a man poleaxed most of his life, as a writer needing to stay in one room and yet who was caught in the contamination of restlessness.

The exact relationship between an author and his book is always a mystery. To analyze that relationship in the composing of such works as *The Waste Land, Coriolanus, Finnegans Wake, Une Saison en enfer,* or *The Tropic of Capricorn* would demand the writing of another book. Miller was often attracted by such a mystery because as a reader he was voracious, gluttonous. At times a mere sentence read in some book would set him off, and he would improvise with words and possibly write several pages from it. He talked that way. A phrase or an allusion said by a friend in a conversation might initiate in Henry an oral discourse that was almost apocalyptic. It might be said that Henry Miller was the author of the original deluge in our day.

An honest study of Miller would be a study of the artist as healer. When he left New York for Paris, he left American numbness and found a new cohabitation with a typewriter, at 18 Villa Seurat. He became in Paris the outlaw who had the world inside him, and who, from then on in the decade of the thirties, disliked moving away from his daily routines of writing, eating, drinking, and making love. He was content, he was even happy if he had enough food. This was his Paris regimen during the great creative decade of his life. As time went on, his books generated all that Henry Miller needed.

A man who sets out to find himself by being a writer comes smack up against language. And after that trauma is passed, that is, after the book is written, he encounters a series of practical problems to which Henry Miller, in his particular case, devoted an inordinate amount of time. He set about getting the book reviewed, talked about, read, praised, censored. He helped create a world around the book when he should have been working exclusively on the next book. Those were his frenzied, megalomanic days.

The danger for a writer is to become too much of a writer rather than becoming more and more himself in life as well as in his books. A serious writer is so much alone that he is always on the verge of losing his mind. He is saved from such a predicament by his book, which is a contact with the human world. But the dilemma soon starts up again because the writer, once his book is published and read, never knows if there will be another book.

Isolation is a precious gift for the writer, and the most dangerous, since it can lead easily to the schizophrenic route. I believe that Henry avoided that route by writing in essentially the same way, in the epistolary style, to his friends, his publishers, his fans, and his attackers. He approached the writing of each book in the same way: novels, protracted essays, travel monologues. His was the undivided self, always acknowledging his weaknesses, always repeating, in a total absence of self-pity, that he was imperfect through and through. He never learned how to lie fallow.

Once *The Tropic of Cancer* was finished and published in Paris, in 1934, Henry's life, until his death in 1980, was characterized by constant writing and constant publishing. His great talent—a kind of miracle—was the skill he had in enlivening whatever he wrote. With someone else there would have been, in the writing, barren wastes of self-questioning and arguments. Not with Henry! Somehow he was able to force hysteria back against the wall and never allow the ceiling to close in on him.

Often in his lonely life, filled with wives and friends and omnivorous fans writing to him from every part of the world, portents would loom thick. But he would know there was always a strange meeting lying ahead of him. The Brooklyn boy living in Europe found new wonders each day. He often collapsed from sheer fatigue, but would recover quickly and then reeled with ideas that might come to him from some new correspondent.

He made friends with a few French writers who appreciated him and believed in him: Maurice Nadeau, Joseph Delteil, Blaise Cendrars. These were not among the most famous of his day, but he had chosen one giant of the past, as Baudelaire had chosen Poe, with whom he felt close affinity: Honoré de Balzac. In letters and essays two titles of Balzac keep returning: *Séraphita* and *Louis Lambert*, Henry's favorites from *La Comédie humaine*, and Henry never forgot that those novels were written at a time of the most sordid financial worries in Balzac's life. He was awed by the gigantic output of the French novelist, and fascinated by Balzac's alternating moods of prophet and clown which he knew to be parts of his own temperament.

Henry never claimed for himself the clearly announced goals of Balzac: the contentment that would come from "glory and love." Despite major differences of background, a lower middle-class Brooklyn life for Miller, and a Touraine-Paris background for Balzac, there were similarities of drive and ambition, and especially a moral phenomenon that characterized the writers: a vision allowing them to perceive, to guess the truth in whatever situation they were writing about. This particular vision is more important than the incoherences in a writer's character, more important than the daily threat he feels of being the prey of excessive ambition.

At times Balzac proclaimed himself a Swedenborgian, and at times Miller called himself a Zen Buddhist or a Gnostic. The protagonist in Henry's books is himself, avowedly so, whereas Balzac created two thousand characters in *La Comédie humaine*. And yet of all those personages, whom he claimed he had observed briefly or lengthily, Balzac himself is the most curious and the most striking, the most romantic and the most unusual. Both novelists were pursuers of dreams, seekers after the absolute. Both never ceased to write, correcting and recorrecting the pages of their proof through which the unity of their sentences and the unity of their work were dispersed. Each man created his own method as inventor and observer, as naturalist following the generation of ideas and visible beings. Both understood and felt the joy of such creation.

At the time of the great upheaval of 1939, Henry pulled up stakes in Paris—he had to—and from then on moved from address to address: Greece, New York, Big Sur, until he settled down for the last years of his life in Pacific Palisades. Balzac stayed in Paris except for brief trips to visit a mistress or to sign for some wildcat financial deal that would only add to his ever-increasing debts. Henry was the American in Paris during the few best creative years of his life. Balzac was the provincial in Paris exposing his lavish tastes in appointments and apartments and style of living, while writing his ninety novels on a small table with its two candles and endless cups of coffee.

As a child, separated most of the time from his mother and father, who seemed to pay him little attention, Honoré was a boarding pupil at the school of the Oratoriens in Vendôme. There it was customary for the priests to use whips and dark cells for recalcitrant boys. Honoré was a model pupil since he disliked corporal punishment. The Brooklyn schools Henry attended were far different, and the boys he knew and went around with gave him an early life of comradeship and a knowledge of the city that Balzac did not have. "La Dilecta" was the name Balzac gave to his first mistress, Mme de Berny. He was twenty-two and she was forty-five, an intelligent woman, *une grande dame*. Their liaison lasted thirteen years. Henry had no comparable introduction to love, which for Balzac was always closely associated with luxury and large estates and wealth.

Each novelist, representative of the prose of his century, functioned as a writer outside the world of poetry. Baudelaire wrote about his contemporary Balzac and admired him, but Balzac was engaged in an art totally different from that of Hugo and Nerval and Gautier. If T. S. Eliot complimented Miller on *The Tropic of Cancer*, Miller himself paid little attention to what was being accomplished during his lifetime by American poets.

Neither Balzac nor Miller was barren for long. Each felt the compulsive need to complete book after book: Balzac, in order to make himself the novelist of the Restoration, the "secretary of a generation," as he once said, and Henry Miller, in order to make himself, not so much the novelist of his generation, as the voice of conscience of his country. Balzac was a man of great passions and of a brief life of only fifty years; Miller, a man of minor passions and of a life of almost ninety years. Whereas Balzac faced criticism and adulation in varying degrees from critics who were astute and learned, Miller faced apathy and censorship from a public of readers hesitant to accept the new openness of his speech and the new verboseness of his style.

Both novelist and philosopher, Balzac was determined to fuse all of his writings into a system. This esthetic determination was accompanied by three very personal, very human dreams: to see published, before his death, a huge edition of his novels; to pay off his debts; and to marry Eva Hanska. When these dreams were realized, he had only four months left in his life, and they were agonizing months of painful illness.

The twenty-year-long story of Balzac's love for the Polish countess was a novel in itself that he lived and suffered through as he, in book after book and throughout a series of disastrous financial enterprises, strove to make himself into the great man of his age, to succeed with the pen where Napoleon had failed with the sword. Stimulated by Eva's first anonymous letter, signed L'Etrangère, he met her first in Neuchâtel in the fall of 1833. Although Count Hanski died in 1841, Balzac did not marry Eva until 1850. After their first passionate meetings in Geneva and elsewhere, there were years of epistolary love, and then when marriage was possible, the countess hesitated: her infatuation had lessened, Balzac's health was poor, and his debts tremendous. A long love story in three acts: passion, the loss of passion, and pathos, which can be followed in Balzac's correspondence.

No single love affair or marriage occupied a comparable expanse of time in Miller's life. The fury and warmth of the Villa Seurat days in Paris caused Henry's suffering in love to be overshadowed by his work and the array of his friends: Anaïs in her cloak, meetings at the Deux Magots, dinners "chez Henriette" on the rue Léopold-Robert, brief appearances of Moricand the astrologer and Soutine the painter. After the war, in 1946, Freud and Miller—briefly—seemed to be the giants of that period. Henry was happy then at Big Sur with his baby daughter Valentin Lepska Miller. From Patmos, Lawrence Durrell wrote to him describing that island of shattering whiteness. And Henry wrote back, in January 1946, "I am deep in Rimbaud." In Durrell's letters he heard of the two Greek writers he had enjoyed knowing (*Colossus of Maroussi*): Katsimbalis and Seferis. Maurice Girodias was reorganizing the Obelisk Press in Paris. All was starting up after the war. In Big Sur Henry was besieged by pilgrims eager to talk with him, satisfied if they could merely touch him. He was an American guru.

A crucial year, 1946, when the effects of the war were being felt: famine reports from Asia and existentialism reports from Paris. Durrell, closer to those reports, was depressed in Rhodes, and Miller, far from Europe in Big Sur, was in high spirits as he worked on *Rosy Crucifixion*. He learned that his book about Katsimbalis (*Colossus of Maroussi*) had in a way saved the Greek writer's life, had helped to set him up as *the* raconteur of Athens.

The thread of experience shines through all the books of Henry Miller. He was never threatened by that permanent danger for American writers: the descent from strength to mannerism, which can be seen in Hemingway, for example. The real American giants, Melville, Whitman, Miller, never did that. They remained fountains running wine.

As the baby daughter Valentin lived through her first year in Big Sur, there were very few intervals of peace and solitude for Miller. In Paris the two publishers Gallimard and Denoël were to be brought to trial for publishing French versions of the *Tropics* and *Black Spring*. "Le cas Miller" was being compared to "le cas Baudelaire" and "le cas Zola." The first youthful imitators of Miller were trying to place their manuscripts. They had not realized that the free and easy effect of Miller's writing was arrived at by endless practice and carefully evolved technique and elision.

By early 1947 Henry was enjoying his view from a new home in Big Sur: a view of sea and sky and stars. He learned at that time that Céline was in prison in Copenhagen, and Man Ray in Paris was reporting on the battle going on between existentialists and surrealists. Russia and America were dividing the world between them. Among the more illustrious visitors that year, Cyril Connolly paid Henry a flying visit.

During the years 1947 and 1948 Durrell was often depressed, and Miller was more and more harassed by fame, obligations, and difficulty at getting to the real work—that of writing. The autobiographical writing, as in the new work *Rosy Crucifixion*, did not change from the earlier books, but style and treatment did change: diffuse, rambling, opaque in varying degrees. By December 1947, he had written 1,000 pages of *Rosy Crucifixion* at a time when André Breton was trying to organize in Paris an exhibition of Henry's watercolors.

His son Tony was born in September 1948. During the next few years there were fewer letters between Henry and Larry Durrell. Their long separation continued. In Latin America and then in England, Durrell longed for Greece and was unable to resist a strong melancholia. Henry, from his fortress in Big Sur, was beginning, as he thought, to push editors and publishers around, until he realized that very little action was taken on his vehement suggestions.

In an issue of *Horizon*, Durrell published a long critical essay on Henry Miller, a serious reassessment and praise. In his comments on the piece, Miller made a few corrections by saying that if he did read Freud, he was more influenced by Rank and Jung. The major influences had always been Nietzsche, Thoreau, Whitman, and especially Elie Faure. He hinted that Durrell might be disappointed by volume one of *Rosy Crucifixion*. A truly prophetic hint.

Not only was Durrell disappointed in volume one, called *Sexus*, he found it disastrous, describing it as "chunks of puerile narrative," "explosions of obscenity." If one followed chronologically this literary friendship, one might well have wondered whether Durrell's diatribe against *Sexus* would not cause the friendship to founder and die. It did not. Henry in fact urged Durrell to write a companion piece to his *Horizon* article and denounce *Sexus* in the strongest possible terms.

I marvel at the gentleness of Henry's reply to his friend and at his quiet self-justification: "I have only this one life to record." He reiterated a belief often stated earlier that criticism of a writer's work never teaches. The writer has to be impervious to all attacks.

From this time on, 1949, when volume two, *Plexus*, was published, the letters became infrequent. In the fifties, with *Justine*, the first of the *Alexandria Quartet*, Lawrence was warmly acclaimed, first in England, and then in America and France. He settled down in Provence, in a small town near Nîmes, and there was already talk of publishing the letters (the volume was not published until 1962). In the last letters from Big Sur, Henry wrote of reading Delteil's *Saint Francis* and being buoyed up by it: "Life is everlasting." As he worked on *Nexus*, volume three of *Rosy Crucifixion*, he told Durrell how his day began at Big Sur by playing records of Monteverdi and Ravel's *Gaspard de la nuit*, and remembering moments of his life in Paris when he sat at La Rotonde.

Recapitulations

The daily adventure of a vocation (students and the new criticism)

In the writing of a memoir, the thoughts of a man, which are for the most part memories, are converted first into notes and then the words of those notes are reset into sentences. My own medium of communication is sentences. The words of these sentences are all the familiar ones, and their subject, in my case, seems always to be related directly or indirectly to a profession I did not consciously choose, but which was there at a very early age and which I merely followed as a natural pattern of existence.

The speech that one uses in a classroom is, on the whole, pedagogical. It has to be that, or almost that, if the service of a teacher has meaning. The texts I try to teach in class appear to my students at first reading very far in time, in style, and in subject matter from their immediate world, from their own way of speaking, and from their major preoccupations. Early in my career I discovered a fact which continues to be valid today: the difficulty of discussing in class what is close, what is serious to me, without disturbing the academic atmosphere.

Candor! That is the enticing word filling my mind as I write this page. A despairing word, too, because candor, that goal I would like to reach in the articulation of a lesson is always too far ahead of me. I have to give up any hope of expressing it and therefore of being it. If I ever did attain to candor, what could it be? I believe I know the answer to that question. Candor would be a quality of the spirit in a man that would never have to retract anything. It would be selflessness, uncontaminated by any impulse of gain.

Only one writer among those I have frequented the most often seems to have approached the goal of candor. Stendhal, the man of many pseudonyms, who left two masterpieces, *Le Rouge et le noir* and *La Chartreuse de Parme,* has given to countless readers like myself a pleasure in the perfection of his art. No episode is overwritten, no character is overdrawn, no useless expansiveness outweighs the writing. (This could not be said of Balzac, and I fear it could not be said of Flaubert, those novelists so often joined with Stendhal.)

Candor in the teacher, candor in the writer: there is not much difference in the impossibility of these goals. Whether literature is being taught or whether it is being composed, it has to stay in relationship with experience. And like experience, it has to manifest a multiplicity of implications. Human experience, after all, cannot be separated from this concept of candor I am trying to understand.

A teacher is more bare, more unprotected when he stands before his class, than a shaman is who uses magic to cure, or a matador who can rely on a piece of red cloth to divert the danger, or even an epiphanizer who makes manifest some vision.

He stands, as I say, vulnerable and naked, because there is no final formulation in teaching. Students count on that; they expect the impossible. Teaching has to be an exchange that can never be concluded at one time. On many occasions in my classroom, a simple question from a student has gone right to the heart of the subject around which I had been wasting my time prowling and parading. And then abruptly, and sometimes impertinently, that question revealed to me the fact that I had not really learned what I had been trying to teach.

At such moments I learn an additional lesson: that patience and mortification are higher parts of life than energy, valor, and wit. We spend too much time in class promising a better lesson tomorrow, promising more exciting things to come. And we easily forget that students will not judge us by promises made and not kept, but rather by our performances of each day, by what is specifically brought to them each day. I try, in each class I prepare, to bring out the intention that I am also working on something unrelated to libraries. My ideal is to listen as much as I speak, to bear witness to a text as much as I analyze it, and finally to prophesy as much as I provide historical data.

Students are writers too, or they become writers. A teacher, a philosopher, should not take himself seriously. But he should take teaching and philosophy seriously. I presume I am trying to say that it is better to be consistent with truth than with oneself. A teacher should be a begetter of books in his students, if not books in a literal sense, then some form of wisdom. Those students whom we see daily, some of whom we know well and look upon as young friends, are actually in a constant diaspora, moving from a cell-like room to an apartment, from a classroom to a dean's office, from a cafeteria to a basketball court, from a library to an ill-lit night dive, from a fraternity meeting to mass (a higher kind of fraternity). They move from their native northern town to a southern retreat in a university and there make plans, constantly revised, for a still more significant diaspora. To Yucatan, perhaps, or Israel, to Caracas or Big Sur.

A teacher is also a reader. Like any freshman he has to read over the text the night before. He is also a critic and a writer, a friend, a rabbi, a priest. The ideal teacher is he who in his life and profession makes all those roles inseparable. Otherwise he will suffer from his own form of diaspora.

I know a brilliant teacher who was asked at the end of a graduate seminar: "Sir, do you regard yourself as a priest?"

My friend replied: "Yes, I do."

Then the student went on: "So, are your students your congregation?"

After a slight pause, the professor replied: "No, my students are seminarians."

Good teachers of literature (this means good teachers of good literature) are unusually obsessed with it. This obsession is a form of enthusiasm that is obvious in a classroom and may appear to some students as silly or even idiotic. But this is in keeping with the tradition of teaching through the centuries. It is far healthier to appear silly and idiotic than merely to mellow.

To be literary, in the best sense, for both teacher and student, is to be engaged in a constant revision of literature, which means to be engaged in following the new creative writing and the new literary criticism of the day. This may help remind the teacher how dangerous it is for a man to be called "rabbi" all his life. It will encourage him to preserve an attitude of receptivity, of innocence before the text. Let the text work on him and on the students before they begin to work on the text. This is one way by which I would attempt to define literary engagement, which is in reality self-forgetfulness.

Beyond the immediate pleasure that can come from the reading and the study of a text: the beauty of its style, its literal and symbolic meanings, its power of revealing some intuition on the mystery of human existence and ambition—behind all that, there is the example of the man who wrote that text, of the author who at a moment in *his* life was able to achieve such a communication to the rest of us.

The example is there, and it may count tremendously for young and old readers. It can point out how a single life is (or should be) a continuous and progressive experience. If progress is made from principles guiding a life, from taste, from objectives, a willful stubbornness is indispensable. Such a life will allow no complacency.

As he reads more and more texts, the student begins to realize that the scope of literature is vast, and he may easily ask: "Is there anything that literature does not involve? How can one define an art that presents individuals, good and bad individuals leading their lives in every country, that gives us pictures of their manners, morals, and societies, and that gives us, better than most historians, a glowing picture of the past?"

As we read literature, it is inevitable that we begin taking attitudes toward it and making decisions about it. The reader becomes critic without having any sense of transition, and before learning any specific technique of analysis he is analyzing the text. When he begins to speak about the text after closing the book, he is a critic, at least an impressionistic critic or a moralistic critic. These two terms, often used today in a derogatory manner, describe the earliest, the most natural, and perhaps the most naive stages of criticism. But I would claim that as the modes of criticism become more sophisticated, more complex, and more metaphysical, those early attitudes toward a text are never totally obliterated. They assume more or less emphasis with the changing modes. Critics as well as novelists and poets are somewhat controlled by their readers.

Is it possible in any one form of criticism to bring together all the questions and all the answers that rise up when a reader-critic asks himself the central conundrum: why is this text—this page of Proust or this poem of Stevens—the way it is? It was written at a given moment in time and thus it must belong to the literary tradition of that time, either in accord with the tradition or in opposition to it. Did this text come into being because of what the author was, the kind of man he was, who writes in this way because of his life, temperament, and obsessions?

A third question following fast on these first two questions would be: is this work the way it is because of an entire society that engenders it? Did it come about as the result of social forces and situations that shaped its characters?

Perhaps—and this is surely a valid fourth supposition—a book is the way it is because of the language of its time. The language of each generation has its own quality and its own code. We are no longer certain of the meaning of some of the words in Dante, in Villon, and in Shakespeare.

After those four questions or hypotheses on why a work is the way it is, a young reader may easily ask why and how is this work valuable? In literature classes today that question is usually avoided. The term *value judgment* is looked upon as somewhat degrading and the new teacher will tend to turn it aside and continue with some form of textual analysis. But close textual analysis in the search for accurate meaning often leads beyond the text to problems best characterized as philosophical, or historical, or sociological.

Long before a literature class was associated with Marxism or structuralism or poststructuralism, its central activity, in English departments particularly, was literary criticism, and this often involved on the part of the teacher and the students responsible attitudes toward problems that were moral, social, political, civic, spiritual, and frankly religious. In any one literature department in universities of any size, there would be, and there is today, a range of attitudes toward criticism and its practices.

Students are often bewildered by such differences of approach. This pluralism in criticism is more and more blatantly announced in a department. To the traditional critics who tend to interpret the meaning of a text are added now exponents of German hermeneutics, psychoanalysis, feminism, semiology, and the most recent and therefore the most revolutionary: French deconstructionism.

A brief and somewhat mysterious jargonlike definition of "deconstruction" would be "a divorce of meaning from historicity." It followed, in 1980-81, a long series of ways of reading a text that began in the forties and fifties with Leavis in England and the New Criticism in America. Then, in the wake of Valéry, Roland Barthes in the sixties appeared as critic-mythographer, an approach which coincided with the structuralism of Lévi-Strauss and the semiotic thought of Derrida and the psychoanalytic thought of Lacan.

From Lévi-Strauss's principle that man is a structure-making animal, subsequent scholars have emphasized the theory that this structure-making impulse is best evidenced in language. The belief that language is a complex structure of signs has led to the study of signs now called semiology. This term is not to be confused with semantics which is a study of meaning. The traditional approach to literature was semantic, but ever since I. A. Richards asked the question: "What is the meaning of meaning?" as far as I know, no clear answer has been forthcoming.

The discipline of semantics, in its attempts to discover the meaning of a text, calls upon culture in general and especially history and psychology. The study of semantics is rich, complex, and, one can easily say, endless. It raises questions of which there is no limit and offers thus far relatively few answers. With the study of signs there seems to be more control, more assurance. The semioticians give every evidence of knowing where they are and what they are encompassing. Saussure, often referred to as the father of linguistics, is behind both the structuralists such as Barthes, and the poststructuralists such as Lacan and Derrida.

Traditionally literature is considered a peaceful, genteel study. But in recent years contending forces have risen up in American and European universities over the definitions of what writing is and what criticism is. There have always been disagreements among scholars over the interpretation of a text, but such disagreements seem mild indeed in comparison with the esthetic and moral concern in the study of literature and the deconstructionists today, who undermine the usual relationship between the author and the reader. The deconstructionists advance not only revolutionary theories of language, but also a nihilistic philosophy of life. They claim that the so-called meaning of a text (the theme of patricide in *Hamlet*, for example) has no relationship with the author's intention.

Any text, *Huckleberry Finn* or *Moby-Dick*, is a network of linguistic conventions, of codes, of strategies, which can be deconstructed and found to reveal interpretations different from the traditional interpretations. This deconstruction, if it is written out, is not only literary criticism but a new work of art. Under the conventional meaning of a text, other multiple meanings are concealed, as well as surprising philosophical positions. Wayne Booth in writing about the art of fiction discusses the plot of a novel. A deconstructionist will tend to speak of "inter-textuality."

Language is fairly strong in both camps, as traditional critics such as Alfred Kazin attack the deconstructionists, and they in turn deride the more classical interpreters. The controversy is ending now, because the words used in the scrap are false or exaggerated. Language has defeated both sides.

Derrida questions the reliability of human communication. He would say that a poet does not express his feelings about objective reality or about his personal reactions to people and emotions, but he is, in his poem, incarcerated within a language made up of signs independent of those meanings the poet feels he is putting into the poem. Language is full of puns not consciously manufactured. Breton's *Nadja* begins with three words: "Qui suis-je?" These would seem to mean: "Who am I?" But they may also mean "Whom am I following?" Both questions are equally applicable to the text of *Nadja*.

Fifty years ago at Cambridge University F. R. Leavis lost his fellowship for attacking the faculty establishment. Today a young authority on James Joyce was denied tenure because of his new wave theories on literature. Colin MacCabe had many sympathizers among whom was Frank Kermode, the most distinguished English don at Cambridge. He lost because his case represented more than himself: the battle between conservatives and experimentalists.

In summary, the problem is: how should English literature be taught? MacCabe describes himself as a poststructuralist but claims that in teaching a literary work he always considers it in its historical context. In his study of Joyce he examined the Freudian influences on the writer and evidently disturbed the Cambridge conservatives when he proposed the theory that Joyce's Irish nationalism was the result of "repressed and repressing masculinity."

Whether the course be on world literature, English or French literature, or comparative literature, the traditional approach is based upon the belief that literature contains eternal moral values. A structuralist view would claim that literature has no such consistency. A novel means different things to different people at different times. A cursory glance at the various interpretations of Rabelais' *Gargantua* since the sixteenth century would substantiate this claim. During the past fifty years Joyce's *Ulysses* has received the largest number of exegeses of any novel ever written, not merely interpretations, but exegeses with as many contradictory theories as those we usually associate with the biblical.

A traditional critic of fiction often has recourse to the life of the novelist and the life of his times in explaining both the meaning and the art of the novel. A large amount of time is often spent in this biographical and sociological approach to a novel. A deconstructionist would counter that a writer is more influenced by his unconscious mind and by the structure of the language he has used than by the life and the times of the author.

To teach successfully is to perform successfully. The good teacher like the good actor is aware of the demands, expectations, hopes, and powers of his audience. Even if he is on one side, as psychological critic or semanticist, he tends to refer to the other viewpoint for contrast and for enrichment, and such a method enhances the performance and transforms the classroom more than ever into a theater.

What is remembered from a class is not literally what is said. The points made about the interpretation of a text or the background of a text are forgotten quite soon by the students. They remember best the skill with which a lesson was organized, the projection of the lesson, the personality or the charisma of the teacher, his enthusiasm, the relatedness he establishes between his subject and their lives, and finally the relation the teacher illustrates between his subject and himself. The teacher is a mystery man. For fifty minutes in a classroom he exists as a human being having a love affair with his subject.

The personality of the teacher carries the subject and is more memorable than the lessons. Sidney Hook, in writing about his teacher Morris Cohen, remembers best his vanity and cruelty. That teacher's role was largely punitive, or at best, hygienic. Alfred Whitehead is best remembered as a sweet English gentleman. He taught at Harvard when I was a student there and I knew of his reputation of giving only A's. One day in the lounge of the faculty club I noticed him quietly writing at a desk. A student came into the room, obviously agitated, and waving a paper in his hand. He approached Professor Whitehead and said, "Sir, you have given me an A- on this paper, and I am discouraged. Should I give up the study of philosophy?"

The venerable teacher asked to see the paper, looked at the top page, and with his pen made a line through the minus sign, changing it into a plus. "There," he said, "that will take care of it. Isn't that better?" And he handed the paper back to the now puzzled student.

Graduate students told me at that time it was hard to recall any specific statements or aphorisms that Whitehead made in class, but they felt a glow from being in the presence of such a distinctive person. The distinctiveness came more from the books he had written than from the classes he taught.

In a recent book, *Portraits of Great Teachers* (edited by Joseph Epstein), homage is paid to such teachers as Nadia Boulanger, F. O. Matthiessen, Yvor Winters, John Crowe Ransom, Hannah Arendt, and Robert Oppenheimer. In many of these cases, real evidence of great teaching is hard to produce. The teaching is usually described as a performing art.

The performance of the teacher is both art and pedagogy. A comparable duality seems to exist for the structuralists and deconstructionists: dogmatic pedagogy in the classroom or lecture hall and the widespread publication of what is now referred to as a "literature of criticism." Graduate students in literature today read extensively in the newer books of criticism, and pay less attention to the basic literary texts. They are not reading those teacher-critics of a few years ago: Wimsatt, Trilling, Burke, and Olson, but are valiantly struggling with such books as Barthes on Balzac ("S/Z"), *Glas* by Jacques Derrida, and Riffaterre's stylistic study of Gobineau. Will this art on art supersede the original? Will the newest book on Milton or Joyce, on Chateaubriand or Proust, make any fresh reading of Milton or Chateaubriand unnecessary?

Exegetical criticism—biblical exegesis such as Saint Bernard's sermons on the Song of Songs—stays very close to the text and repeats the text word for word. T. S. Eliot's criticism, coming before the advent of the New Critics and the newer critics, does not stay close to the text, but makes pronouncements about the text. He was, for two generations of teachers and scholars, an inspiring moralistic critic. The New Criticism of Ransom and Brooks followed Eliot's seminal essays with their close analysis of a text that avoided sociological and anthropological commentary. Then the new criticism or structuralist criticism involved the text and several other complementary subjects, as we read in Barthes' *Sur Racine* and Serge Doubrovsky's *La place de la madeleine*. Barthes focuses steadily on the father-son relationship, on the son's need to slay the father, in his *Racine*. And Doubrovsky studies the son-mother relationship in his interpretation of Proust.

Such books, and others that have followed them or appeared contemporaneously—Gilles Deleuze's *Proust et les signes,* Richard's *Le monde de Mallarmé,* Genette's *Figures,* with its essays on Proust—are forceful literary expressions in themselves, holding their own as works of art beside the authors they study. A brilliant essay of Oscar Wilde, "The Critic as Artist," published in the volume *Intentions,* is revindicated by such creative criticism. Ever since Wilde first made the claim that the writings of the critic—Plato, for example, in his dialogues— can equal the creativeness of the dramatist or the novelist, the theory grew in force, first in an underground manner, to surface today in a thoroughly outspoken manner. If Oscar Wilde were living today, he might classify as outstanding creative criticism such books as Harry Levin's *Gates of Horn,* René Girard's *Le sacré et la violence,* Austin Warren's *Rage for Order,* Francis Fergusson's *Theory of a Theater,* J. E. Rivers' *Proust and the Art of Love.* I would too, and I would add, with my own predilections, a few others: James Boon's *From Symbol-*

ism to Structuralism (1972), Northrop Frye's *The Great Code* (1982), Hugh Kenner's *Joyce,* and, going back a few years, Sartre's *Qu'est-ce que la littérature?* (1948)

Turmoil is apparent today in criticism, but there is turmoil also in contemporary fiction. The abstract form in the writing of structuralists is often difficult to follow, and one is inclined to call it "metacriticism" that has cut itself off from the kind of elucidation earlier critics strove to reach. But I can remember such accusations once leveled against Kenneth Burke and even R. P. Blackmur. Those critics and I. A. Richards, whose *Practical Criticism* appeared in 1929, more than fifty years ago, were all teachers training students to avoid making stock responses to poems. In those days students read more willingly, more avidly, the major literary texts, whereas today in colleges the tendency is to read fewer novels and poems, and to read the major contemporary critics. The movement is away from a humanistic culture and toward an urgency to enter the ranks of literary technicians.

A few stalwart critics among us, Denis Donoghue and Frank Lentricchia, for example, remind us of the formative pressures always at work on society that are reflected sooner or later in the creative art of our day and in the critical writing that considers it. I imagine that the last two decades will be eventually classified as the richest and the most confusing of critical history in America and Europe. "History" is perhaps the wrong word to use, because criticism during these years has been affected by what one camp of doctors would call an antihistorical virus.

In his book *After the New Criticism,* Lentricchia sees Northrop Frye (*Anatomy of Criticism,* 1957) as among the first to consider a literary text as a self-contained structure and thus question the existence of an author's voice, individual and characteristic, within the text. Alienated in this way from the author, the text is also alienated from history. Without any historical dimension, the text enjoys a new kind of freedom. It is indeterminate.

Michel Foucault refuses to see any continuity in history. This effectively parallels Derrida's denial of the writer's presence in his work. When joined together, the theories of these two critics erode the systems of metaphysics which in our western world have protected such concepts as "meaning," "presence," and "history."

The changes that have taken place in theories of the critics themselves, the turnabouts and the varying emphases in the movement of structuralism and poststructuralism, make one hesitant to grant allegiance to any one theory. Such a query arises naturally with the publication of a book by Philippe Sollers: *Vision à New York* (1981). It is a series of conversations with an American professor about Sollers' work, and especially about his novel *Paradis* (1981), a text without punctuation, paragraphs, or chapters. Sollers is the director of the periodical *Tel Quel* which has gone through many changes since its beginnings. In the early issues *le nouveau roman* and structuralism were analyzed and defended by the staff and the contributors of the magazine. In the seventies an emphasis on poststructuralism and a dissatisfaction with Marxism prevailed over most of the articles.

Sollers, whose writing often seems gratuitously hermetic, was one of the first to look upon structuralism as a new "establishment" and therefore worthy of being denounced. *Tel Quel* reflects the rapid turnover of interests and the ever-changing cults: Moses replacing Mao, for example, attacks on the *états-Unis*, and praise for American campuses where Bernard-Henri Lévy and other *nouveaux philosophes* are read. Prophets from the Old Testament and epic heroes are revealers of truth according to Sollers. Each of his new books is more forbidding than the others: *Nombres* of 1968 and *Lois* of 1972 and *Vision à New York* of 1981. His masters are certainly Freud and Lacan, and the gnostic view grows clearer. It is difficult to know whether Sollers is writing the psychoanalysis of himself or of our present world.

What is literature? This is the persistent question raised by structuralism, and it may be answered, in time, thanks to a renewed study of language—language seen as the common denominator of myth and symbol, of ritual and archetype, of ambiguity and time. The academic world is no longer a body of scholars with their students. It is a widespread, deep-rooted malaise. I would say the same about science. No longer can we separate a scientific culture from a humanistic culture. There is only one culture.

Structuralism began with a haughtiness and a tone of absolutism that characterize new revolutions. Today it is fragmented, divided into heresies and orthodoxies that will bring about its death. Not its death, perhaps, but its metamorphosis. And yet it has raised the leading questions that have to do with the survival of literary study today. The leading books of this movement are courageous attempts at showing how a text may be read, analyzed, interpreted, understood.

French intellectual *snobisme* is incorrigible, but I think most of us have learned to live with it. The arrogance of some of the semiologists often appears to me as a mask disguising their own trepidations. The poets these new critics look at the most steadfastly—Mallarmé, Nerval, Rimbaud, Max Jacob—were all seekers after a valid meaning of poetry. They were awed by the age of the language they used in their verse, and felt they half-understood the meanings of the words they placed in strategic positions in the poems.

But the structuralists, despite their dogmatic tone, meaningfully continue in the tradition of the symbolists, and beyond the symbolists, in a more purely philosophical sense, in the Platonists' tradition as well. The search of the poet in his composition is similar to the search of the structuralist in his criticism: the effort to reach the unknown behind the visible, the extraordinary behind the commonplace. It is the effort to hear, not the purely lyrical, nor to see the purely picturesque, but to experience a sudden "illumination." Rimbaud's word is the most accurate.

Catholicism

To the Dante class in January 1973 I welcomed back familiar faces. Two sets of friends, for example, for whom the study of literature was important: Frank Abetti and Bob McCutcheon in row one; Bill Singer and Robert Worster, row two. Frank's Italian sounded more authentic than mine, and I had him read a few passages, to the delight of the class. His Italian grandfather had been a professor at the University of Florence, and his father who lived in this country had taught his children, without their realizing it at the time, the last line of the *Inferno*. On Sunday drives, at the end of every tunnel, as the daylight appeared, Mr. Abetti would recite:

E quindi uscimmo a riveder le stelle.

Each time, as the end of the tunnel came in sight, the children would nudge one another and wait for, and always hear, Dante's line about emerging from Hell and seeing the stars again. Throughout the semester Frank told me he waited impatiently for us to reach—at the very last class—the ultimate line of the poem.

On the first meeting of the class more students turned up than had formerly enrolled. There were sixty-three seats for fifty enrolled students, but before the class began all seats were occupied. There must have been thirteen who came to look me over before signing up. I placed one loose chair in the aisle of the last row and it was taken by a heavy-set black-haired fellow who throughout that first class kept a large book opened on his knees. His pale face seemed to me the face of a reader, but his body could be that of a football player. At the end of the class he stopped by my desk to ask in a quiet voice if he could use the edition of the *Inferno* he was holding in his hand. It was Singleton's edition which had not yet come out in the American edition. The student had bought it in England from where he had just returned after a semester in an English university.

Those were the first words Ken Hill and I exchanged. Gradually through that spring semester I began to appreciate his knowledge and love of literature, and his knowledge of . . . every other topic we happened to touch upon in the course of conversations casually carried out whenever we met on the campus. Everything was mysterious about him. His accent was not of the South although he was born and lived in Whiteville, North Carolina. When, on one of our earliest talks, I expressed surprise at his being a member of a fraternity, Delta Sigma Phi, he gave me a direct, cogent explanation. "My inclination," he said, "would be to read all day and night. I felt I must do something to initiate a few human contacts, so I joined a fraternity, and I am enjoying it."

In the fall course on symbolism I welcomed back into the English section several who had read Dante with me. Ken Hill returned and brought with him a fraternity brother, Steve Leatherman. On one early morning visit to my classroom Steve told me that Ken was secretary of Delta Sigma Phi and was delighting the fraternity every Sunday night when he read the weekly report and put it into a different literary style each time: biblical, Shakespearean, Joycean, etc. The brothers had realized Ken's extensive readings and were often consulting him for help in their papers. To acknowledge their brother's accomplishments they had begun to call him "Flash."

The French section of symbolism was the first advanced course for a football player, David Schmit, a large red-haired fellow whose enthusiasm for French was awesome. When I learned inadvertently that he was a member of Ken Hill's fraternity, I one day, to test him out, referred to "Flash." He showed due surprise at my knowledge of the secret name. He praised his brother's intellectual prowess, but he did remind me that he was taking the course in French whereas Flash was taking it in English.

One Sunday at the eleven o'clock mass celebrated in the Divinity School chapel, close by the large Duke Chapel, I noticed both David Schmit and Flash. Ever since coming to Duke I had heard mass on the campus. Zener Auditorium, a large classroom in the psychology building, had been until recently the room used for Sunday mass, but the number of Catholic students had grown, and by 1973 two masses each Sunday were said in York Chapel.

On leaving the chapel that Sunday, Flash and David greeted me, and that evening David came to visit me to talk about religious matters and Baudelaire! I remembered how in explicating passages in Villon and Pascal, in the introductory course, he had demonstrated some knowledge of Church doctrine. After a pious Catholic upbringing, he was feeling, in his second year at Duke, misgivings about his faith. This was a familiar situation to me, and it usually involved on the part of a student questions directed to me about my own faith and my visible attendance at mass on the campus. The questions always seemed justified to me and my answers so sketchy, so unsatisfactory, that I often wished I felt the initiative to write out a more complete analysis of the role of religion in my life.

When in my twenties I became a new Catholic, I felt the experience of joining a world institution and a supernatural world that represented stability existing within the more familiar world of change and indecisiveness and hesitation. And yet in the two steps I had taken from the Baptist Church of my childhood to the Anglicanism of my college years, and then from Anglicanism to Catholicism in my first years of teaching in Vermont, I had never at any moment felt I was rejecting or repudiating a religious belief or practice.

I felt at each of those decisions in my life, as I still feel today, that I was carrying forward all that I had learned and believed, moving into a wider context, understanding more fully historical Christianity, commiting myself more firmly to the past as well as to the present and the future. In a word, I was convinced that by taking the third step in my religious life, I was joining the universal church. I wanted not parochialism, not nationalism, but Catholicism in its sense of universality. I still believe today that Roman Catholicism bears with it Judaism, Protestantism, and other forms of orthodoxy, and gives them their fullest meaning.

At the time of my conversion, in the 1930s, when I was studying the catechism, I was also avidly reading Chesterton and Belloc, and especially, in French, Pascal and Péguy. I found the arguments of those writers strong and personal. They had sought and found in Catholicism the same fullness and stability that I was seeking. But then, during those years of the thirties when I had in a personal sense discovered an inner peace and satisfaction I had never known earlier in my life, I became aware, largely because of the tragic news reaching us of the Spanish Civil War, of a momentous controversy being waged within the Catholic Church itself, a struggle which in political terms was left wing versus right wing, or liberal thinking versus conservative or even reactionary thinking.

This political controversy involving the Church seemed to be a contradiction of the powerful unity, the universality, I had hoped to find. I had to learn at that time the hard lesson that at every turn of history, the Church is challenged, and often by forces within it—by brilliant men and women who participate in its communion.

In an effort to understand these hard problems, I came to the writings of Jacques Maritain and to his example as a Christian thinker. I found him to be a compassionate and committed man. When I first read him, he was, like so many French intellectuals at that time, fully concentrated on the suffering and the confusion of the Spanish Civil War. But behind the immediate problems of that crisis, I could see that Maritain was following the progress of Thomistic thought. No, he was not following it, as I first imagined, he was creating the progress by applying the principles of Saint Thomas to our world. To reach and preserve, even briefly, the peace promised Christians, vigilance and strength—combative strength—and prayer were needed.

I learned that Maritain's was the vocation of the philosopher, that of being witness to the world in its meaningful presence, and of welcoming the world by means of a language that attempted to reveal the truth of the world. He provided me at that time with the philosopher's understanding of humanism. History, for Maritain the humanist, is the long road taken by man from the moment of his fall to the moment of his redemption, and which will continue until he is transfigured in the vision of the Godhead.

On countless occasions Maritain said that new applications of the principles of Christianity are necessary today. His entire work might well be defined as the carrying out of this belief, the effort to explain once again the foundation of Christian thought and theology, and at the same time to explain why, in the light of today's history as well as of past history, the Christian can never feel totally at ease in the temporal and eternal aspects of Christianity.

The vibrant pages which Jacques Maritain devoted to the place of Israel in modern history form only one example—but deeply characteristic of this philosopher—of the solicitude and the personal suffering he felt for the race of man. He saw the plight and the struggles of Israel as stimulating the entire movement of history. Maritain explained the waiting of the Jews and their anxiety as signs that they refuse to receive the Incarnation into their hearts. But these passages on the "mystery of Israel" through the ages are applicable to any single Christian soul who holds back something in his own nature that should be offered with the total gift of himself.

The history of man seen as two simultaneous and contradictory forces: the deadening, heavy weight of sin, on the one hand, and the illuminating spirituality of grace, on the other, is a Thomistic interpretation for which Maritain discovered vigorous, fresh applications. In all of his books, he never ceases evoking the presence of the Church in the history of mankind. History, he would say, is written under the permanence and the will of God. His plan is immutable, and it allows the free will of man even to do wrong. With every problem that Maritain touched, he ended by fusing into an organic growth the supernatural life of the Church and the temporal life of the world.

Concurrently with my reading of Maritain, I read also Mauriac and Bernanos, novelists and polemicists strongly critical of reactionary thought expressed by their fellow Catholics. The years leading up to the Second World War were years of vehement controversy when Catholic writers were either liberal or conservative. The French Dominican newspaper *Sept* represented the extreme left-wing Catholic view, and it was suppressed. I am not sure what impressed me more: the views expressed in that weekly publication or the submission of the writer-priests to the decree of their order in Rome.

After the tragic years in France of the Occupation and the Resistance movement, I became more aware of the dilemmas facing priests in France as in every other country. I reread *Journal d'un curé de campagne* of Bernanos and began to see the priest as a leading contender for the tragic hero in today's society. The movement of the worker-priests (*les prêtres ouvriers*) seemed to grow from the dynamics of the Resistance in France and the realization that the Church was fast losing out to communism in the working class. As long as it lasted, especially in France and Spain, it seemed to me an extraordinary human and spiritual adventure, an apostolic adventure, a dialogue carried on between a priest and his fellow workers in a factory. A priest was more than a man attached to a monastic order or to a parish. He was a man dressed like other men, working hard to bridge the gap between the working class and the Church. Would he be pulled back into his parish and forced to wear a cassock and a biretta? Would he be humiliated and repudiated by his fellow workers when they learned who he really was?

In opposition to the rigors of Church discipline and hierarchical order, the worker-priest remained faithful to his people. During those years when his fate was being questioned, I often repeated to myself a line from the Book of Deuteronomy. God, having grown weary of the repeated infidelities of the children of Israel, said to Moses: "I am giving them up. Come with me and from you I will raise up another people." Moses' answer to God was sublime: "Lord, I will not go without them."

Then, fifteen or twenty years later, with an abruptness comparable to the student rebellion of 1968–69, the Church appeared threatened with question after question: the celibacy of the clergy, birth control, abortion, the liturgy of the mass, the folk mass, gay marriages, lack of vocations. These questions, still uppermost in our minds, are all related to the upsurge of activism in the late sixties. As we moved into the second half of the seventies and beyond, there was little activism, but greater cynicism, growing fear of economic collapse, and signs of a new kind of warfare such as the bombing of a crowded New York airport during the holiday season. Esoteric cults trying to replace the Church continued to proliferate.

Violence and racism are intrinsic to human nature. Within our memory, the spirit of a Gandhi was opposed to violence and racism when he preached that a society is most viable when it exists for its children. And for centuries now the Christian spirit has been preaching that no society is worth fighting for unless that society exists for its weakest members. The most depressing event to me of the 1970s was the amnesty for draft resisters announced by the president of the United States. This amnesty was not only unacceptable, it was outrageous and immoral. It meant that official America, the government in Washington, still considered these young people criminals and law-breakers. They were few in number, but they were the real heroes of the day when they put their lives on the line in order to bring to an end an obscene, disastrous, lingering war. Yes, they were the heroes who should have been welcomed home. The criminals were the architects of the war who prolonged it year after year. Only a few Christian leaders spoke out in defense of those exiles: men like Father Philip Berrigan and the Rev. William Sloane Coffin. Only a few voices representing religious convictions were audible at that time, but the power of God starts with tiny beginnings.

What is the role of the Church, what is its reality for me, what is its supernatural reality from the viewpoint of a lay Catholic? I would like these few lines I am writing to be a testimonial to all those men and women who are concerned with religion today, who are seeking to understand the eternal role of the Church as the guardian of truth and the ways of remaining within the truth.

I like to think of the Church as that place where history is recapitulated every day, history which in its highest sense is man's search for God. And at the same time it is that place where heed is paid to the changes in society, in morals, in behavior, and in attitudes. Thus the Church is the present as well as the past and the future. The Catholic lives in a historical Church which goes back at least to the days when God carried on a dialogue with Moses.

In my twenties, at a time in my life when I was looking for arguments and justifications, the most overwhelming proof of the sanctity of the Catholic Church was for me the historical fact of the large number of saints it has guided and sponsored and finally canonized. A host of men and women, modest, selfless, and God-loving, who would not have lived in the way they did, if it had not been for the Church. As a child I learned to say "Paul" in speaking of the apostle, but as soon as I became a Catholic I learned to say "Saint Paul," and today when I hear "Paul" used by my Protestant friends and students, I realize that no longer can I speak in that way.

What are the principal sources for these lines I am writing, for this recital of belief? My own experiences in religion, the Bible, some writings of the Church Fathers, Saint Augustine in particular, and the language and forms of the liturgy as I have known it in the past. Finally, in acknowledgment of old and cherished debts, let me repeat here the names of three French writers who are almost part of my daily life: Pascal, Péguy, and Maritain, and six other writers, read more intermittently, but who have helped me to reaffirm and understand my own convictions: Graham Greene, Bernanos, Mauriac, Simone Weil, Pierre Teilhard de Chardin, and Flannery O'Connor. In reading the published letters of O'Connor (1979), I was moved to see her many references to the same writers.

I confess that the list is weak in theologians and scholars. Instinctively I tend to read and reread those writings that come from a personal experience in religion. But every Sunday when I stand at mass with my fellow-believers to recite the Creed, I feel I am retracing a way that starts with my faith at that moment and moves back into its doctrinal expression. For forty years I have tried to live as a Catholic in a non-Catholic world, especially the last fifteen years when I have lived in North Carolina, which is the lowest of all fifty states in Catholic population: one and six-tenths percent.

What is the Church, then? Not a notion, certainly. A fact, rather, a divine fact. The Church is the people of God, living, walking with God, from one end of the Bible to the other. There is another way of describing the Church: the body of Christ. It is a concrete community of men, women, and children living today or who have lived in the past, and who are attentive to the revelation made by the prophets and by Christ.

Etymologically doesn't *ecclesia,* the Latin word for "church," mean a "call," a summons spoken to all by God? Once in the desert God spoke to his people from a cloud, once from a burning bush to Moses. Today he may speak to a child trying to find words for a prayer, or looking at a sunset, or listening to words of an aging grandmother. The Church then is a convocation, a calling together of all those who believe and expecially of all those who have heard God's voice. The Book, preserved by the Church through the centuries, tells us all, Jews and Gentiles, who we are. It tells us that after the Passover (*la Pâque*), after Easter (*les Pâques*), we move into eternity. We belong to a Church that is in movement toward eternity.

The history of the Christian Church does not begin with the earliest communities of the first and second centuries. It begins with Israel of the Old Testament. It begins as far back as we can go in recorded history with a consciousness of a continuity. The earliest Christians, those who first called themselves Christians, accepted without any questioning the inheritance of the chosen people. They accepted it as a totally spiritualized and spiritualizing inheritance.

That inheritance was the meetings of God with the great patriarchs, meetings that had been sealed and consecrated by the alliance with Moses on Mount Horeb. God was intimate with his people at that time. The author of Deuteronomy, in chapter seven, speaks of that intimacy, of that love of God for his people. Even if Israel is small among the nations of the world, it is the chosen people who were redeemed from the bondage in Egypt. The pious Jew reading the history of Israel in such accounts as those of Esdras and Nehemiah can still read how the domination of the chosen people is to become universal because of the mercy and faithfulness of God. Leader will succeed leader and finally be called the "one shepherd," the messiah. The plan of a theocracy is there, indeed a universal theocracy.

The early Christians did not deny their Jewish origins. Israel was the guardian of the Torah, the law. The Jews of the first century adopted and even invaded the Gentile world without in the least rejecting their own world. Saint Paul's cry, which we read in his letter to the Romans (11:1), "I too am an Israelite, from the posterity of Abraham, from the tribe of Benjamin" is echoed by a recent pope: "Christians are spiritually Semites." Even in his vocabulary, with such often-recurring words as "the seed of Abraham," "Israel," "people of God," "circumcision," the old and the new are joined in the writings of Saint Paul.

The history of Israel and the history of the early Church as recorded in the Old and New Testaments are accompanied by a listing of promises or privileges. At the end of the mass, when we stand as the priest raises his hand and makes the sign of the cross over us who have been united momentarily around the sacrament, I often feel that in the formalized benediction we are receiving the promises made to Abraham. The tabernacle of the Jews is there over the altar in the box where the sacrament is kept. If the altar is improvised in a room or in a field, then the tabernacle is the chalice or whatever receptacle holds the wine as it is changed into the blood of Christ.

Whether God is in a column of fire, or in the tabernacle of the temple, he is the center of a worship organized around the Psalms and the writings of the prophets. Nothing of the past is rejected. The Christian community was once and for all time designated in the words of Saint Paul: "You are the people of the patriarchs and Christ." And these very words are repeated by the priest at mass. Israel was the seed of the Church. The prophets of Israel once spoke of the future domination of God over all peoples. They used the phrase, endlessly repeated in the New Testament, "the kingdom of God," which still today remains awesome, mysterious, indecipherable. They are the words printed on the pages of our Bible, and comparable to those hieroglyphs carved on the stones of the pharoahs that puzzle scholars today. John the forerunner said it: "The kingdom of heaven is near, repent." (Mark 1:15; Matthew 4:17)

The story of Pentecost is the story of Jerusalem. It has always seemed to me totally Judaic and the fervent sign that the Church did not break with Israel, but took it over as its rightful past, as its solely legitimate future. The setting was a holy day in Jerusalem when the apostles, representing the consciousness of the second generation, were gathered together in one place. Pilgrims in large numbers, and dressed in colorful costumes, were there too when the noise of the wind was heard, and the Holy Spirit, in the visible form of tongues of fire, entered them all. They "shared" languages. The gift of tongues was the mark of the Church's universality at that precise moment in time when the Church of Christ was born (Acts 2:14). When Peter called for silence and spoke of the mission and resurrection of Jesus, he referred to the prophecy of Joel. Three thousand were baptized on that day, and therewith the Church was added to the Israelite collectivity.

A community is of course an assembly of individuals who "hear" the same words. From the vocation ("call") of Abraham to the conversion of pagans, the ministers of the Church endlessly repeat to each individual: "The kingdom of God is within you" (*regnum Dei intra vos est*). But that "kingdom" is not as discernible an event as Pentecost was. When the Pharisees asked Jesus when the kingdom of God would come, he replied in the words I have just quoted, and which Abraham must have felt, that the kingdom of God is already here in you. Young Catholics today are united in groups around what they call Pentecostal charisma. The original Jerusalem Pentecost is repeated over and over again whenever there is an assembly in the name of Christ, whenever the same spirit, the same charisma touches everyone. At that moment of togetherness the Church is founded once again.

Charisma has to serve the group. First, it served the twelve at Jerusalem, and then the three thousand, and soon after that the pagan-Christian community founded by Saint Paul, and today the pentecostal communities at Tysé in France and a few Newman clubs in American universities.

Pentecost was a historical event following the teaching of Jesus on the allegory of the vineyard (John 15:1–8). Unless there is a concrete society (with branches growing out from the trunks), how can a man experience what Jesus promised in the form of a command: "Love one another as I loved you"? Jesus himself was the worker in the vineyard, the worker-priest in the mine, as he formed his disciples and made new recruits among pariahs.

Beginning with the year 1973, outside the classes on Dante and symbolism, conversations with students at times hit religious problems so squarely that I wished I had more competence, more theological knowledge than I had. For myself I summarized the liberal religious viewpoint which I heard from Protestant and Jewish students, and even from Catholic students, in this way: man has never fallen, man never incurred guilt, man is ultimately perfectible by his own works, his own efforts. It was hard to argue against this, and I usually ended by stating my own view, which is the orthodox view: man has fallen and he is perfectible only by God's grace, and not by his own efforts.

A Catholic has to have strong nerves to speak about Catholicism in North Carolina, or, for that matter, in any of the states, because it is an immigrant church here. It is painful to acknowledge the vulgarity in the Church, its lack of scholarship, its lack of intellectual honesty. We are a church of sinners in which Christ is crucified by all of us. It does little good to remind skeptical friends as they dig into you with pointed jibes that Peter denied Christ three times and could not walk on the water by himself. Ours is not an age of great Catholic theology. Protestant theologians are more perceptive and more alert than Catholic theologians today. The Jewish theologian Martin Buber, in such a book as *The Eclipse of God*, offers a powerful adjunct to orthodox theology.

The reading and the teaching of Dante always restored for me the Catholic sense of history: everything a man does in his life moves him toward his true end in God, or moves him away from it. Everything is ultimately redeemed or lost. Hell and paradise are eternal places and eternal concepts. We were created to love God. The experience of love requires two beings, and then it requires man's free will. The will to reject or to love.

Index

Wallace Fowlie is the author of many books: scholarly studies on Proust, Rimbaud, Mallarmé, Gide, Claudel, Stendhal, and Dante, as well as *The Letters of Henry Miller and Wallace Fowlie, Characters from Proust* (poems), and *Journal of Rehearsals: A memoir* (Duke University Press), for which he received the first Harold D. Vursell Memorial Award, given annually by the American Academy and Institute of Arts and Letters "to single out recent writing in book form that merits recognition for the quality of its prose style."

Wallace Fowlie is James B. Duke Professor Emeritus of French Literature, Duke University.